THE NATURE OF HUM
TURKISH VILLAGE

TURKISH VILLAGE

Arthur **Paul** Stirling

Lecturer in Anthropology
The London School of Economics and Political Science

SCIENCE EDITIONS®
JOHN WILEY & SONS, INC., NEW YORK

CONTENTS

TABLES

MAPS AND DIAGRAMS

PREFACE

Traditionally, anthropological field work has involved the adventure and physical discomfort of living in remote places, and at the same time, the intellectual surprises and emotional upheaval of making oneself, even partially and temporarily, a part of a relatively closed and culturally strange society. Some of those who nowadays work in familiar or in industrial societies may miss something of this experience; but although Turkey is a modern European nation and Islam is in many ways close to Christianity, Sakaltutan and Elbaşı provided my wife and myself with plenty of adventure, and an indelible experience, both intellectual and emotional, of adjustment to the day-to-day life of a culturally alien community.

The whole research project was made possible by the grant of a Senior Studentship from H.M. Treasury, and I am most grateful not only for the studentship, but also for the understanding way in which it was administered. My major debt of gratitude is to Professor Evans-Pritchard, who welcomed me into the Institute of Social Anthropology in January 1948, gave me encouragement in my plans, and supported my wife and myself with professional guidance and personal friendship. We should like to thank warmly Professor Fortes, who gave us much of his time, and also, for friendship, instruction and many profitable discussions, Professor Max Gluckman and the other members of the Institute between 1948 and 1951, both staff and students.

My friends, both colleagues and students, at the London School of Economics have of course done much to teach me and supply me with ideas; in particular I should like to thank Professor Firth and Professor Gellner for reading the manuscript and making helpful suggestions, and Professor Schapera who performed this task twice on different versions, surely a rare service to a junior colleague. Many people have helped with preparing the text. In particular, Miss Dorothy Thompson,

Mrs Marjory Taylor and Mrs Ingrid Lyles helped with the typing, and Mrs Eunice Wilson of the L.S.E. Geography Drawing Office offered professional advice as well as skill in preparing the maps and diagrams. Mrs Pamela Hunter and Mrs Marion Horn kindly read through the manuscript for editorial comment.

It was our good fortune to have for our first teacher of Turkish Professor Fahir Iz, then a lecturer at Oxford, and he and his wife have proved permanent friends. Through him we met Professor and Mrs Aydın Yalçın whose family in Ankara offered us the hospitality of their home, and who gave us many introductions to their friends. We enjoyed warm hospitality from Ankara University through the kindness of the Rector, and among many friends on the staff I should particularly like to mention Professor Irfan Şahinbaş, who taught us Turkish. Dr H. Z. Koşay, of the Ethnological Museum in Ankara, and Professor Z. F. Findikoğlu, of Istanbul University, were unfailingly kind and helpful.

Arrived in Turkey, we received great kindness and much practical help from members of the British Council and the British Embassy, and I should like to acknowledge the friendly co-operation of the British School of Archaeology in Athens, and the personal kindness of the Director, Seton Lloyd, and his wife. We were fortunate also to meet in Ankara Professor and Mrs Richard D. Robinson, whose knowledge of Turkey, and whose enthusiasm for our studies have been invaluable.

Our field work was aided in many practical and indispensable ways, and our spirits periodically revived by friendship and comfort at the American School and Clinic at Talas. Mr and Mrs Paul Nilson and the School staff were kindness itself, and Dr and Mrs W. L. Nute Senior nursed us through dangerous illnesses, freely opened their private home to us, and helped us immeasurably by their knowledge of the area, and their co-operation in dealing with the problems of our village friends.

To the Turkish Government we owe gratitude for permission to work in a rural area, and for much help and co-operation. I should also like to thank the two Valis of Kayseri during our field work, and all their officials in Kayseri, Talas, Bünyan and Elbaşı.

But our greatest debt, plainly, is to the people of Sakaltutan and Elbaşı, who made welcome two total strangers who came to pry into the life of their villages, and did a vast amount by their affection and practical help to support and assist us. In the seas of snow, to use their own phrase, on those open hills, in the winter of 1949–50, the help of the villagers was a condition of survival. These are friends we shall always remember with pleasure and gratitude.

A NOTE ON TURKISH WORDS

The modern Turkish letters are pronounced more or less as an Englishman would expect, with the following exceptions:

c — as *j* in *jam*
ç — as *ch* in *chapter*
ğ — barely pronounced at all; tends to lengthen the preceding vowel.
ı — (distinct from i) rather like the indefinite unemphasised vowel in English, e.g. *tion* in *fraction*.
ö — as *eu* in French *veut*
ş — as *sh* in *shop*
ü — as *u* in French *rue*.

I have spelt most Turkish words according to the current Turkish spelling, including some Islamic terms more familiar perhaps in an anglicised form of Arabic, e.g. *Evkaf* for *Wakf*, *Şeriat* for *Sharia*. A few words are half-way between English and Turkish. I have arbitrarily decided in some cases that they can be treated as imports into English – vali, vilayet, kaymakam, imam, Ataturk – and put the rest into italics, giving them if necessary Turkish plurals.

NAMES

All villagers' names are fictitious. The letters which follow them in brackets indicate their patrilineal group (pp. 162ff.)

A NOTE ON MONEY AND MEASUREMENTS

MONEY

From 1950 to 1952 the official rates of exchange were

> T.L. (Turkish Liras) 7.8 to £1
> T.L. 2.8 to U.S. $1.00

These rates are somewhat unreal. Black market rates were much higher, and what counts is purchasing power in relation to certain needs. But some indication of value is desirable and I have given rough equivalents in round numbers in sterling and dollars where I have had to refer to Turkish currency.

MEASURES

For local land measures, see p. 52. Officially, 1 dönüm = 1 decare. I have given rough equivalents in acres and in hectares in most cases.

Transactions in grain are conducted both by weight and by cubic measures of volume. This creates some problems; but since none of the quantities are more than estimates, I have accepted the village statements of equivalence to the metric system. By chance, standard four-gallon petrol cans (five American gallons) are used as measures of volume, so that conversion is simple. I therefore give quantities in British and metric measures, where appropriate.

CHAPTER ONE

TURKEY

Introduction

In less than twenty years, between the late nineteen-thirties and the fifties the views of Western intellectuals on the future of mankind underwent an extraordinary revolution. Between the wars, most Western people took for granted the gulf in way of life and standard of living between Western Europe and its emigrants and trainees, and the poverty-stricken rest of the world. If not eternal, the difference was fundamental and apparently unchanging. Only the Japanese had succeeded in demonstrating that industrial society could be transplanted without a European ruling class, and this was regarded as a special case – almost unfair. No one dreamt of hundreds of millions of Asians and Africans driving their own cars to work in their own industrial cities. It was not yet customary to measure national success in terms of the annual rate of economic growth, and few had thought of arguing that a completely industrialised world, far from rivalling Western industry, would provide that industry with vastly increased markets.

In the nineteen-twenties, a whole generation before problems of backwardness had been rechristened problems of development and aid programmes and agencies had sprouted in all parts of the world, when most of the West still knew little and cared less about the millions of Africa and Asia and their poverty, Turkey attempted to westernise its institutions and its economy. Turkey was one of the very first 'developing territories'.

The thoroughness with which Turkey's legislative and administrative reforms reproduced their European models is startling. By the nineteen-thirties the Turkish Republic could claim: a modern European legal system; an independent judiciary; women judges, members of parliament, doctors and scientists; a secular outlook free from fanaticism; and the beginnings of industry. All this has been described in a number of books, the titles of which imply renewal and transformation: the Western phoenix springing from the ashes of oriental defeat.[1]

In these books Turkey is a land of contrasts: the ox-cart beside the combine harvester; the bride in her traditional costume carried to her groom, not on a white horse but in a shiny American taxi. They imply that the quaint and retarding old customs are disappearing before the modern rational revolution. But no author has yet been able to restrain himself from assessing the success of the revolution and perhaps offering advice on how to do it better. No one has asked precisely and objectively what happened to the traditional life of the four-fifths of Turkey's population who work the land and live away from the larger towns and cities and who were forcibly subjected to ideas and reforms modelled on the ideas and institutions of their ancient enemy, infidel Europe.

Social anthropology began as the study of small-scale, preliterate societies. In these studies, anthropologists learned to place strong emphasis on a long period of intimate acquaintance with one particular community of the society under study. These thorough and detailed studies produced remarkable results, which were not only ethnographically rich and accurate but also stimulated new ways of analysing and interpreting social data. Naïve and hopeful, I came into anthropology with the idea of applying similar methods to the study of complex, literate societies with recorded histories, and I chose Turkey for my field more or less by chance. In spite of a training in philosophy and history, I was a beginner in thinking systematically about the problems of society, and I accepted, perhaps rightly, the view of my teachers and colleagues in anthropology that an intensive immersion was the best way to achieve understanding of any society.

How was I, singlehanded, to apply this method to a whole

[1] E.g. H. Armstrong, *Turkey in Travail: the Birth of a New Nation* (1925); Edib Halide, *Turkey Faces West* (1930); H. E. Allen, *The Turkish Transformation* (1935); E. Jaeckh, *The Rising Crescent* (1944); I. Orga, *Phoenix Ascendant* (1958).

nation, whose population ranged from Paris-educated intellectuals to nomadic tribes and isolated, illiterate villages; from Muslim divines to agnostic engineering students; and which contained manifold ethnic and cultural varieties among even its rural and pastoral populations? Add to this problem that I had had a little over a year to learn anthropology, Turkish, and all I could about modern Turkey and the Ottoman and Islamic civilisations out of which it had grown. The task I faced when I set off for Turkey in 1949 appears almost laughable.

But in fact a possible solution was not difficult to find. The kind of research for which my brief anthropological training had fitted me was the study of a small and relatively close-knit community. At the same time, the greatest gap in our knowledge of Turkey was, and still is, how the villagers live. I therefore chose to study one village thoroughly and a somewhat different village in rather less detail.

Although it was not possible to choose a 'typical' village, because no such thing exists, it was at least possible to avoid choosing villages with obvious peculiarities. I set out to find an orthodox Muslim, Turkish-speaking village of modest size, fairly far away from the direct influence of the cities, on the plateau which forms the largest part of Anatolia. My final choice was unscientific. When the staff of an American school and clinic situated in the right kind of area, near Kayseri, generously offered to provide a base, and to help with some acute practical problems, my wife and I accepted with gratitude and enthusiasm.

I was in Sakaltutan from November 1949 to August 1950, my wife joining me in March. It had an excellent water supply, more or less regular lorries into Kayseri, and eleven other villages within an hour and a half's walk.

In 1951 we returned to the area. From August to November we lived in the second village, Elbaşı, some five hours' walk east of the first, and, in the summer vacation of 1952 I returned alone to this village for two months. I chose Elbaşı because it appeared to provide certain contrasts with Sakaltutan, being richer, more dependent on agriculture, more sophisticated, and less isolated. It was also the centre of the District, *Nahiye*. In fact, as it turned out, it was the similarities which were the more impressive.

The Ottoman Empire

The westernising revolution of Kemal Ataturk's Republic has its roots in the series of reforms and changes which are conventionally said to begin with the new model army, formed by Selim III (1789–1807), because of the serious defeats of Turkey at the hands of Russia in the wars of 1768–74 and 1788–92. Perhaps the most critical event was the defeat in 1826 of the Janissaries, the Sultan's unruly praetorian guard, by the new model army of Mahmud II (1808–39) (Lewis (1961), p. 77).[1]

During the nineteenth century, partly under the influence of the spontaneous spread of ideas through personal contact and study, partly under direct political pressure from the Western powers, the central government made periodic attempts to introduce Western political and social institutions by promulgating decrees which there was little or no machinery for implementing. The model, Western Europe, was itself in a state of violent and accelerating change. Concepts such as universal suffrage, education for all and equal rights for minorities, were developing in Europe spontaneously and indigenously, in a close relationship to the new technology, and to the new forms of society it rendered possible. These ideas, wrapped up with, and based on other older Western notions, such as secular legislation and secular justice, were to be applied from the top downwards, by order of a centralised authority, to a society whose social structure and morality were fundamentally different from those of Western Europe.

The central government, in the name of enlightenment, justice, liberty and efficiency, was forced into an unprecedented absolutism. Yet the imposed changes either caused unanticipated and complicated results far from the legislator's intentions, like the 1856 Land Registration Act, or else had little or no effect, like the 1878 Constitution. But it is pointless to discuss these attempts at reform in terms of rationality and success. They were the reactions of the ruling class to new social situations, and symptoms of profound social changes, the course of which they did no more than influence. The reactionary régime of Abdul Hamid from 1878 to 1908 did little to slow down these

[1] Lewis (1961) gives an excellent account of pre-Republican Turkey.

4

social changes, though it did inhibit both government reforms and overt radical opinion.

The splendid confusion of ideas held by the Committee of Union and Progress which combined to overthrow Abdul Hamid and ruled Turkey from 1908 until the end of World War I, embraced pan-Ottoman parliamentarianism, rights for minorities, pan-Islamism and pan-Turanianism,[1] together with a flavouring of Liberty, Equality, Fraternity and a practical admixture of Turkish nationalism and Prussian absolutism. The political unit to which these ideas were to be applied contained numerous violently nationalist minorities, Islamic as well as Christian, each as much against its neighbours as against the Turks, and in many cases so dispersed and mixed territorially that, once the system of the independent 'millet'[2] of the Ottoman Empire was abandoned, no satisfactory political substitute could be found. Moreover, the vast majority of the inhabitants on whom this hotchpotch of political and social ideas was to be imposed were illiterate peasants, many living in places inaccessible to wheeled transport, for whom government meant the tax collector and the drafting officer, both foreign and hostile meddlers with village life. Few of the minor officials who would be responsible for the detailed administration and application of the 'reforms' had any knowledge of the models on which they were founded, or any comprehension of the purposes they were intended to achieve.

The founders of the Republic, headed by the great figure of Mustafa Kemal, were the heirs of this confusion. Historical events had solved some of their problems and given them the means of solving others. The European Christian peoples and the Arabs were now entirely independent of them. The end of the political power of the Sultan and Caliph and the break-up of his dominions meant the end of any serious political pan-Islamism. Pan-Turanianism was pointless in face of the Russian

[1] A movement to unite politically all the Turkish-speaking peoples of Central Asia, then under Tsarist rule.

[2] Non-Islamic communities were outside Islamic law. They enjoyed some degree of political separateness and internal autonomy under their own religious leaders, albeit as second-class citizens. The criterion of membership in such a community was not place of residence, but religion. The word *millet* is now the standard word for nation.

Revolution and the relative weakness of Turkey. The agreement with Greece over the exchange of populations (1923) and the flight of most Armenians rid Turkey of any numerically significant non-Muslim minority. Nationalism became the driving principle of Ataturk's party, a nationalism directed at raising the prestige of Turkey by efficient Westernisation rather than by an attempt to recover the Empire. Confusions remained, for example between the glorification of everything Turkish, carried to the point of xenophobia, and an open admiration for the technical and social achievements of the West; or between an anti-religious secularism, and a pro-Islamic hostility to Christianity. Vast administrative and social problems also remained. The illiterate peasant majority was unconcerned with, or hostile to social reforms, and the minor local officials were ignorant of the purposes and functioning of Western institutions, and incapable of administering new laws and regulations based on them. Nevertheless, so many of the confusions and problems of the Young Turks had disappeared or been cleared away, that it was possible to tackle seriously the task of converting the new Republic into a modern national state on the Western model.

Ataturk, to use the surname he adopted later, had established himself as a military commander of outstanding ability during World War I. In 1919 he was sent to the Third Army in Anatolia, as Inspector-General, to supervise its disarmament on behalf of the Sultan's government. Five days before he landed at Samsun, in May, Greek troops, with British and American naval support, landed at Smyrna on the pretext of preserving order, but in fact for reasons of international jobbery. Ataturk at once set about organising nationalist opposition to the Sultan and the Allies. His Nationalist movement secured an official General Election at which it won a big majority. The elected Assembly, meeting first unofficially in Ankara, drew up a National Pact, (17th February 1920) (Toynbee (1923) pp. 207–10) demanding full sovereignty for a new State to include all territory of the Ottoman Empire not containing a majority of Christians or Arab-speaking Muslims, and the withdrawal of all foreign troops. They then went on to Istanbul to meet as Parliament, but their attitude was not sufficiently submissive, and the Allied authorities occupied Istanbul and arrested many

6

of them. Ataturk had with prescience stayed in Ankara. He at
once organised a new Assembly and an alternative government
– the first Turkish Grand National Assembly. In August 1920,
the Sultan's government signed the Treaty of Sèvres with the
Allies. This Treaty, which would have reduced Turkey to the
north-west corner of Anatolia, and divided the rest of her present territory between Greece, Italy, France and an independent Armenia, roused a fresh wave of nationalist fervour and
determination. By this time Turkish irregulars were engaging
Greek troops advancing eastwards from Smyrna. The war in-
tensified and became a fully organised campaign. After a
desperate defence during 1920 and 1921, the Nationalists,
strengthened by steadily improving organisation, by the departure of the French and Italians from Cilicia and Antalya
respectively, and by the support of the new Soviet government,
launched an offensive against the Greeks, who were growing
weaker as time passed, and drove them into the sea. An
armistice on Turkish terms was arranged in the autumn of 1922.
In October, the Ankara government declared the Sultanate at
an end and the last Sultan, Mohammet VI, fled in a British
warship. His son remained as the Caliph of Islam, shorn of
political powers. Ataturk's right-hand man, Ismet Pasa, later
to be called Inönü, in tough negotiations which lasted till 1923,
won practically all the points of the National Pact of February
1920.

On the 29th October 1923 Turkey was declared a Republic
with Ataturk as President. Only in the light of the power and
prestige which Ataturk acquired during these events can his
success in carrying through his staggering programme of
Westernisation be understood. The victory of the Turks over
the Greeks restored their morale. Indeed, the villagers today
do not think of the First World War as a defeat at the hands of
the Allies, but as a victory over the Greeks.

Republic and Reform

From October 1923 until the end of the Second World War
Turkey was a one-party state, virtually under the control of a
dictator. The organisation which began as a nationalist movement against the Allies in 1919, was re-christened the Republi-

can People's Party and became Ataturk's organ of control and propaganda. The most serious opposition at this time was from organised religion. In 1924 both the Caliphate and the Ministry of Şeriat (Islamic Law) and Evkaf (Pious Foundations) were abolished, and schools and law courts secularised. In the following year, the Kurds revolted under a Nakşibendi sheikh. The revolt was suppressed, but Ataturk took the opportunity to increase his hold over the state machinery. All dervish orders, which were widespread in Turkey, were made illegal, and their premises closed. To make clear to the people what he intended, Ataturk next decreed the abolition of the fez, currently the symbol of Muslim superiority over the infidel, and its replacement by infidel hats, henceforth to be the symbol of Turkey's identification with Western civilisation. This measure was imposed with firmness – in a few cases even ruthlessly. In 1926 the Ottoman codification of Islamic law, which was still in force for all personal matters, was replaced by a slightly emended translation of the Swiss Civil Code. At the same time the French-based Ottoman codes of commercial and penal law were also replaced by composite codes based mainly on German and Italian models. In 1928 the sacred Arabic alphabet was made illegal and replaced by a Latin script, which is in fact better adapted to the needs of the Turkish language. In the same year Islam ceased to be the established religion of Turkey. Nominally, in five years, the country had adopted an entirely new constitution, within a new set of frontiers; crushed the power of the vested interests in the established religion; separated Islam from the state; changed completely the system of law, and introduced a new way of writing.

Obviously, the implementation of the new institutions, which at first existed, not in people's behaviour, but merely on paper, was not a matter of overnight transformation, but of years of learning and adaptation. The process is still going on. But these were no passing gestures of transitory enthusiasts; the work that was done has remained.

The early reforms were socially fundamental, more so than anything that has followed. But westernising activities did not stop with the introduction of the new alphabet and legislation; they have continued up to date and are likely to persist. In order to explain what had happened, and to spread knowledge of the new ideas, the Republican People's Party launched, in 1932, a programme for establishing Party clubhouses, called People's Houses, in all townships of Turkey. These were intended as general adult education centres and for indoctrination in the new ideas. In many cases, minor Party branches were established in the villages, and up to 1950 nearly all village headmen and schoolmasters, and a good few others, declared themselves supporters of the R.P.P., but often without much knowledge of what this implied, beyond the fact that the Party was the Government.

It was not until the nineteen-thirties that a serious attempt to establish industry was made. A five-year plan was announced in 1934, to include sugar, cement, paper and textile factories, coal and metal mining, and a steel mill; and a further plan on similar lines was announced in 1938. The Second World War put a stop to these activities, but after the war, with foreign, largely American, aid, further ambitious plans for increasing industrial output, improving transport, and raising the productivity of agriculture were put into operation. Private capital played a relatively restricted part in development. Progress was slow. Official estimates show no significant rise in per capita national income from 1938 to 1948. (Istatistik Bülten No. 27, Ankara, May 1956, quoted in Robinson (1956) p. 178.)

It is difficult to state in figures the relative importance of agriculture and industry round about 1950. Some eighty per cent of the population worked in farming, forestry or fishing. (International Bank Report (1951) p. 16.) Official figures show agriculture as producing almost exactly half the national domestic income, (Istatistik Bülten No. 27, Ankara, May 1956, quoted in Robinson (1956) p. 178), but very probably they make no allowance, or an inadequate allowance, for the large amount of agricultural produce consumed on the spot by its producers without ever reaching the market. Moreover, part of the national income not attributed to agriculture is directly concerned with buying, selling or transporting agricultural products or in some sense serving agriculture. From 1927 to 1955 (Turkey: Census 1955, p. XLIV), within two or three per cent, three-quarters of the population lived in villages; besides these, many of the small places classified as towns are large villages; and even the major towns like Kayseri have large farming minorities. Thus undoubtedly agriculture is by far the most common occupation and by far the most important source of income. It is true that in the area in which I worked – and without doubt in many other parts of Turkey too – some villages exported non-agricultural migrant labour in order to supplement an agricultural income insufficient to maintain the village population. But this phenomenon is not large enough substantially to qualify what I have just said.

At least among the educated city-dwellers, Turkey has developed more than a superficial respect for a Western type of one citizen – one vote elected parliamentary democracy, with guaranteed civil and political rights. From the beginning the Party firmly declared its belief in liberty and the rule of law. Such professions may seem to go ill with a one-party system and the absolute, and at times arbitrary, rule of Ataturk. But he made a great point of separating military and civil office, and established a truly independent judiciary. In form at least, the constitution was democratic; a single assembly was elected by universal suffrage, and in turn elected the President, who chose the Prime Minister, and approved the appointment of other ministers. The President could be overruled by the majority of the Assembly. 'All citizens are endowed at birth with liberty', and all the usual rights – freedom of speech, freedom of the press, freedom to travel, and so on – were listed.[1]

After Ataturk's death in 1937, Inönü took his place as President. An attempt in 1931 to found a loyal opposition party had been abandoned. In 1945 permission was again given for the foundation of other political parties, and among others the Democrat Party was founded, mainly by defection from the R.P.P. (Karfat (1959) Chap. 5). In the election of 1946 it gained only some sixty seats out of about four hundred and eighty. But the Democrat Party set to work to build up an organisation, and to campaign for reform of the electoral law. This reform was carried out, and the election which I witnessed in 1950 was fair and satisfactory to all parties. The R.P.P. was defeated, and handed over power to the Democrat Party after twenty-five years of rule. It seemed that a two-party system had been established over-night.

[1] The constitution was abolished after the *coup d'état* in 1960. The new one is more complex but, in theory, at least equally liberal, and safer.

The new government deliberately set out to please the villagers, partly by a more tolerant treatment of religion, partly by a more friendly attitude on the part of its officials towards villagers, and partly by reducing taxation (p. 75). Economic expansion, pursued by inflation, brought a sharp increase in village earning power, and the party won an even greater victory in 1954. But the Government had begun to hamper the opposition and even to interfere with the judiciary. Economic and political troubles increased, and the party's ten years of rule was ended by the 1960 *coup d'état*. The army claimed that it had intervened in the defence of genuine democratic rule by representative government, and the military junta revised the constitution, conducted elections and handed over to a civilian government in October 1961. Yet the political situation continued to be uneasy.

Government

Turkey is divided into provinces or vilayets, numbering sixty-three in 1950, each under a vali, appointed by the central government. Each province is divided into smaller areas (sing. *kaza*) varying from four to sixteen or so per province, centering on towns, and each under a centrally appointed kaymakam who nowadays must be a university graduate. The *kaza* is divided again into districts called *nahiye*, containing a number of villages, sometimes as many as twenty, under a *nahiye müdürü*, a townsman who should be a high school graduate and is appointed by the vali.

The vilayet has an elected assembly, of which the vali is ex-officio chairman, and which has certain limited powers and local duties. But, except for the law courts, practically all matters are under the control of the vali, who has an impressive array of officers under him – finance, education, agriculture, public works, security – though many departments are responsible also to their own chiefs in Ankara. His officers also directly administer the central *kaza* which surrounds the main town of the vilayet. The other *kazas*, each under its own kaymakam, have a much smaller number of officials. The number of *kazas* to a vilayet varies – in Kayseri, it was six.

The district officer or *nahiye müdürü* has no one to assist him

11

save a sergeant or corporal of gendarmes. The rural areas are policed by a corps of gendarmes, which is part of the army permanently seconded for this purpose. The NCOs are regulars, but the men are conscripts, villagers like the people they police. Very often the district officer is posted to a village where he is without the company of any of his own social class. Kaymakams and valis form a branch of the service of the Ministry of the Interior, but the majority of district officers are casual government employees who vary greatly in quality, and who have no hope of promotion to the next grade in the service.

The village, the smallest recognised political entity, chooses its own headman and council of elders. The relationship between the villager who is acting as headman, and the urban-bred district officer who is his immediate superior, is the critical point in the rural administrative system – it reflects the break between the educated and largely Europeanised townspeople and the still largely illiterate and traditional peasantry.

Towns, among which are classed many small entirely village-like district centres, have an elected mayor and council, under the supervision of the vali or kaymakam as the case may be. Town wards have headmen, but these are far less important than the village headman, most of the work being done by the mayor.

Government is highly centralised. Officials are appointed or at least approved by Ankara, and most major matters, for example, disputes between a vali and his elected council, must be referred back to the capital. Initiative, in fact, still comes mainly from the top downwards. What is not expressly permitted is generally assumed to be forbidden. Even in the judicial system disputes of importance before civil courts have to be referred for decision on documentary evidence to Ankara.

Between attempting to carry out orders which pour from above, and dealing with matters which well up from below, senior officials tend to be extremely busy. Most doors, even the vali's, are permanently open, and no one works on a strict timetable or a system of appointments. Relatively little business is done by letter. The office of a vali, kaymakam or senior official is liable to be full of people from his immediate juniors in the hierarchy to patient embarrassed villagers, all trying to catch the great man's attention to extract a decision, a signature or a favour. The whole system gives the impression of being highly hit and miss, of decisions taken *ad hoc;* a system in which the word of one having authority counts far more than written laws and regulations, and in which getting things done depends on influence or on making a tactful nuisance of oneself in person.

Efficiency commonly declines with distance from – or rather with difficulty of communication with – the centre. Such a decline is inevitable, the more so with a highly personal and *ad hoc* system. Moreover, all officials hate rural isolation and scheme for transfer to greater comfort and urbanity. If we may assume some correlation between success and efficiency, then on average the more remote the post the less efficient the incumbent, from valis down to village schoolmasters.

The dependence on personal authority and the decreasing efficiency as one moves away from contact with the bright lights mitigate against the effects of a highly centralised system. The more foolish or tactless rules and regulations promulgated by the centre may be unknown, and if known safely ignored, by dozens of local officials and local communities. Indeed, it is surely this built-in inefficiency, which was greater in the nineteen-twenties, that saved the revolutionary reforms of Ataturk from provoking effective opposition. People did not know, or did not understand, or did not care what the central government was doing.

CHAPTER TWO

THE SETTING

Kayseri and the Two Villages

Turkey is almost all mountains. From the Aegean coast the land rises rapidly to about three thousand feet (1,000 m), and thence the bumpy, arid plateau stretches eastward for some five hundred miles till it merges into the eastern mountain ranges. High mountains guard the northern and southern coasts, stealing the rain before it reaches the plateau. The rain that does penetrate falls unevenly, sometimes in cloudbursts which destroy standing crops and wash away top soil. Capricious weather often undoes the farmer's work, and disappointing harvests are frequent. Summers are hot and dry, winters intensely cold, with snow sometimes lying up to three months. As one goes east, this tough climate grows tougher.

Kayseri lies in the centre of Turkey, in one of the large plains sunk in the plateau. It had been and still was in 1950 a central point in Turkey's transport system, since the main railway and roads[1] from Istanbul and Ankara to both east and south ran through or very close to it. Besides its commercial, agricultural and administrative importance, Kayseri had in 1949 the largest textile mill in Turkey, built in 1935 with Russian help under the first five-year plan. In 1950 it had a population of 65,000 (Ann. Stat. 1951).

Immediately south of the town, the land rises towards the solitary, volcanic peak of Erciyas, 12,860 feet high, but otherwise the country is typical plateau in all directions. The broad valley in which Kayseri lies runs north-east from the town, carrying the main road and railway to Sivas and the east. This

[1] The new roads which now link Ankara with eastern Turkey and with Adana do not pass through Kayseri.

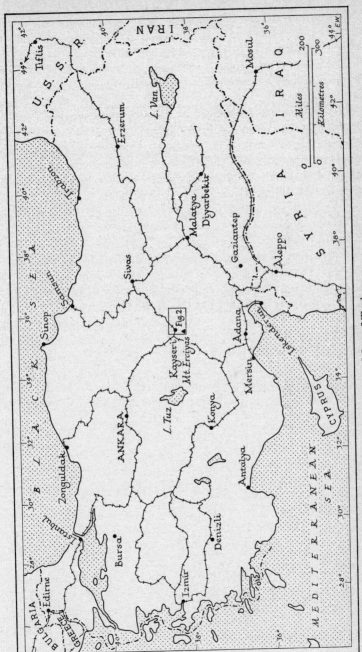

1 Map of Turkey

valley is bordered to the south by an escarpment, along which nestle a number of relatively accessible and prosperous villages. The most southerly of these, only five miles from the town, is Talas, *nahiye* centre under the central *kaza* of Kayseri province. Talas is mainly an agricultural village, but also partly a dormitory suburb of the city and partly a centre of the motor transport business. Its former large Christian population drew a flourishing American Protestant mission centre to the village in the nineteenth century. Forbidden by law to proselytise, and much reduced in scale, the mission now runs a boarding school for Turkish boys and a medical clinic for the local people, especially the villagers.

Sakaltutan is fourteen miles farther east, the last village of the Talas *nahiye*. Only two years before our arrival, a rough village road had been made just passable for motor traffic, joining Tomarza, the next *nahiye* centre out, in the *kaza* of Develi, to Kayseri. Passing through the village to the north of Talas[1] this road climbed across steep valleys and sharp hills as far as Sakaltutan, which lay at the foot of the slopes rising towards Erciyas, at about 5,500 feet, some twenty miles from Kayseri. Thence the road swung south-east round the base of the mountains and slowly fell towards Tomarza.

Another fork of the road, also just passable for lorries, branched off at Sakaltutan and ran slightly north of east, down into a wide valley, through three or four villages until it reached Elbaşı, the next *nahiye* centre, at about 4,000 feet, and only about four miles from an alternative main road from Kayseri, through Bünyan to Pınarbaşı. Elbaşı was attached administratively to Bünyan, about fifteen miles away, and over forty miles by the main road from Kayseri. In village terms, Kayseri to Sakaltutan was six hours, Talas to Sakaltutan four or five hours, and Sakaltutan to Elbaşı four or five hours. Although the lorries and the new roads had rendered this way of measuring distances obsolescent, it was still the normal way of talking about distances.

Sakaltutan was of medium size—about one hundred households and just over six hundred people. Elbaşı was well above the village average for the area, with over two hundred house-

---

[1] In 1952 this road was rebuilt to run through Talas itself.

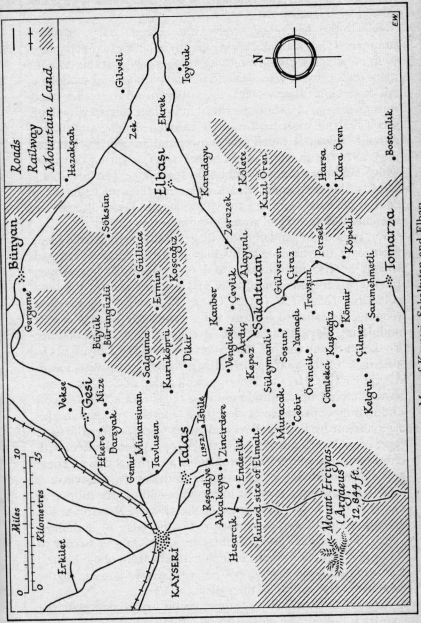

2 Map of Kayseri, Sakaltutan and Elbaşı

gives an easily worked rock for cave-making. Willows and straight poplars, so common in the villages of central Turkey, grow along the stream in considerable numbers and give it the distant appearance of a green oasis in a treeless waste.

The disorderly array of flat-roofed and irregular houses in local stone give the villages a half tumble-down appearance. This impression is not altogether false. Much new building is in progress, and many older houses have been abandoned, and their valuable roof timbers removed. On closer inspection, most of the houses are occupied and solidly built. The streets are haphazard – people have built as and where they chose. In both villages, and especially in Elbaşı, many of the new houses are well away from the village centre, and some of them have their own wells, being too far from the village fountains.

The village mosques were in neither case remarkable. They looked from the outside like larger versions of village houses, except that an outside staircase ran up to roof level, ending in a platform covered by a small pinnacle which constituted the minaret. Inside, the floor was covered with rugs, where the faithful came shoeless to perform their ritual prayers or to listen to the Holy Koran.

Many villages now have one red-roofed school building, conspicuous with its new white walls. But Sakaltutan had not achieved this distinction; its school building was a stone, flat-roofed building, two unused rooms of which became my home.

Elbaşı, by contrast, had four public buildings; an old flat-roofed stone school dating from the nineteen-twenties, a new red-roofed school, a house, not occupied, for a village health officer (*Sıhhat Memürü*) and an older tin-roofed building which acted as headquarters for the *nahiye*, and housed four gendarmes and a sergeant.

Village Houses

The stone houses vary in size and layout, depending mainly on the size of the household and its wealth. One or two families in Sakaltutan still lived in caves. One cave had been newly made for a young couple. Caves, after all, are not only cheaper, but better insulated against heat and cold, do not leak in heavy rain – most flat-roofed houses do – and require no upkeep. The earlier inhabitants of the village probably lived in caves or houses with their animals at one end and themselves at the other, but only one or two households still had this arrangement. Most houses have caves behind or below the house, where animals are kept, and straw for winter feed is stored. These often have clear signs of previous habitation.

Every village home has a main living-room, called in this area *ev*, the normal Turkish word for house. In this room is the fireplace, a beehive-shaped oven called *tandır*, let into the mud floor, supplied with draught by a built-in pipe. The opening at the top is at floor level, and normally covered with a large flat stone – a deadly trap for babies if this stone is inadvertently left off. The ovens provide for warmth and cooking, burning dried cakes of cattle dung mixed with straw, which will smoulder for hours. When the *tandır* is first lit in the morning the room is filled with dense acrid smoke and everyone crawls, or walks around bent double, until it has cleared through the hole provided in the roof.

The *ev* is the scene of all household activities. Here are shelves of earthenware vessels and tinned copper pots and pans. Great wooden chests store the family supply of grain and flour. An upright loom serves for the women to weave woollen rugs, saddle bags and grain sacks. Round the oven, when guests call or the women have time to sit, are spread mats and rugs and cushions. Rolls of bedding – mattresses, quilts and pillows – stand in a neat pile, or sometimes in a special recess.

This room is the province of the wife of the household head, where she sleeps with her husband and at least her younger children. Her own chest, which came with her when she married, holds her own and usually her husband's personal possessions, safely under lock and key. No man enters the *ev* of a household other than his own unless he is very close kin – even a first cousin of one of the couple might hesitate – unless he has very special business, when he will knock and call out to give warning.

Almost all homes have more than this one room. Most are entered through a high-walled courtyard, and off this or behind the *ev* are a stable, a cave or building that acts as a barn, and possibly other storage rooms. A second *tandır* is normally placed somewhere out of doors, but sheltered from direct rain. Junior married couples should and normally do have their own room where they sleep with their children, and keep their personal possessions.

The wealthier homes, and some of the less wealthy, have also a special room for the men of the household, where they sit in the evenings, brew coffee or tea if they can afford it, and entertain neighbours and guests. These rooms are much more luxuriously furnished. They invariably have a built-in *sedir*, a divan which runs right round the walls, or in the older design, run like tramlines facing each other along one side of the room. Originally these rooms were heated by open hearths, but in the last ten or fifteen years these had been ousted by small sheet-iron stoves. The divans are covered with rugs, carpets and cushions. The floors are usually of stone, or even wood, and the windows are large, by village standards. The few really large rooms of this type in each village are used for weddings and other large-scale entertainments, and are often approached by a small ante-room in which coffee is made on important occasions. The villagers call these 'guest rooms' *misafir odası* (sing.) or more simply just *oda* (room). These are in fact much more than guest rooms. But since they correspond roughly to similar rooms – or tents – in other Middle East societies, which are usually called 'guest rooms', it is perhaps best to use this term. In contrast to the main living room, (*ev*), the guest room (*oda*) belongs to the men and should preferably stand apart from the rest of the home, or have a separate entrance, so that male visitors see nothing of the home at all.

Village History

Sakaltutan is not an old village. On the meadow is a tomb or *türbeh*, said by the villagers to be that of a Muslim commander named Mehmet Miktat, killed in a battle with Byzantine forces. There is another small burial ground said to contain the bodies of martyrs who died in this battle. Some marks on rocks in another part of the village were said by the present inhabitants to be tombs left by a previous Christian village on the site.

The present village was probably founded by people from villages nearer Kayseri, who had first made a temporary summer camp there for pasture, and later decided to settle permanently and plough. All the villagers could tell me was that four brothers founded the village, though no one could give their names or genealogical link with the present inhabitants. The longest genealogies were six generations above elderly living men. Assuming that the first man named was, as they claimed, born in the village, and that a generation averages about twenty-five years, this would take us back over two hundred years without arriving at the original four brothers. The local sergeant of gendarmes commented that Sakaltutan was not an old village, and guessed two hundred years – which may not be far out.

Elbaşı is undoubtedly much older. Again, no one knew much about village history. One village story of an imperial visit implied its existence in the reign of 'Murad Padishah', presumably Murad IV, who reigned from 1623 to 1640. In recent times, it has been an administrative centre, and several recent ancestors of village households were said to have held the office of local müdür. It certainly has a good deal more land than most other villages in the area.

In both villages, the population has apparently expanded rapidly in the last generation and is still increasing. Sakaltutan, now just over one hundred households, is remembered by old men when it was only sixty households, and a middle-aged man in Elbaşı spoke of a population of four hundred and fifty in his childhood, whereas it now has about twelve hundred. In Sakaltutan, this increase was natural. The three most recent male immigrants were two old men and a middle-aged man, all of whom had been brought to the village as children by widowed mothers. Apart from similar cases of casual immigration through some kinship connection, Elbaşı had eighteen refugee households descended from war refugees from Eastern Anatolia, who had failed to return home in 1877 and 1915, following the Russian invasions. But in general the male population of both villages was remarkably stable, many men having their houses on the ancestral site, and almost all in the ancestral village.

Education and Urbanity

Although, weather permitting, three or four lorries on their way to Kayseri ran through Sakaltutan every day, it was still

23

in 1950 a remote village. It had no telephone, and in the winter was often snowed up for two months or so. The winter of 1949 to 1950 was severe and no lorries passed from the end of December to the end of March. Elbaşı, close to a metalled road, with no hills close by, was cut off only for a few days at a time.

Sakaltutan was still completely a village. During my stay, no one had had more than three years of the most elementary type of elementary schooling (p. 275). Some of the older men could read the old script, and many of the younger ones could read the new Latin script. Plenty of people had been away to live in towns for months, even years at a time, and three villagers had been on the pilgrimage to Mecca. But they remained villagers, whose central interest was the village. Even Ahmet (K) the schoolmaster had been born and bred in the village. Following his military service, he had been given a few months' training under a special government scheme. He enrolled a fresh class of mixed age every three years, so that he only had one class at a time. His last class before he was replaced in 1951 by a young, trained, schoolmaster (p. 275), included a few girls. Only one woman in the village was literate.

Elbaşı was more sophisticated. Quite a number of its in-habitants could read, including a few women. It contained a local tax collector, whose two sons were officers during their military service, an inspector of village schools who had con-siderable knowledge of the world, and one man who worked in the Kayseri central offices; and it had produced about six village schoolmasters trained in the Village Institutes (p. 275f.), three of whom taught in the village. It is also said to have pro-duced its own local District officers and other local officials in the past. One man, Kara Osman (Ax), whom I met when I was still in Sakaltutan, was of great wealth and power. He is said to have been a friend of Ataturk and to have held the whole area 'in his hand'. I never questioned him closely, for he died just before I began work in Elbaşı. But presumably he had been the local ruler – officially or otherwise – during the disturbed days of the early twenties.

Elbaşı's greater wealth, education and outside contact seemed to make surprisingly little difference to the way of life of the majority of its population, and the two villages were for the most part remarkably alike.

Typicality

One comment on my work which I hear from all directions is that I cannot generalise from these villages since I have no way of knowing whether they are typical. This objection would hardly deserve a reply were it not so frequently stated. In the first place, I do of course know from visiting, travelling and reading that they are typical in almost all respects of the area in which I worked, and in many if fewer respects of most Turkish villages.

But the whole implication of this objection is mistaken. I have not set out to make general statements about all Turkish villages and do not pretend to. The anthropologist, by his detailed field work in one community, is able, explicitly or otherwise, to offer a model of social structure of this community. The chosen community cannot possibly be 'typical', because there is no such thing. But the model is bound to throw light on other similar communities, either because the model fits and enlightens, or because the points at which it does not fit, in so far as they are not explicable by elementary common sense, suggest new problems. Of course, had I been five people (or twenty-five, for that matter), capable of working in five sharply different villages simultaneously, the study would have been more informative. But I am only myself.

CHAPTER THREE

VILLAGES AND HOUSEHOLDS

A Summary of the Social Structure

One major problem in giving or following any ethnographic description is the order of presentation, since an adequate understanding of any one institution presumes a knowledge of other institutions in the same society. I hope I have overcome this difficulty by offering my summary here instead of at the end.

The village itself is the most striking social group. No village forms part of any larger indigenous organisation. All the villages in the area, and indeed in most of Turkey, are self-contained clusters of buildings, separated from each other by stretches of unfenced land. To walk from one to the next may take half an hour to two or more hours. There were two villages within half an hour of Sakaltutan, and another nine within one and a half hours.

Each village is composed of distinct patrilineal, patrilocal households. Although several households often occupy one block of buildings, the physical and social boundaries between them are never vague. Village and household are the main social units. Newly married women apart, everyone must belong at one time to one and only one village, and to one and only one household.

Every village is divided into a number of quarters or wards (*mahalle*). These have no clear boundaries and are not corporate. People acknowledge loyalty to their quarters, and may speak of fights in the village as fights between quarters. Because close neighbours often intermarry, and close agnates and sometimes other close kin live near each other, these quarters often have some kinship unity as well. In Elbaşı, several quarters were actually called after lineages. Close neighbours, whether kin or not, will tend to form informal groups for recreation and conversation

Last of the important groups in the village is the lineage. This group consists of a number of households, the heads of which are descended patrilineally i.e., strictly through males only, from a common ancestor generally three or four generations back. These households normally form local clusters. The rights and duties of membership are not precisely defined, and the degree to which members are committed varies greatly between individuals. The main function of the lineage is the protection of members from aggression by supporting them in quarrels. Yet not all household heads are members of lineages, nor do all lineages that could be defined genealogically constitute significant social groups. Most of those who are not committed lineage members are among the poorer and less powerful stratum of village society.

Apart from membership of these groups, a person's position in the network of interpersonal relationships is mainly determined by the obvious factors—sex and age, kinship, occupation and wealth; and to a lesser degree by piety and learning, by personal honour, and for a man, by the range and strength of his urban contacts.

The sexual distinction is, as one would expect in an Islamic society, strongly emphasised, and for most normal social life the sexes are sharply segregated. Age is not a criterion for any formal groups, but it carries respect and authority.

Kinship relations are both the most intimate and intense and the commonest type of social relations. The personal kin ties of men through men form the core of the lineage groups. Extra lineage kin ties form strong and numerous relationships between both households and individuals. This kinship network extends from village to village and provides vital channels for all sorts of activities – economic, political, religious – and for the arranging of marriages which will in turn forge new kin ties.

Distinctions of wealth are not conspicuous. All households in both villages appear at first sight to live in much the same way. All who can, work. There are no permanent rentier households, though one or two elderly men are supported largely by their sons, womenfolk and share-croppers. The wealthiest and most urbanised households have a comfortable sufficiency, while the

27

2*

poor are badly housed and clothed, and underfed in all but good years. But though differences in wealth are not conspicuous in the way of life, they are of great social importance. The rich are the leaders of the village; they receive deference, carry weight in village counsels, employ their neighbours, and are able, by gifts and loans, to exercise influence and even direct control, especially among their own kin.

Religious learning carries high prestige in the villages. Many village boys receive some kind of special religious training either informally from kinsmen, or from special schools in the towns. A few of these may become village imams; others live a normal agricultural life, but with a special reputation for learning and piety. How far a man succeeds in exploiting this prestige for gaining power and wealth seems to depend on personality and circumstances.

Other non-agricultural occupations and skills are structurally of minor importance. Most specialists are part-time, owning or at least wishing to own land; there are no social groups based on occupations such as the castes of Indian society, nor are craftsmen treated as outsiders.

Urban contacts have probably always conferred great influence and prestige in the villages, chiefly, of course, because they imply influence with officials, an influence often overestimated by villagers. Traditionally, it is likely that the main channels for social promotion lay through the official religious hierarchy. Nowadays, in a village like Elbaşı, and even in many poorer ones, people have sons, brothers or affines who are traders or officials, sometimes of fairly high standing, in the urban world. These links give great prestige in the village. Where they exist in numbers as in Elbaşı, they seem to be leading to the beginnings of a class structure in the village.

But only the merest beginnings. Village society seems in the past to have had a highly mobile ranking system, with a marked absence of inherited rank. In every generation, each household split, dividing its land at least among the sons, sometimes among both sons and daughters. The richer a man, the more wives and therefore the more heirs he would be likely to have, so that in general there was a tendency for each young married man to find himself on his father's death with a fairly modest amount of land, and thus bound to start building up afresh on his own account. In a situation so open, one would expect that occasionally a particular man by skill and luck would establish considerable personal pre-eminence, and stories about the great villagers of the past are current in most villages. But it seems equally true that the successful men did not found dynasties. Their sons normally began again with, at the most, a short lead over rivals.

Village Solidarity

People belong to their village in a way they belong to no other social group. On any definition of community, the village is a community – a social group with many functions, not all of them explicit, and to which people are committed by birth or marriage, and bound by many ties.

None of the geographical or administrative units larger than a village is in any way comparable. The villagers do, of course, see themselves as belonging to a vaguely defined district, and to the Province of Kayseri. Men in the army or working away in the cities often form friendships and groups along the lines of locality of origin, but the actual units of administration, *nahiye*, *kaza* and vilayet as such have no social relevance outside their administrative functions.

The virtues of the village are an eternal topic of conversation with outsiders, and of banter between men of different villages. Every village has the best drinking water, and the best climate. One village, which stored winter snow in large deep wells, and drank all through the summer the stagnant water which resulted, pleaded the superiority of their water as an argument for my moving in at once. Every village is more hospitable, more honourable, more virile, more peaceable, gives better weddings, than any of its neighbours. Other villages are savage, mean, dishonourable, lying, lazy, cowardly. Neither Sakaltutan nor Elbaşı found my choice of themselves surprising, but everyone else found it quite incredible.

Each village possesses a territory, recognised by the State as its administrative area, over which it exercises *de facto* pasture rights. Villages normally own common land, and sometimes meadow or crop land which can be let; but in the Civil Code it has no rights to land within its territory owned by individuals, and unoccupied land belongs to the State.

For the village, this territory is much more than an administrative area, – it is a symbol of village identity (de Planhol (1958) p. 340). If any other village attempts to use land lying within the village boundaries, people mobilise rapidly and are quite prepared to fight, with fire-arms if necessary. Even incursions by other villages' flocks or herds cause at the very least militant indignation. On one occasion, Sakaltutan animals crossed the frontier to Süleymanli, and the Süleymanli headman who happened to be passing on a horse, struck the shepherd in charge with his whip. Many Sakaltutan men talked of immediate armed attack. However, they were restrained by wiser counsel. I never witnessed mobilisation of this kind, but it is clear that all members are expected to defend the village regardless of the quarrels which constantly divide them. Not even lineages cross village frontiers, so that the village from the outside presents a solid front of loyalty. Its members are ready at all times to defend both its reputation and its territories.

This outward solidarity is matched by what one might call internal intensity. Village populations are highly stable. Almost all men and more than half the adult women in a village were born there. If we could measure the intensity of social relationships in terms of emotional strength, of the number of rights and duties involved, and of the frequency of contact, we would find that all residents except the more newly arrived wives had their more intense social relationships almost exclusively inside the village. Of course, many indispensable and controlling economic and political relationships lie outside, but these are not intense in the same way. Even beyond their own immediate circle, all the villagers belong to one another. Even enemies inside the village are intimate enemies.

Village Organisation

Since the village is a community – a group with a multitude of functions and involvements for its members – it is not surprising that a number of offices and corporate rights and duties are attached to it. Roughly, these are of two kinds, the formal institutions laid down by the State, and the informal institutions run by the village for its own purposes to meet the actual needs of its members.

The actual power relations within the village, and the relations between State and village will be analysed later (Chapters 11 and 12). Here I only set out the organisation of the village.

Administratively and legally, the village is ruled by a head-man, elected every four years up to 1950, now every two, nominally by secret ballot; all persons over eighteen can vote. He is expected to receive all public visitors, especially officials; to help keep order and bring criminals to justice; to take care of public property – for example the school; to draw up electoral lists; to countersign all official applications for government seed, bank loans and such; to see to the registration of births, deaths and marriages; to report the arrival of strangers, the occurrence of epidemics, and other untoward events, and so on. He is in short the agent, guarantor and communication channel for all village business with government. This post is not sought after.

The council of elders is elected with the headman, and its size depends on the number of the inhabitants. Sakaltutan had four councillors, Elbaşı six. Each council is covered by a like number of reserves, also elected, who take the place of the full members if they are unable to attend meetings. The elder who receives most votes in the election is automatically deputy head-man, and so on down the list. The council is supposed to meet at least every month and to discuss all village business.

It would be rash to state that these councils never meet. The council in Sakaltutan did not meet during my stay, and the only function attributed to it by villagers was the supervision of the assessment of contributions to the village chest. People said the Elbaşı council did meet, but it did not do so regularly, and it did not to my knowledge supervise assessment. Certainly the councils did not function as the main decision-making body of the villages. No one took the slightest interest in their election, or attached any importance to their activities. Instead, when something called for corporate action in a matter which the villagers considered important, the senior heads of households and lineage segments assembled either spontaneously, or on the initiative of any leading villager with sufficient prestige. Such a meeting has no formal standing, no constitution, no procedures, and no responsibilities. It can only occur if the matter is im-portant enough to draw together important people. It serves as a means of thrashing out public issues, and letting the headman know what people think, but the interpretation of what is said and the tactical assessment of what is possible and desirable remains in his hands.

Every village is compelled by law to levy a local tax, *Köy Salması*, and to raise a fund, the Village Chest, *Köy Sandığı*. Out of this, the headman draws a small allowance for entertaining visitors, and meets other expenses, such as keeping school equipment and other village property in order, and clothing and sometimes paying the village watchman. The village households are divided into four tax assessment classes. This assessment is mainly based on the amount of land held, but other circumstances – the number of animals owned, the number of grown working men, and the number of mouths to feed – are also taken into account. The poorest households are excluded altogether.

In Sakaltutan the assessments of the four classes were T.L.15, T.L.12, T.L.8 and T.L.5 per annum respectively, in Elbaşı T.L.15, T.L.11, T.L.7 and T.L.4. This fund is the only officially imposed institution which arouses real interest, and, with the offices of headman and watchman, comprises the only area of genuine overlap between village institutions and State-imposed ones. It is the subject of continual argument and accusation, and very difficult to collect. In 1953, many headmen were still not literate, so that even those who wished could hardly keep adequate records. Accusations of eating the village chest are therefore inevitable, universal, impossible to disprove, but undoubtedly wildly exaggerated, and probably often unfounded.

Villagers claimed that even if the council of elders did nothing else, at least it met to assess the contributions to the chest. Obviously, where the assessing authority, the headman, is a neighbour of no particular eminence or authority except for his temporary office, individuals who feel over-assessed are likely to argue, and any obvious anomaly will arouse jealousy and protest. But I have a strong impression that once established the assessment was changed little from year to year, and that changes were normally left to the headman. In general, the headman consults members of the elected council if they are friends of his, if they can actively assist him, or if they represent sections of the village capable of making trouble if not consulted.

But very much the same applies to any leading villagers, whether council members or not.

In almost all cases I came across, headman and elders were young or middle-aged men. Senior and outstanding men did not hold office themselves, though very often their sons and younger brothers might.

All villagers must also by law appoint a watchman, a *bekci*; he is a sort of policeman, supposed to act under the orders of the headman. He is also expected by the authorities to act as a messenger, and is continually going back and forth between the District Office and his village. He is chosen by the headman, for a year at a time, on so lowly a salary (T.L. 300–100, £37 10. downwards, in 1949–52) that only the poorest and most incompetent villagers will normally take on the office. The watchman in most villages acts as a servant to the headman, and is often to be found making his coffee, running his errands or even chopping his wood. The Sakaltutan watchman collected his dues in kind himself, household by household.

Apart from this legally required set of institutions, every village has a number of its own officers and servants to meet the needs of a farming community, mostly herdsmen. Two or more special watchmen are usually appointed to guard the harvest for the village as a whole. These are expected to, and do, run foul of the herders, whose animals frequently maraud the standing crops. Elbaşı also appointed two men to supervise the allocation of water during the months of June and July when demand is high and supplies are low.

Most of these are chosen by village elders, among whom the current headman has the most say. But the shepherds are appointed by leading sheep-owners. All are paid directly in cash or kind, household by household (pp. 58ff.).

The village is then a corporation, with both official and unofficial servants, and an official and in a sense an unofficial income. The state-imposed general village fund is clearly alien, and so far the traditional arrangements for traditional village servants have not been brought into the new scheme. The traditional method has the advantages that village servants are responsible for collecting their own dues, and that people pay in proportion to their use of the services.

People still regard themselves as dependent politically on the village for defence against other villages, although the vastly increased efficiency of the national maintenance of order has largely rendered this dependence obsolete. But if political dependence is minimal, economic dependence on the village is still very real. Shepherds and watchmen and common pastures are indispensable. Refusal to allow a man to use them would cripple him. Moreover, the annual switch from one side of the village territory to the other ties all the villagers to the alternate year of fallow (p. 48). The introduction for example, of a revolutionary crop cycle is impossible without disrupting the whole village farming system. Meanwhile, the legal freehold of land is subject to the *de facto* common right of the village to pasture flocks and herds on it every other year.

Other Villages

Loyalty to the superiority of one's own village did not prevent the existence of a rough hierarchy of prestige among the villages of the area. This scale was not openly discussed, but was expressed in discussions of marriage, in the respect in the area accorded to the leaders of certain villages, and in the consensus of scorn for some of the poorer and remoter villages. The evaluation is not consistent, nor does it follow a single and simply applied standard. Perhaps the most commonly expressed pair of ideas, or rather those which command most general assent, are *medeni*, 'civilised', on the one hand, and *kaba*, 'coarse', or *vaksi*, 'wild', on the other. *Medeni* implies good order, urban manners and style of living, and the absence of violence. It is sufficiently vague to allow people systematically to avoid admitting inferiority in specific cases. Yet in general the villagers often bewail their backwardness and lack of *medeniyet*.

Villages with a tradition as administrative centres, with greater wealth, and which had possessed distinguished men with urban influence, ranked higher on this scale. The differences between villages were particularly related to the treatment of women. More 'civilised' people keep their women more closely confined and give them less work, especially less agricultural work. Where the differences were marked, decent families would not consider letting a daughter go to a less civilised village. For example, women from the villages nearer

Kayseri spoke of the Sakaltutan area as *köy* 'village' and would not consider going among such people as wives. Differences in standards of formal politeness among the women of different villages were readily noticeable. Of course, every community has a lowest stratum including the very poor and girls whose reputations had suffered, and these might be given to inferior villages.

Differences of prestige among neighbouring villages did not prevent a great deal of social intercourse. People visit, hire craftsmen, seek advice on religious or technical problems, commission magical services, borrow money or food, search for oxen to buy, buy up animals for market, take grain to be milled. In the past, before the petrol engine, longer journeys, especially journeys to town, compelled the traveller to put up for the night with kinsmen or friends on the road. Now people congregate in the villages which serve as boarding points for lorries and buses to Kayseri, gossiping and often visiting as they pass through. The villages are too similar in production for intense economic exchange between them, but social contact is nevertheless constant and lively.

Beyond the occasional conflict over territory, and some traditional enmities, political relations between villages as groups are unimportant. In this area, all the villages were sunni and Turkish-speaking, so that the issue of ethnic or language differences did not arise. No one village nowadays has the slightest hope of dominating others, whatever may have been the case in the past. Fighting is rapidly suppressed by the gendarmerie. Feuds did not seem ever to be pursued between whole villages.

Household Types and Numbers

The villagers say that a house, *ev* or *hane*, is a group of people whose food is cooked in common. Common cooking implies a sharing of resources produced or earned by the members, that is an economic unity.

The villagers are right. This economic unity is the most fundamental fact about a household. Only through membership of a household does an individual take part in the economic life of the village. Otherwise survival is possible only by begging.

Yet this economic emphasis is perhaps misleading. Membership of a household is also a condition of social recognition as a member of the village. Only one or two old widows living alone are not members of households, yet even they are relics of past households; they are able to survive only as dependents of current households.

The household's economic organisation is aimed, next to survival, at providing the means to nurture and train the recruits on whom the continuity of the village depends. Within it, the intensely emotional relationships of the processes of physical and social reproduction are contained and controlled.

Authority and responsibility within the village are also largely a household matter. A man is in charge of his wife and children and their dependents, and responsible to his neighbours for their good conduct. Descent is patrilineal. Sons are expected to remain with their fathers until the father's death. Thus the household ideally contains a man, his wife or wives, his married sons with their wives and children, and his unmarried sons and daughters.

Logically, of course, households need not contain families. In fact, almost always and almost everywhere, they do. In these villages all members of a household are always close kin – except, very rarely, for resident servants (çirak). Such domestic groups are often called 'families' and distinguished according to their composition into nuclear families, extended families, joint families, compound families and so on. But the word 'family' is also needed to refer to the social group of father, mother and children, and sometimes grandchildren, without entailing common residence. It seems to me clearer to use the word family for very close kin, whether or not they reside together and to use the word household for the residential domestic group.

Where others have talked of simple and joint families I shall talk therefore of simple and joint households. Households which contain one married couple I shall call simple, those with more than one married couple, joint. In this context, I reckon widowers and divorced men whose children are living with them as married couples, partly because such widowers are almost always actively seeking remarriage, and partly because a wifeless man and his children form an autonomous domestic unit in a way that a husbandless woman and her children do

36

not. Widowers apart, households which contain no married couple I call fragmentary.

The villagers themselves have no word corresponding to the English word family.[1] The standard Turkish for this is *aile*, but in the village *aile* was one of the several words used for wife. Instead they used the words for house, *ev* and *hane*, in the general way in which I use household. These words are of course also used of the physical structures so that a man could say to me, 'I have three houses, but we are one house.'

The following tables set out some facts about the population of the two villages, and the distribution of types of households. I cannot claim that small errors have not occurred. Since the

Table 1

HOUSEHOLDS AND POPULATION BY NUMBER OF PERSONS PER HOUSEHOLD

No. in Hshd.	Sakaltutan 1950				Elbaşı 1952			
	No. of Hshds.	Per cent	No. of persons	Per cent	No. of Hshds.	Per cent	No. of persons	Per cent
1	2	2	2	—	4	2	4	—
2	5	5	10	2	8	4	16	1
3	11	10	33	5	27	12	81	7
4	12	11	48	8	37	17	148	12
5	18	17	90	14	35	16	175	15
6	20	19	120	19	36	17	216	18
7	11	10	77	12	29	13	203	17
8	10	10	80	13	14	7	112	9
9	7	7	63	10	14	7	126	11
10	2	2	20	3	6	3	60	5
11	3	3	33	5	—		—	
12	—		—		—		—	
13	2	2	26	4	1	1	13	1
14	1	1	14	2	—		—	
15	—		—		2	1	30	3
16	—		—		1	—	16	1
17	1	1	17	3	—		—	
Total	105	100	633	100	214	100	1,200	100

[1] Yasa (1957) p. 110 reports a similar lack in Hasanoğlan.

Table 2

DISTRIBUTION OF HSHDS. AND POPULATION BY HSHD. TYPES
(KINSHIP OF MEMBERS TO HSHD. HEAD)

Hshd. Type	Sakaltutan 1950				Elbaşı 1952			
	No. of Hshds.	Per cent	No. of persons	Per cent	No. of Hshds.	Per cent	No. of persons	Per cent
Simple[1] Hshds.								
Married couples	4	4	8	1	7	3	14	1
Married couples, children	54	51	301	49	114	53	605	51
Married couples, husband's mother	1	1	3	0	5	2	15	1
Married couples, husband's mother; children	9	8	52	8	10	5	64	5
Father with children, no wife alive			—		2	1	6	1
Married couple, children and other kin	4	4	30	5	7	3	37	3
Married couple, husband's younger siblings	1	1	3	0	4	2	19	2
Married couple, husband's younger siblings, mother	2	2	11	2	7	3	48	4
Totals	75	71	408	65	156	72	808	68
Joint[1] Hshds.								
Fraternal joint	3	3	20	3	2	1	17	1
Paternal joint, no grandchildren	6	6	44	7	18	9	122	10
Special paternal joint,[2] no 'grandchildren'					1	—	4	—
Paternal joint, with grandchildren	15	14	141	22	21	10	167	14
Special paternal joint[2] with 'grandchildren'	1	1	8	1	6	3	57	5
Totals	25	24	213	33	48	23	367	30
Fragmentary[1] Hshds.								
Widows with children	3	3	10	2	6	3	21	2
Widows living alone	1	1	1	0	4	2	4	—
Widows living alone (son in vlg.)	1	1	1	0	—		—	
Totals	5	5	12	2	10	5	25	2
Grand totals	105	100	633	100	214	100	1,200	100

details were gathered over a period, as the opportunity presented itself, and not by a systematic census on a given date, the stream of births, marriages, deaths, and divisions of households altered the facts as they were collected. Errors on this scale clearly make no difference whatsoever to the general description and analysis.

The two villages are remarkably similar. For Sakaltutan, both the median and the average number of persons per household coincide at six. For Elbaşı, there is no clear median, households of four, five and six being roughly equal in numbers, and the average is 5·6. Proportionately, there are fewer large households, only ten per cent of the population living in households of ten or over as against seventeen per cent in Sakaltutan. In both villages, most people live in households with populations of between four and nine – seventy-six per cent in Sakaltutan, eighty-two per cent in Elbaşı.

The distribution by household types is also remarkably similar in the two villages. Only two per cent of people live in fragmentary households. Roughly one-quarter of the households are joint and roughly one-third of the people live in joint and two-thirds in simple households.

At first sight, since joint households are clearly stated by everyone to be the ideal, the proportion of people living in them appears remarkably small. The apparent inconsistency is not due to non-conformist behaviour. The cases of premature separation, that is, of sons leaving the paternal home and setting up independent households, are more or less balanced by the number of delayed separations, that is, fraternal joint households. Only three heads of households in Elbaşı, and eight in Sakaltutan were sons separated from living fathers, and if all had returned home, the number of joint households would have increased by only one in each village.

Notes:

1. Simple household – one with one married couple.
   Joint household – one with more than one married couple.
   Fragmentary household – one without a married couple (p. 36).
2. These include married couples in which the husband is not the true son of the household head, e.g. son-in-law, or a kinsman informally adopted. In some cases, the offspring are not strictly grandchildren.

The simple households which contain the majority of the population are not deviant from the ideal. They have simply failed so far to achieve it. By the ideal, each household should grow by the birth of children, then by the marriage of its sons, and finally by the birth of grandchildren. On the death of the head, it splits into its constituent families, each of which should then repeat the cycle. Even if this scheme worked perfectly, there would always be a considerable number of households in the village, say half, in what one might call the pre-joint stage. In practice, the scheme seldom works perfectly. Household heads may die prematurely, leaving unmarried children; the child death-rate is high, and so is the rate of infertility and miscarriage among women. A man may beget a run of daughters. And occasionally, of course, a son may leave home on or very soon after marriage, usually because of trouble with a stepmother. Moreover, I was often told that the generation which would have provided the grandfathers and heads of joint households in 1950 had 'remained at mobilisation', that is they had not returned from the wars in which Turkey was involved almost continuously from 1911 to 1922.

If the death-rate among the senior generation had been abnormally high, the village, like the rest of Turkey, is now experiencing a population explosion – a sharp drop in the death-rate, especially among children, with no fall in the birth-rate. Thus at the moment, the villages have young people recently arrived at the age of marriage in numbers which are out of proportion to the supply of senior men. This means that the proportion of simple households is higher than it would have been had the death-rate remained constant.

The Elbaşı figures present one other curious feature. Nineteen out of forty-six 'paternal joint' households contain no grandchildren. When we compare this with only fourteen simple households lacking children, the figure seems even more surprising. In Sakaltutan, the figures are similar, though less emphatic. Six out of twenty-two paternal joint households lack grandchildren, while only six out of seventy-five simple households are without children. The reason is not far to seek. In all cases in which it is possible, married life begins under the roof of a senior kinsman of the husband, in most cases that of a father or married brother. It therefore creates, or increases the size of, a joint household.

The successful begetting of children is not easy, especially for young men. The wife is often very young; the husband is often away on military service or migrant labour a good deal in the early years of the marriage; gynaecological troubles are common, and gynaecological services limited; infant death-rates are still high. But after a few years, a man with no sons will take steps, first with treatment, both medical and magical, and later, if need be, by trying other wives. In the long run, nothing is more important than begetting a son. Thus the younger the husband, the more likely he is to be part of a joint household, and the less likely he is to have successful children. The large number of childless couples in joint households illustrates the delays and difficulties of successful procreation.

The small number of fragmentary and exceptional households are similarly due in most cases not to whim or deviance but to biological failure. The death of women and children, serious as it is, does not usually disrupt the household, because they are replaceable. A bereft husband normally remarries at once. A bereft father begets more children. One widower in Elbaşı maintained a womanless household with his young sons, but he was the only example I came across. On the other hand, I heard a story in Elbaşı of an old man who lost his two sons in a snow-storm, and immediately took a widow to wife and begat two more children, one of each sex. His age varied between sixty and ninety in different versions of the story, but his son and stepson were living evidence of its general truth.

The death of the household head is more devastating. Solutions of the problem are various. If he leaves sons old enough to work, the sons normally remain together at least until they and their sisters are all married. Their mother is unlikely to remarry.

A widow with younger children suits her circumstances. If she remarries, she may leave the children with her late husband's agnates, she may take them to her new husband, or she may leave them with her own father and mother. She may marry her late husband's brother, or some other kinsman of his. If she does not remarry, she may either remain in her husband's house and struggle to bring up his children there, with the help of her own or her husband's agnates; or she may return to her father's house.

If a couple fail to produce a male heir, they may take on the son of a close kinsman, normally a sibling's child of one of the parents. Adoption is not recognised in the Şeriat, and villagers do not take formal legal proceedings for adoption, though this is possible under the Turkish Civil Code.[1] But normally the inheritance of such adopted children is not questioned. One elderly couple had taken into their house and married to each other two adult grandchildren by previous marriages. The groom was daughter's son to the old man, and the bride son's daughter to the old woman. I knew of several cases of a man giving a son to his brother; in one of these the adopted boy had married the only daughter of his adopter. In such cases, the kinship terms are not changed. The adopter is called *'emme*, father's brother, not *baba*, father, by the adopted boy. It might be argued that this is not really adoption; but the adopter takes over full responsibility and thus artificially creates a family. Girls are never adopted; daughters are not structurally necessary to the continuance of the household.

Adoption is never thought of as a means of taking care of orphan children. These are common enough in the villages. They are not normally sought after, though sometimes a household will welcome the increase in the labour force which orphans bring. Since orphan boys normally separate from their foster-parents as soon as they are married, and thus do not provide foster-parents with the basis for a joint family, they are less rewarding than natural sons. In the past, orphans seem very often *de facto* to have lost their rights to their father's land, but in recent cases this does not appear to have happened. Girl orphans are not wanted and are still sometimes sent away by their foster-parents to middle class urban families as servants, in return for which their employers marry them off to respectable urban working class boys when they reach adolescence.

Only the lame, the blind and the idiots fail to marry, and not even all of these. One girl was married to a mentally defective kinsman to provide a means of taking care of him. Normally the unmarried remain in the household of their closest agnates.

Very rarely, a man may marry uxorilocally. Usually, this

[1] Haci Osman (H) of Sakaltutan told me that he intended to adopt legally the small orphan son of Ibrahim, whom Haci Osman had informally reared as his own heir. Ibrahim died in the spring of 1950.

implies no more than going to live close to a wife's household, and co-operating with her kin. All migrations of men between villages involved this relationship. In these cases, the dependence of a man on his wife's agnates is obvious. Where marriage takes place within the village, cases of uxorilocal marriage are more difficult to define, because a range of degrees of intimacy with wife's parents is possible. Apart from adoptions, where a young man takes over, through his wife's inheritance, her father's land, I knew of only two cases where a man had actually resided in his wife's natal household. Both were refugees with no kin and no property in the area. The term for a man who marries this way, *iç-güvey*, 'in son-in-law', has a decided flavour of mockery and scorn.

None of these exceptional cases involve any deviation from the rules which govern the normal cycle of household growth and division. They are simply adaptations to meet unusual circumstances, and all, given normal health and normal reproduction, will turn again into normal, and, if possible, joint households.

The patrilineal joint household is then the ideal at which all are aiming; moreover, most villagers live in such a household for at least one period in their lives, perhaps for two or three different periods. The reasons why such households are in a minority are far more physiological and ecological than social. In a sense the patrilineal joint household is not only the ideal, but also the typical village household.

CHAPTER FOUR

THE VILLAGE ECONOMY

Land Use

The village lives by growing crops and keeping animals.
Mixed farming, which I call agriculture, though it includes
horticulture and animal husbandry, is the main source of income and the main occupation. Everyone has some direct connection with it, and almost everyone puts work on the land before
any other kind of work, emotionally, morally and in practice.

Both villages grow mainly cereals. In Elbaşı, the commonest
is wheat, as in most plateau villages; in Sakaltutan, exceptionally, rye, though both villages grow both. They also grow some
barley, and a crop of mixed wheat and rye, which produces a
flour considered specially appetising for bread-making.

Yields are poor. People do not normally express these by area
but by return for seed sown. Estimates for normal yields varied
considerably, and the different types of measurement involved
made comparisons unreliable. Five for one was generally agreed
to be the figure in Sakaltutan, though in fact in 1949, 1950 and
1951, the harvest was considerably below these modest expectations. In Elbaşı yields seemed slightly higher, and in 1951
and 1952, Elbaşı had satisfactory harvests. Normal yields appeared to be about eight cwt per acre (one metric ton per ha.)
in Sakaltutan and perhaps about ten cwt in Elbaşı ($1\frac{1}{4}$ metric
tons per ha.).

Agricultural efficiency is further impeded by the familiar
problem of fragmented holdings. The pattern of fragmentation
varies between the more distant, less fertile land, where some
villagers still retain fairly large fields, and the valuable well
manured land close to the village, where the pieces may be
minute. This difference is readily explicable in terms of the

44

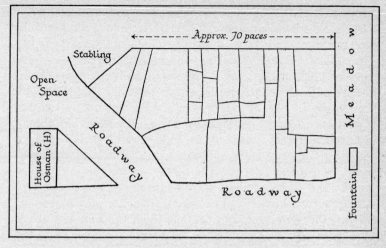

4 Sketch of a divided field

history of village land holding, discussed in Chapter 7. A typical
example of fragmentation is shown in Fig. 4.

In Sakaltutan, many households were making, or had
recently made, small walled gardens for themselves, usually a
patch of land near the village, in which they grew vines, fruit
trees and vegetables. These were said to be at most ten years
old, but in spite of doubts about the long-term success of these
in so severe a climate, more and more people were following
suit. Another recent innovation was the planting of potatoes
and onions for the Kayseri market. Ground peas (*nohut*),
lentils, fodder crops and even a little irrigated alfalfa immediately below the meadow were also grown.

Elbaşı had fewer and even more recent gardens. It had the
advantage of irrigated land, but most of this seems to be used
either for alfalfa, for water meadows or for growing rather more
successful cereals.

In both villages, almost all households aimed to produce a
surplus of cereals for sale, and after the harvest the village
hummed with activity as everyone jostled to get his own grain
sacks on the lorries before his neighbours. In Sakaltutan, and
for the smaller and poorer households in Elbaşı, the habit of
cash-cropping was a new one, developed under the stimulus of
a government guaranteed price for grain. The first aim of

45

cultivation is still to produce food for one's own household.

Animals are an equally vital part of the village economy. For draught, the villagers used mainly oxen and water buffaloes. The milk of the cows of both is a valuable item of diet, very often eaten as yoghurt, and their dung is the main source of fuel. Occasionally they are sold for meat, or ceremonially eaten in the village. In Elbaşı, in recent years, horses have partially replaced oxen as draught animals. People say there are about a hundred teams of horses in the village now, though oxen or water buffaloes are still commoner. Most households own a few sheep, and many own small flocks. In Sakaltutan, one or two men owned flocks of up to forty or fifty, and in Elbaşı one or two up to two hundred. The sheep, (the *karamanlı* breed), are small, hardy and have large fat tails. They are kept as much for their milk and their tails as for their wool and meat. Chickens are to be seen everywhere – scavenging in the latrines, or messing in the houses. Some people keep pigeons for meat and manure.

Agricultural Work

The technical processes in Sakaltutan are still almost entirely traditional. The plough in common use is the usual light wooden Middle East plough (Morrison (1938) Chap. II, figs. 21, 23; Aran (1938) p. 86, fig. 33), seed is sown by hand, reaping is done partly by sickle, which the women wield, and partly by the scythe, a fairly recent innovation used almost exclusively by men. Villages to the east were in 1950 said still to be using only sickles. The crops are threshed by driving a special sledge, the underside of which is studded with flints, round and round over the grain. It is drawn by oxen or horses, or even by donkeys. This not only threshes, but chops the straw up fine. Straw is always stored and fed to animals in this chopped form. People were incredulous when I said that animals in England eat straw in the stalk. They winnow simply by tossing the chopped straw, chaff and grain into a breeze. Transport is by two-wheeled ox-cart, similar to those depicted on Hittite monuments. The axle turns with the solid wheels, making a screeching squeak against the frame if the cart is loaded. Eight households had European-type steel ploughs in 1950, but did not seem to make much use of them.

The bulk of the work in Elbaşı is done by identical methods. The number of steel ploughs is very much higher, however, and many are used. Many households have horse-drawn four-wheeled carts. Kara Osman (Ax) (p. 145) had introduced machinery some years ago; an old combine harvester was rusting away in a corner, and one of his sons ran the tractor. Now tractors and combine harvesters are available for the villagers to hire. By 1952, one villager had purchased a new tractor and set of machinery under the government easy credit scheme. When combine harvesters are used, the straw has to be chopped up afterwards by traditional methods.

During the winter months, weather conditions make outside work impossible. The women are busy in the houses, using time spared from the daily cooking and cleaning for weaving, mending, knitting and spinning; but for about four months, from the end of November to the end of March, the men have no work to do but feed and water the animals, which are kept in the stables and fed on straw, eked out with some meal or bought feed.

As soon as the spring comes, the men get busy. The oxen weakened by the long winter must be got into training for work, and spring ploughing and sowing must be done. The ox-herds and shepherds take charge of the animals. The sheep are lambing and in each household a woman must be ready at midday to milk the ewes. Ploughing and sowing of spring wheat and barley is immediately followed by the ploughing of the year's fallow, which goes on perhaps into May, even until June, depending on individual circumstances. Meanwhile, the vineyards must be dug over, and potatoes and other vegetables sown. Most of this latter work is done by women.

In June, all the grasses and weeds growing in odd places among the crops are cut for hay, again mostly by women. During late May and June the men are comparatively idle. In July the harvest begins, first with vetch and lentils, then with the main crops of rye and wheat. Threshing follows the reaping; reaping, threshing, and storing together last for about two months, two months of ceaseless activity for everyone; a whole household frequently works right through a moonlit night.

In September the pressure eases. As soon as rain falls on the hard baked ground – even before, if the rains are late – the men must plough again and sow their winter rye and wheat. By November there remains for the men only a visit to town to lay in supplies of coffee, paraffin, salt and so on, and perhaps cheap vegetables for the winter months of isolation, and then idleness again until the spring. One villager, unsolicited, told me that the peasants only work for four months a year – a month in the spring, a month in the autumn, and two months at the harvest. He was overstating his case and, as someone commented, in two months' harvesting they do four months' work; but the idea of having, like an English agricultural labourer, to work for wages day in and day out all the year round was greeted with horror.

In all the villages of this area, a two-year fallow system operates. One-half of the village land is sown one year, and the other left fallow and used for pasture (de Planhol (1958) pp. 317 ff.). The village herds and flocks are transferred from one side to the other after the harvest, to glean the harvested fields and eat the stubble. Soon after the completion of the harvest, autumn ploughing and sowing on the fallow land begins; the fields from which the crops have been reaped become fallow for the next year. This system prevents any individual from planting the same fields in successive years, except for a few walled fields immediately adjoining the village, where manuring and special crops make it agriculturally advantageous, and the animals can easily be kept off. Each man farms his own plots quite independently of his neighbours, so that he is free to plough and sow when he wishes, and to sow what crops he pleases. He may, should he wish, miss one or more turns of the cycle; that is, he can leave land fallow for three, five, or more, years instead of one, so long as he sows it in a year when it is part of the village pasture. On the other hand, he dare not lag behind his neighbours at the harvest, lest the flocks and herds are turned on to the land before his crops are reaped and away.

Land Tenure

Each village has a territory surrounding the village settlement, over which it has formal administrative rights. This territory acts as a symbol of village political identity. The economically important common rights to this territory are pastoral, though these are not explicitly recognised in the Civil Code. Flocks and herds of villagers are pastured free only within village territory. Sometimes villages own patches of mountain pasture not contiguous with their main territory (cf. de Planhol (1958) pp. 293 f.). All villages are zealous in keeping other villages' animals out of their territories. The boundaries are known, and since 1924, they have been required to be registered with the local District Officer. Before this, boundaries seem to have been much vaguer (Aran (1937) p. 26; Yasa (1957) p. 18), depending on the coincidence of local memories and traditions, and sometimes with unclaimed land forming a buffer. Since the population and the cultivated areas were smaller, the land available for pasture was greater and the likelihood of clashes between villages therefore less, though undoubtedly disputes and fights over this issue occurred, as they still do.

Anomalously, under the present law, the cultivated land within the village territory belongs outright to its private owners, who can dispose of it as they choose. In practice, land is not often sold, and when it is, it is normally sold to close kin or to neighbours. I can recall no instance of village land being sold to a complete outsider (p. 127). Moreover, the exercise of the individual rights involves *de facto* co-operation with other villagers. The land can only be cropped in alternate years, in accordance with the village fallow system described before. Success depends on the protection of the village herdsman and watchman, and only a resident owner or tenant can be sure of this protection. Some land in most villages is in fact owned by outsiders, but almost always by close kin of village families. One or two people living in villages near Sakaltutan worked land inside the Sakaltutan territory, if it was not too far from their own homes, and similarly some Sakaltutan men held and worked land in other villages. In other cases, kin living elsewhere, who had inherited rights to a share of land, let it on a share-cropping basis to their kin in the village and came annually at the harvest to collect their share of produce.

Besides cultivated land, house sites and land in the settled area are owned privately, and occasionally water meadow or threshing sites are also so owned.

Close to every village are areas of meadow for casual grazing, and places for threshing. In Sakaltutan one patch of land above the village was known as *harman*, the threshing floor, and another patch below, better watered, was called *çayır*, the meadow, but both were used by all the villagers for both purposes. Both areas were village common land. In Elbaşı there was also a patch of common meadow used for both purposes, though much threshing took place inside the village area on privately owned patches of bare rock where grain could not be lost in the dust, and much of the extensive area of water meadow was also privately owned. People sometimes stick to the same site on common land for threshing year after year, but no fixed rights are recognised. Some villages also communally own cultivable land or cropped meadow which is hired out to village tenants. The proceeds go to the village chest.

The rest of the land within the village territories is used for pasture by the flocks and herds. Most of this is waste land – rocky slopes and bare hill tops – but it usually includes, in dells and valleys, patches of richer watered pasture. Technically, such land is the property of the State, but this provision has almost no practical consequences. Villagers can in fact plough it up and thus in time establish rights to it, if the rest of the village takes no steps to prevent them.

In Sakaltutan, almost all land worth having which was not essential for pasture had already passed into private hands, but there is still occasionally trouble because someone encroaches on fertile village pasture. In Elbaşı, whose territory is much larger, only in the last few years, with the great increase in cash cropping, had the village combined to prevent members from ploughing land as they wished. In the recent past, only members of the village community, or men with some village connection, were permitted to acquire land by this method, and casual strangers were prevented, informally but effectively, from settling in the village for this purpose, except for refugees (p. 23). This *de facto* right to take over unused land was an important addition to the joint rights which the villagers had over their territory. Once this encroachment is permitted, the village as a corporation eventually loses legal control of the land.

Full legal title to land can be established in three ways. A man may be the holder registered in a formal title deed, called a *tapu;* he may hold tax receipts, showing him to be the owner;

or he may be able to show that he has been ploughing the land for twenty years.

Among the villagers, though people sometimes claim to hold the deeds, no one appears to take them very seriously. When land changes hands at the death of the owner, or by purchase, people do not go through the costly bureaucratic and legal procedure of altering the deeds, so that these are normally out of date.

Tax receipts are much more important. The land had been assessed for tax about 1938, by visiting officials working with the headman and a committee of villagers. Recognition as owner both by the State and the village is binding, unless misappropriation is subsequently established in court.

The legal provision that any land held in undisputed possession for twenty years becomes automatically the legal property of the possessor is known to the villagers, but not regarded as of much importance. In fact, it provides the main basis for rendering legal the *de facto* situation. What matters to a villager is simply whether he can in practice plough a certain piece of land without trouble, and this depends not on his legal rights, but on the acceptance of his customary rights by his local community. Only when he is challenged is a villager interested in establishing legal rights, in order to be able to defend himself with the power of the State. By this provision, his undisturbed holding, outside the law, of a piece of land for twenty years automatically confers full legal rights should he require them. To establish formally evidence of such rights is, however, costly and complex, unless he is prepared to wait for the next tax assessment and declare the land for tax for ever after. For this reason, most villagers do not have established legal rights to all the land they regard as theirs.

Land Holdings

The land owned by members of a household is worked communally by them under the direction of the household head. Most land belongs to household heads, but women may own in their own right; and sometimes stepsons or a brother's child living in a household may own part of the household land.

Household holdings of land vary greatly. In Elbaşı a few

3

households were well-off for land but most of the household holdings of both villages ranged from moderate to very poor. I did not attempt in either village to measure holdings, and I found people unwilling, and often genuinely unable, to give accurate figures of their extent. Sometimes they gave figures for the amount they worked in a single year of the two-year fallow cycle, sometimes they included their holdings 'on both sides'. Where the household land was owned by more than one person, or where some land was legally owned and additional land had been acquired by ploughing village pasture or borrowed for share-cropping, it was not easy to sort out the meaning of the figure I was given.

To make matters worse, the units of land measurement are by no means fixed. The common unit is a *dönüm*, (from *dönmek* – to turn) traditionally the amount of land a man can plough in a day. The government has fixed the *dönüm* for official purposes as equal to one decare, about a quarter of an acre. But the village *dönüm* varies not only from village to village, but also from man to man, and field to field. Most informants in Sakaltutan and the surrounding villages said the *dönüm* was forty paces by forty paces, but in Elbaşı people said sixty by sixty or eighty by eighty, and one man even said a hundred by a hundred. They had not, I am sure, grasped that the smallest of these areas, very roughly one decare, is about one-sixth of the largest. Informants stated that a village *dönüm* was twice or three times a government *dönüm*. I have therefore taken the Sakaltutan *dönüm* as two decares (half an acre), and the Elbaşı *dönüm* as two and a half decares (five-eighths of an acre). I managed to get an estimate in *dönüm* for every household in Sakaltutan, and these I give in Table 3. In Elbaşı, only a minority of households gave me such estimates, but by use of the village system of classes for assessment of village tax (p. 32) I have worked out figures in which I feel reasonable confidence.

The total quantity of land a man owns is not, of course, a direct index of his wealth, since land varies in value. But it can be fairly safely assumed that the greater part of the village arable land is poor and dry, and that with a few exceptions the valuable irrigated and manured land is roughly divided among the owners in proportion to their total holdings.

Table 3

CULTIVABLE LAND BY HOUSEHOLDS IN SAKALTUTAN

Households	Dönüm	Decares	Acres
6	0	0	0
10	1–5	1–10	1–2½
9	6–15	11–30	3–7½
31	16–30	31–60	8–15
31	31–50	61–100	15½–25
11	51–80	101–160	25½–40
5	100–150	200–300	50–75

Table 4

ESTIMATES OF CULTIVABLE LAND BY ASSESSMENT CLASSES IN ELBAŞı

Assessment Class	No. of Households in Class	Dönüm	Decares	Acres	
No assessment	14	—	—	—	(1)
IV	62	30–60	75–150	14–38	(2)
III	70	40–70	100–175	25–44	(3)
II	42	70–100	175–250	44–62	
I	26	80–200	200–560	50–125	(4)

Notes:

(1) Landless households; and those owning little, and unable to work it themselves – for example, widows.

(2) Includes a few with little or no land, which either share cropped others' land, or practised a regular craft or trade.

(3) Includes a few with more land.

(4) One or two have even more. Up to his death in 1951, Kara Osman (Ax), held 'more than 1,000 *dönüm*'; even if these are 'government *dönüm*' he held over 100 ha.

Share-cropping and Renting

Land is no good unless it is worked. To work it, manpower, draught animals, tools and seed are all necessary. For want of one or more of these owners are sometimes forced to leave land uncultivated. If the land is sufficiently valuable it is often hired out to a neighbour on a share-cropping basis. The terms are fairly standard, though details may vary. The owner pays all taxes, is expected to help with the harvest, and takes half the crop and half the straw. The share-cropper supplies animals, equipment and labour in return for the remaining half. Seed is usually provided by the owner, but whoever provides it is entitled to deduct an equivalent amount from the winnowed grain before the division. Share-cropping is arranged *ad hoc* and partnerships vary greatly from season to season. It is not a system of permanent landlord-tenant relations. There is no definite date for fixing contracts and neither side has any right to continue the arrangement beyond one season. It may of course be renewed annually, and may in some cases continue for years, but fluctuations in man- and ox-power in one household or the other, dissatisfaction with each other's conduct, or some change in the social situation is always liable to upset it.

Whereas land in Sakaltutan was short, in Elbaşı it was plentiful. Share-croppers were easy to find in Sakaltutan, and many people were keen to take on more land if they could get it. In Elbaşı, on the other hand, most agricultural households had land, and the total amount of available land in proportion to labour and oxen was greater. In consequence share-croppers were difficult to find, and they would not take on the poorest land at all since the half of a poor yield did not repay the labour and expense involved.

Those who put their land out to share-croppers are not necessarily the well-to-do. They include the aged, the sick, the widows, or those who have lost or been forced to sell their oxen or are short of seed. In many such cases a kinsman works the land, and may claim that he is doing so as a duty rather than for his own benefit. Others let out their land to free themselves for some other occupation.

Correspondingly, those who take on share-cropping are not the poorest village households. To share-crop a man needs

54

Table 5

OCCUPATIONS: SAKALTUTAN 1949–50

Total adult working male population
(approximately 16 years and above)   171

Occupation	Main Source of Income	Supplementary to work on the household land
1 Full time farmers (including casual unskilled labourers primarily occupied in farming)	72	

2 Men employed in the village or in neighbouring villages.

	Main Source of Income	Supplementary to work on the household land
Headman	—	1
Watchman	1	—
Herdsmen	4	3
Mason	—	3
Pedlar	2	—
Unskilled	2	Many
Entrepreneur	—	3
Carpenter	1	1
Teacher	—	1
	10	12+

3 Migrant workers	Main Source of Income	Supplementary to work on the household land
Plasterer	19	7
Mason	3	4
Carpenter	2	2
Plumber	1	—
Painter	1	—
Vegetable seller	2	1
Factory worker	5	—
Cook	1	—
Porter	2	—
Unskilled	12	15
	48	29
Total of Groups 2 and 3	58	41+

Note:

These figures are based on my notebooks. The balance of 41 men without a 'Main Source of Income' are unmarried youths, mainly living and working in their fathers' households. A few may be unskilled workers whose temporary migrations I failed to record.

resources – oxen and supporting manpower. In fact most share-croppers are middle range land owners who prefer to take on more land rather than supplement their income by other means.

Fixed rents for land are known, but rare. They are much less profitable, but have the advantage that the tenant cannot cheat. Owners of land in other villages who let to people they do not trust and cannot watch sometimes prefer them.

Labour and Services

The agricultural economy creates demand both for agri-cultural labour and for a number of specialised services. Other demands arise from more elementary human needs, more especially houses, domestic utensils and clothes. Some of the village population lives by meeting these demands, both by production and trade.

Almost all the work of cultivation is done directly by the household labour of the owner or share-cropper. Only rarely, because of an emergency or miscalculation, or in order to avoid the need to share-crop, does anyone employ agricultural labour. Other jobs – the commonest is building – are available from time to time. Usually the poor or landless take such employ-ment, but people with some standing in the village will work if they have the opportunity, and are short of money for a specific purpose. In 1950 the rate was T.L.1½ a day, plus food, (3s. 9d., U.S. $0.55) about half the rate for casual labour in the towns.

At harvest time the situation is reversed; the demand for labour is intense. Those who have no harvest of their own may work on a contract for those who have large harvests, either for a share or for a fixed quantity of grain. Others work on a daily basis. As much as T.L.5 (12s. 6d., $1.80) was paid for a full day's reaping.

Prosperous households had another method of recruiting labour. Young men or even married couples were taken on as servants (*çirak*) on a yearly contract for their keep and a small emolument in cash (p. 61). One orphan from another village was *çirak* in Elbaşı, and one young man of Sakaltutan was *çirak* in a distant village. Another orphan had been *çirak* to at least two village households before his marriage. In the recent past the system seems to have been far more common.

The decline of the *çirak* system is a symptom of the decline in the availability of casual labour. This decline is relative; Turkey still has a problem of under-employment. But the demand for migrant labour and the spread of cash-cropping have undoubtedly used up some surplus labour in the villages. Allowing for the usual misrepresentation of the past, comments in Elbaşı indicated clearly that not long ago casual labour was much more common, and many more households lacked the resources to cultivate in their own right.

Besides better-off individuals, the community itself is an important employer, needing herdsmen, guards, and, in Elbaşı, water supervisors.

The duties of the village herdsmen vary with the type of animals and the season. In Sakaltutan two shepherds and two boy lamb-herds are appointed in the spring, but in the autumn, when some of the sheep are sent away to pasture elsewhere, one of each is sufficient. Goats are herded with the sheep. One man is responsible for the cows for about eight months from spring to the first snow, and a boy looks after the calves and asses. Two ox-herds work from the spring until the beginning of the harvest, taking the oxen off by night to pasture and returning them to their owners at daybreak ready to work. The water buffaloes are separately pastured in the same way. Thus a total of six men and three boys are employed for a limited period in the course of each year.

The arrangements in Elbaşı are similar but on a larger scale because the village owns far more animals. They have, for example, eight shepherds and four lamb-herds as well as separate herdsmen for horses and foals. The total number employed in a year, again for varying periods, is about twenty-four.

In both villages the village as a whole employs the herdsmen for all animals except sheep and goats. In Sakaltutan they appear to carry out their duties according to their own intelligence, but in Elbaşı the headman exercises a definite control over them, directing them daily where to take their herds. The shepherds in Elbaşı are employed on a private basis by leading households in each part of the village, and lesser men attach their sheep, according to convenience and social ties, to whichever flock they choose. In Sakaltutan the two main quarters, each acting jointly, engaged a shepherd and a shepherd-boy each in the spring.

In almost all cases the herdsmen are paid *per capita* by each household which sends animals to their herd, and the amount is settled by bargaining as so much per beast. Ox-herds are paid more because they work at night though for less time. Roughly it works out at about T.L.280 (£35, $100) for a session. Some villages had in 1950 recently changed over to the payment of shepherds by fixed sums in money, which they still collected themselves by dividing it among the owners according to the number of animals. In these cases T.L.300 (£37 10s., $110) was becoming the standard rate.

Just before the harvest each year field watchmen (sing. *tarla bekcisi*), are appointed to patrol the ripening crops. These are responsible to the headman and were also paid about T.L.300 for some three months' work. In Sakaltutan in 1950 no watch-men were appointed, possibly because the headman did not bother; the reason given was the poverty of everyone following the disastrous harvest of 1949.

For a brief period in June when water is in demand before the harvest, two men are appointed to see fair play over water rights. The system has four branches, and in 1951 people using the water had to pay the overseers 10 *kuruş* an hour so that they received T.L.4.80 (13s., $1.80) per day each, which was good by village standards.

The village watchman received at most about T.L.300 a year, less than T.L.200 in Sakaltutan, which was sometimes paid in cash from the village chest, and sometimes in kind, household by household. Village watchmen cannot, in their year of office, migrate or work regularly because of their duties, but most pick up casual jobs and work at the harvest.

During 1949 to 1950 only one man in Sakaltutan received a government salary. This was the teacher (p. 275) and he was only paid T.L.40 (£5, $14) a month.

Elbaşı had rather more officials. Apart from the *nahiye müdürü* himself, there were the three schoolmasters, the rural school inspector, known as a 'travelling headmaster' (*gezici başöğretmen*), and the secretary of the Credit Co-operative, in effect an official of the Agricultural Bank. There was also a village secretary (*köy katibi*), who was secretary in theory for a number of villages, and was paid by small contributions from each for doing very little indeed.

Crafts

The production of other goods in the villages is limited, but a small range of skills is found, and these play some part in the economy.

One skill is practised in almost every household in this area, namely weaving. The local wool is too coarse to make into clothing but it does make excellent rugs (*kilims*), saddlebags and grainsacks. The wool is washed, spun, dyed and woven exclusively by the women, and it is rare to see a woman relaxing without a spindle in her hand. Almost every household has a simple household loom, at which the girls work when there is nothing else to do, learning the traditional patterns from their mothers. Every girl is expected to weave for her own trousseau, and her skill enhances her bride-price. Carpets are also woven by hand in many villages but this is a more skilled job. No household in Sakaltutan, and few in Elbaşı knew how to weave carpets; this skill is usually a sign of greater wealth and prestige. The village supplies its own needs: the saddlebags and sacks with their gay colours are everywhere in use, and every guest room is carpeted with village-made *kilims* and carpets, but a great many are sold as well. Allowing for the cost of the wool, which would have been sold raw, and for the dyes which have to be purchased, the profit per day's labour is exceedingly small. On the other hand this work is all done by women in time when they would otherwise be idle. Weaving is peculiar in being the only craft practised by women, the only craft which produces for export from the village area, and the only craft which processes raw materials produced by village agriculture.

Traditionally many villages in Turkey must have grown fibres and, with the help of home-produced wool, made at least some of their own clothing. Some distant villages in the area were known to weave cloth, but all the cloth in the villages I knew is now factory produced. The women make it up into clothes for themselves and their menfolk. Occasionally people

3*

bought ready-made, new or secondhand clothes in Kayseri, especially men's trousers and jackets. Although much sewing goes on in the villages no household in Sakaltutan, and only one sophisticated household in Elbası, owned a sewing machine.

The most common male crafts are those of mason, carpenter and smith. A lot of new building is going on in the villages, partly to provide for an expanding population, partly to replace old houses whose lack of amenities is no longer acceptable. The demand is steady. All villages contain some skilled masons and almost all new construction is built by them. During my stay only one unskilled man built anything for himself. It was a small guest room and its rather amateur appearance provoked mild scorn. Clearly one needed a professionally built house for prestige. Houses need doors and windows, and in special cases wooden floors, and these needs are met by village carpenters. Smiths make tools, nails, hinges and so forth, put metal tyres on cartwheels and shoe horses.

The masons in the two villages always worked on specific contracts. No one lived entirely by the craft of mason. This skill lent itself to export, and masons were potential migrants, though one or two who built village houses had never been away to work in town. The masons were paid about T.L.5 (12s. 6d., $1.80) a day when working in the village, three times an unskilled labourer's pay and about half what they earned in town.

Sakaltutan contained a family of carpenters. The father Ziya (S), vigorous but no longer young, had learned his trade as a young man outside the village and his three adult sons were all carpenters too. He himself no longer migrated but his sons did. He was kept busy all the time by orders, from other villages as well as Sakaltutan, and often worked away in his *oda* while neighbours came to sit and talk. He was always ready with a lecture on the virtues of hard work, and the need to maintain his family in decency. His brother farmed their joint patrimony, though they had separate households. He never disclosed what he earned but he certainly did not under-value his services, and would not have accepted less than the rate for skilled work. Just before the harvest his family and that of a rival carpenter, his father's brother's son, who normally migrated for work, were busy making threshing sledges. The putting of the flint teeth into these is said to be highly skilled work. Enquiries about profits brought very varying answers, but even the more modest estimates gave a profit over materials of a good T.L.10 per sledge, and set one day as the time to make one; T.L.10 a day is twice the normal village skilled rate.

Elbaşı contained no full-time carpenter, but did have a full-time smith. His father was alive, and in 1951 to 1952 he was still sharing a common household. After much humming and hawing he said he thought he made about T.L.200 (£25, $70) a month: the income of a lowly government official.

Elbaşı had a number of other specialists. Two barbers and a man who made sheet iron cooking stoves lived by their trade. A piper and a drummer made enough in the winter wedding season, eked out by watching the village fields in the summer, to make a decent living. Others, another stove-maker for example, shoe repairers, and a cave digger combined their speciality with working their land, and some did odd jobs for neighbours rather as a favour. Similarly one man in Sakaltutan, who was an expert glass-cutter, did odd carpentry jobs, while another welded rubber shoes.

These craftsmen then range from the man who happens to have a reputation for performing some particular service, and will do it if asked, to full-time skilled craftsmen who live by their craft. Where skills overlap those of migrant labourers, for example masons and carpenters, a man may live mainly by migrant labour and practice his craft in the village in only a desultory way.

Traditionally skills were learned by a period of apprenticeship: (çirak, p. 56) boys lived with and worked for a craftsman, picking up the trade from him. Others recently have learned skills in the army, and now the government runs special short-term mobile schools in selected villages for boys to learn the elements of woodwork and metalwork. One such course came to Elbaşı in the autumn of 1951. Otherwise skills are passed from father to son or sometimes taught to other close kin.

One new skill is popular among the young men: şöför or lorry driver. A Turkish driver needs to be able to do his own running repairs without help from roadside garages and without a supply of standard spare parts, so this skill is not easily mastered. Although it is common for a driver to work on a lorry that passes through or is owned in his own village, these driver-mechanics are perhaps more properly classed as migrant labourers.

The villagers are visited by travelling craftsmen of various types: tinsmiths, sawyers who make planks from baulks of timber for the carpenters, smiths who specialise in shoeing oxen, and so on.

On one occasion, a troop of Abdaller, a wandering ethnic group rather like gypsies, came to Sakaltutan and camped on the meadow for about three days, selling and repairing sieves which are much used by villagers for a variety of purposes.

Retail Trade

Even the traditional economy of the village was far from self-sufficient. Cloth, iron, timber, string and thread, utensils and tools, tea, coffee, sugar and its substitute, *pekmez*, (boiled down grape juice), were always imported, and probably other odds and ends, including local fruits and vegetables in season. Now the volume and the variety of retail goods are much greater and they are supplied by three main sources: shops in the villages, itinerant traders, and merchants and shopkeepers in the towns.

Elbaşı was blessed with a number of general shops. Of these about four seemed to be permanent businesses and another half a dozen to be intermittent. A man who happens to have or manages to obtain credit may buy a small stock of retail goods and sell them off, spending the money as he goes along. At the end of the period he has no means of replacing the stock, and the shop closes. These short-lived enterprises may sell only a few lines; fruit in season is common. The more permanent shops stock salt, sugar, sweets, soap, matches, cigarettes, paraffin (kerosene), notebooks, cloth, especially white cloth for making shrouds for the dead, sewing cotton, buttons, combs and so on – the typical stock of a village shop. Much of the business is done for grain, and much of it on credit. It is the difficulty of refusing a neighbour credit in the first place, and of collecting debts in the second, which sinks many intermittent shops.

When I first went to live in Sakaltutan it had no shop at all, though one or two had existed. One man borrowed the capital from me to buy a small stock of apples and *helva*, a sweet made of nut and honey, but this enterprise was very short-lived. In January 1950 a stranger, a son-in-law of a villager, set up a temporary shop for the winter months only, and the following year Haci Osman (K) established a permanent shop (p. 71).

The rapid rise in national income from 1950 to 1953, combined with the beginning of serious inflation, brought much more money and some increase in real income to the villagers, with a resulting increase in the demand both for manufactured goods and a wider diet. The number of shops in the area was steadily increasing.

I found it difficult to assess how profitable the shops were. Their prices were higher than town prices, because apart from the costs of transport, they worked on a higher profit margin on a lower turnover – though I am not sure that village shop-keepers could buy wholesale as cheaply as town retailers. The acceptance of payment in kind further increased the shop-keeper's margin because he priced grain below what he would sell it for. Against this the impossibility of refusing credit and the difficulty of collecting debts made it a doubtful means of earning a living. The more temporary shops were usually run by poor men, but several of the permanent shops were sidelines run by the better-off. Full-time shopkeeping seemed to provide no more than a modest standard of living.

Small retail trade was also carried on by numerous pedlars. These varied considerably. In Sakaltutan two of the poorest villagers used to bring donkey-loads of fruit or vegetables in season, combs and other cheap odds and ends to Sakaltutan and other villages, exchanging them for eggs and grain. Pedlars of this type are mostly villagers. Even this enterprise required a minimum capital or credit with a merchant, and some degree of judgement of the market.

Besides these, more specialised pedlars and travelling sales-men would arrive, from towns or from more prosperous villages nearer Kayseri. Some sold earthenware pots; others, more prosperous, sold cloth, usually carried by horse; others traded in oxen. This last was a more complex business, involving long-term credit. Oxen cost even then from T.L.200 to T.L.800 a pair, (£25-£100, $70 to $280), and the payments were usually spaced over three years.

Anything imported into the village can be bought more

cheaply in town. Most household heads have occasion to go to town from time to time, and bring back supplies with them. The lorries and buses which run in from the villages will carry more or less any load at a fairly modest charge, and the household income comes in large bursts. It is therefore possible for even a fairly poor household to lay in considerable stocks. Indeed, it is essential in Sakaltutan to find money for winter supplies after the harvest since the road to town is usually blocked completely to wheeled traffic for up to three months.

Trading in town is not entirely simple. Villagers are suspicious, perhaps rightly, of traders, and in spite of the arrangement of the market by which most of the streets are devoted to a single type of shop with full-scale competition, villagers normally have their known friends to whom they always go. These may allow them credit. One village or one set of kin and neighbours tends to concentrate on the same merchant so that he has a good deal to lose by failing one of them. People use the town merchants mainly for large orders and major purchases. Before a wedding, for example, all the necessary cloth, clothes and extra food are bought on an expedition to town. When I gave a feast to the village to mark my departure, I was taken into town to buy rice and other necessaries.

Migrant Labour

One major village export is labour. Villages vary greatly in the numbers who migrate and in their degree of skill.

One extreme is represented by a band of villages nearer Kayseri with an established tradition of building labour. In one of these I was told that all but six households lived by migrant labour, all the adults being skilled migrants who were away from home from April to December. The Kayseri region has a national reputation for skill in building. One of the villages near Talas produced Mimar Sinan, architect of the great mosque of Süleyman the Magnificent in Istanbul.

Elbaşı stands at the other extreme. With as much land as its working population could comfortably cultivate, it had only a small trickle of migrants, and many of these were only away for short periods between the busy seasons.

The villages around Sakaltutan fell between these two types.

Land shortage here is fairly recent and, combined with the opening of communication, has led to the spread of the Kayseri tradition to these villages but on a smaller and less systematic scale. From Table 5 (p. 55) it is clear that the two main categories of migrants are building trade craftsmen and unskilled labourers. In this list, which is made up only from my notes of comings and goings during my stay, those listed under main occupation include both household heads who have little or no alternative source of income, and those who either own land which is let to share-croppers, or are members of land owning joint households to which they contribute cash and in which they have full rights to support. The first are likely to stay away from the village for nine months each year, the second may well return to help with, and in some cases also to watch over their share of, the harvest. Those who combine agriculture and migration are even more unpredictable in their comings and goings. Indeed, every adult male is a potential migrant if misfortune or special needs drive him to earn outside the village.

Thirty-nine men were skilled building trade operatives. Plasterers predominated, I was told, because this was the easiest skill to pick up. The first plasterer in Sakaltutan, Hasan (V), had learned his trade ten years before from a friend, and had then taught his kin, and thus the skill had spread through the village. Almost all the plasterers were young men and recent recruits to the trade.

Labour for building is apparently recruited by a hierarchical system of contracting and subcontracting, so that there are often several levels between the contractor who undertakes to build a building and the workman who puts the bricks and plaster together. Thus, finding regular work depends on establishing and maintaining contacts with people in the next level above oneself. At least two men in Sakaltutan were one level up from the bottom in this system; they took on large amounts of work from contractors and then subcontracted part of it to their friends. A position at this level gave a man much greater continuity of work, higher profit, and the power to dispense employment to his neighbours and friends.

The ordinary skilled men also worked on contract. They claimed to be able to earn from T.L.7 to T.L.12 a day (17s. 6d. to £1 10s., $2.40 to $4.20); the standard answer was T.L.10.

65

This is more than three times the earning of an unskilled labourer, and twice the earning of a craftsman in the villages. (By 1955 these earnings had doubled.) In theory, then, by working every day a man could earn T.L.300 a month. Against this, living expenses were estimated at about T.L.40 a month. But work it seems was almost always intermittent and undisciplined. The men had, or took, many free days when they were not merely not earning but spending. But they did send or bring money home, and T.L.100 a month (£12 10s., $35) seemed to be about the expected savings of a skilled man.

The other large category of migrant labourers were the unskilled. *Amele*, the normal word in use in the village, distinguished these sharply from the craftsmen, *usta*. The rewards were comparatively puny – T.L.3 a day (7s. 6d., $1.00). Men away as labourers lived harder and spent less, and generally seemed to save at the rate of about T.L.50 a month. Many of those listed as unskilled migrants were casual labourers in the building trade, often boys, with one eye firmly on becoming an *usta*. Only a few, too old to learn a skill, or too stupid, were compelled to try to keep a household largely by unskilled labouring alone.

Climatic differences in agricultural seasons have led to traditional seasonal migrations of agricultural labour in many different parts of Turkey, quite apart from migration to the towns (de Planhol (1958) p. 172). In 1950 to 1952 some people from Sakaltutan, Elbaşı and the surrounding villages went down to the Kayseri plain, to work there on the earlier harvest. Some even went as far as the Adana plain south of the Taurus Mountains. Probably this type of migration was formerly more important and has declined with the increase in the population of the plains, the increase in alternative possibilities for migrant labour, and the beginnings of mechanisation (Faculty of Political Science, Ankara 1952). For those few who still go, this shortlived and well paid migration is worth while, coinciding as it does with the lull in work in the upland villages before their own harvest begins, and requiring only skills that every villager is bred to.

Five other villagers had established other occupations for themselves. Two were porters in Kayseri. Turkish towns are full of porters who will carry more or less anything anywhere.

They are organised, and only recognised members are permitted to ply for hire in the streets. But though better than casual labouring, it is lowly, chancy, and not normally a lucrative occupation. More interesting were the two men who had worked their way as stallholders into the marketing of vegetables in the fashionable part of Ankara. This is also a closed group, entered presumably by personal contact and perhaps a period of apprenticeship. Apparently it was the source of a variable but on balance highly satisfactory income. Both men had switched to this occupation from that of migrant craftsman. One other had recently returned to the village after two years away as a cook, at a salary said to be T.L.150 a month.

Under the first Turkish five-year plan, 1934 to 1939 (Herschlag (1960) pp. 104–5) factories had been deliberately sited in the hinterland in order to spread the social effects of industry as widely as possible. In 1950 the Russian-built textile mill at Kayseri was still the largest in Turkey, though larger ones were by then under construction. The factory employed about three thousand workers. Wages increased with length of service and included a number of special benefits: childrens' allowances, marriage bounties, barracks for village men who had left their families behind, and free medical services and amusements. Five men worked in this factory. The wages paid were much less than those of casual skilled work, but the steady income year in and year out made it attractive. The men normally returned to the village on Saturday and left again on Sunday evening or Monday morning. The discipline and the severe limitation of family life were the main drawbacks. Wages varied from about T.L.60 a month for a floor sweeper, barely a living wage even for a villager, to T.L.150 for a machine operator with long service.

This external income had several effects on the village economy. Primarily it injected a large quantity of cash. People said that money had formerly been rare in the villages, and most economic exchange was carried on in kind. Now a considerable number of households prefer to meet their obligations with cash. Secondly, some of the money earned outside is spent in the village on employing labour for housing, or buying food from neighbours. Thirdly, it may in some instances provide capital for new types of enterprise (pp. 70 ff.). Fourthly, the migrant craftsmen return to the village with urban accoutrements: suits, shoes, watches, pens. They tended to furnish their homes with more comfort and modern gadgets. Sooner or later this is bound to stimulate the general level of village demand, though apart from improvements in housing, this process had hardly begun in 1952.

In Elbaşı, the range of jobs was similar. Apart from several building trade craftsmen, there was a man who had been a clerk in Istanbul, a member of the locally recruited Kayseri Watch (a body which assisted the state urban police), a Kayseri carter, and one or two porters. Others went off casually as unskilled labourers, though in Elbaşı casual jobs inside the village were more readily available.

Recruiting is partly a matter of messages reaching the village through established channels, and partly a matter of casual decision. The better known and more skilled regulars sometimes receive explicit invitations from friends. The rest rely on rumour and general gossip about the possibilities in various parts of the country, or simply go off to search. The general election of 1950, for example, slowed down construction work, and people returned to the village saying there were no jobs. On the other hand the building of an airfield by foreign contractors at Adana in 1952 stimulated a minor exodus of hopefuls.

Permanent migration to town was rare in both villages. In Sakaltutan the only cases were those of men who married town women. Even those who were most at ease in the town economic system kept their wives and families in the village. The advantages were partly economic. A roomy village house costs little to build (p. 90), and almost nothing to keep up, whereas a town dwelling of any kind would involve rent, and probably squalor as well. A village family with land would be usefully occupied and provide many of its own needs, and even one without land could earn staple foods by working for neighbours, especially at the harvest, and buy more cheaply than in town.

Social factors were clearly important in keeping people rooted in the village. Most of them, even the young ones, preferred to return where they belonged, among a set of people they had known from birth, permanent neighbours, brothers and sisters, cousins and affines, with all the restraints and conflicts involved. Young men accepted the village system of marriage; and marriage brought them additional ties to the village and a dependent wife exceedingly unwilling to move to town, where she would be almost totally lacking in the skills and social training necessary to running a home and maintaining neighbourly relations.

The villagers are bound to the village by strong social ties, and there is no economic advantage in breaking these. But as village population grows the numbers dependent on cash from outside also grows. I divided the households of Sakaltutan up into four groups:

> 49 depended entirely on their land, or used other sources only to a minor degree in emergencies;
>
> 16 derived the main part of their income from work outside the village;
>
> 22 normally used both these sources;
>
> and 13 derived their income largely or wholly from work inside the village.

The boundaries between these divisions are not clearly cut, and the classification depends solely on my own estimate. It is obvious from these figures that the village relied heavily on outside income for survival.

Economically the present system of migrant labour has great advantages. It does not diminish agricultural production, because most households with even a modest holding of land see to it that it is well used, at least by village standards. On the other hand the fact that many of the village men are both farmers and migrant labourers gives the village economy a flexibility which acts as a two-way insurance. When the harvest is poor, more men migrate for work outside. When the work is in short supply, workers survive by returning to village homes stocked up with food in the traditional fashion. Even when a bad harvest and a mild national recession coincided in the summer of 1949 the flexibility still had advantages. Some of the regular migrants with a fair amount of land returned to live off their land, but at the same time some of the poorer farmers succeeded in bridging a serious gap by finding unskilled jobs away.

However, although skilled rates of pay produce good incomes by village standards, and although the village is now economically dependent on outside income, skilled migrant labour is neither liked by those who do it, nor admired by those who do

69

not. Within the village it is ownership of land which counts, and agricultural income which matters. Money, they say, is soon spent, and who knows if work will always be available? But land is an assurance of food, come what may. The trappings of sophistication – suits, watches and fountain pens – have some appeal, but a scruffy old man who has land and works it well carries much more weight in the village than an elegant young *usta*. Young men enjoy the liberties of the city and the feel of cash in their pockets, but the older men almost unanimously declare that they would far rather stay at home with their families and farm their land, if only they had enough of it to be worth farming. Even if some say this only because they feel they are expected to, this response to expectation is in itself significant. For all its glitter even migrant labour is only an expedient to meet the shortage of land, and not desirable in itself, nor seen as a permanent part of a new way of life.

Village Enterprises

Most villagers conceive of the economic order as fixed, and have no thought of permanent changes. Nevertheless in most, if not all villages, a small number of men are endowed with the necessary resources for, and capable of, trying out new ideas.

The most obvious type of experiment is a shop. The permanent shops in Elbaşı were fairly new enterprises and, as I have said (p. 62) intermittent shops were common. Probably at least some of these were intended to be permanent, but the entrepreneur lacked the necessary skill and experience. Elbaşı contained one café, also a new enterprise, where a few men played cards, back gammon and dominoes and drank tea and coffee.

On a much larger scale was investment in lorries. I was told that, when the road from Tomarza through Sakaltutan to Kayseri was opened in 1947, the first men of Tomarza to put lorries into service had made fabulous profits. The idea caught on rapidly; the number of lorries increased and the fares and freight charges fell. By 1951 some operators were already arguing that, in the long run, charges were too low to cover depreciation. The roads were appalling, and the level of preventive maintenance as low as the level of mechanical ingenuity in keeping vehicles on the road was high.

One other form of enterprise was developing at the time of my fieldwork: diesel-powered flour mills. Traditional mills had been water powered, and the nearest to Sakaltutan was about four hours' walk away in a village blessed with enough water to run seven mills. Just before my arrival a diesel-powered mill had been set up in Tomarza. In 1950 a number of men of Süleymanli, Sakaltutan's nearest neighbour, had combined to put up the capital for one in their village. While I was in Sakaltutan another was built there and was in operation in 1951. By 1952 a man returned from the Argentine had invested his savings in yet another in a village between Sakaltutan and Elbaşı.

The details of capital and running costs and the income from these mills varied greatly every time I tried to get information. The Süleymanli mill was financed by nine shares, but some of these in turn were divided among two or more partners; the total capital cost of the mills seems to have been about T.L.20,000 (£2,500, $7,000). The shareholders originally tried to run the mill entirely by their own labour, dividing responsibility into nine, like the shares; three men on duty, six off. Since the mills ran all day and all night after the harvest, it is not surprising that they found this very hard work and rather unsatisfactory.

The main mover in the Sakaltutan mill seems to have been Haci Osman (H). He admitted to disappointment in 1952 and again in 1955, because the running costs and repairs had been more than he had expected, but he said by 1955 that most of the debt had been cleared, and he looked forward to an income of about T.L.500 per annum as his share. I never obtained a reliable statement of the shares but a considerable part of the capital came from Kayseri. Haci Osman's wife's brother, head of a leading village household, also held a share. Haci Osman ran a shop by the mill, profiting by the throng of people. It is plain that the mills were a fairly satisfactory investment.

The traditional mills used to charge one-twentieth (five per cent) of wheat and rye milled, and one-fifteenth (6⅔ per cent) of barley. The mills began by charging the same, but by 1955 they were charging six per cent for wheat and rye, and nine per cent for barley. People said the new mills produced finer flour, and of course they saved those who lived near them hours of carting, journeying and waiting.

71

In the past, Kara Osman (Ax), the large landowner, had run a tractor and a combine harvester. He had not only used them locally, but had taken them every year to Adana south of the Taurus to hire out. They were still lying derelict in the village. By 1955 another villager had bought himself a tractor and a set of farming tools with government credit and he used them not only on his own land but, for a rent, on his co-villagers' land.

The headman in Elbaşı and one or two of the wealthier villagers in the next village had shares in a hotel in Ankara; and in another village near Sakaltutan the leading households, two brothers, had inherited a small hotel in Kayseri from their father. One of the itinerant carpenters and his plumber brother talked of setting up a workshop in Sakaltutan and actually began excavations, but did not pursue the matter. There was also talk of a small textile mill. Köse Mehmet in Elbaşı had made, so he claimed, a success of sheep breeding, and discussed establishing with his savings a 'scientific-modern' grocery shop in Kayseri, or alternatively, a poultry farm. But he knew that he lacked the necessary knowledge to make either thrive.

It is often said at many different levels that, like other so-called under-developed low-income countries, Turkey lacks capital. Yet the rate of economic development in these villages was restricted far more by inexperience and technical ignorance than by shortage of capital, and also perhaps by fear of regulation and bureaucratic interference. If there had been clear opportunities for profit, in enterprises in which villagers felt they had the necessary experience, then a much higher rate of investment would have been forthcoming. On the other hand their expectations of profit are high. People do not think in terms of investing money and drawing a modest percentage as a permanent income. They expect to recover invested capital, and reckon as profit any surplus over and above this which eventually accrues. A probable rate of return of less than thirty-three per cent gross is unlikely to attract investment.

Marketing

It seems highly probable that, before about 1925, little was sold or bought for cash by any but the most prosperous and powerful villagers. With more land per household, supplies per head of staple grains and milk and meat products must normally have formed a larger part of a less varied diet. More clothes were produced in rural areas. Bride price was paid in gold and silver currency, and wealth was stored in gold coins worn as ornaments by the women. On the whole, most villagers marketed little direct, and most of what they did market was bartered with visiting traders for various necessities; or sold to the tax collectors; or to village leaders who could organise expeditions large enough to be safe.

Nowadays, money is a regular part of life in the village, and every household has urgent cash needs. It is simple for any villager to market his goods direct, so everyone sells as much as he can. By far the greatest part of the exports is grain, which is transported safely by lorry and sold direct to the government Office of Soil Products, *Toprak Mahsulleri Ofisi*, known in the village as *Ofis*.

Following a disastrous world fall in wheat prices in 1930, the government authorised the Agricultural Bank to buy cereals at a price to be decided by the cabinet, and to store and mill them. In 1937 these functions were transferred to a new organisation, the Office of Soil Products. During the Second World War the Office expanded its activities enormously both in range and quantity. After the war, it reverted more or less to its former functions, but has since been expanding its organisation steadily, taking each year an increasing percentage of the marketed cereal crop.

Each year, as the harvesting ends, the village lorries run a flat-out service to the nearest depot of this agency; villagers vie with each other to get their sacks of grain on to the lorries, and day and night the village is full of argument and bustle. At the depot, officials examine each sack for quality and dampness, and eternal wrangles go on over the grading, which determines the price. In spite of these disputes, and although the grading appears to depend on the officials' personal judgement, I never heard of any villagers complaining of corruption.

This major annual marketing apart, there is a constant stream of minor exports from the villages, mainly during the summer months. From Sakaltutan potatoes, onions and ground peas (*nohut*), for example were taken to Kayseri and sold privately in the market.

Livestock also provided a number of commodities for sale. The sheep provided wool, marketed direct in Kayseri. Finished carpets, rugs and bags were also sold in Kayseri direct to the retail shops. Cheese was sold, and people in Elbaşı sold sheep's milk to itinerant collectors while the ewes were in milk after the lambing season. Lambs, mainly the male yearlings, were sold for meat. No household breeds cattle deliberately for market, but calves surplus to needs are sold, sometimes to neighbours, sometimes to dealers, sometimes direct in Kayseri. Eggs are mostly bartered in the village, but a man going to town often takes eggs and a chicken or two to sell. The system is flexible, since the household can consume more or less, and is free to time the sale of livestock and their products to suit its needs and interests. Animals represent a sort of bank balance.

No one in the village runs a regular business as a dealer in major supplies such as seed – this is either part of last year's crop, or obtained direct from the local branch of the Ministry of Agriculture – or fertiliser, which is not used. One or two men, however, traded intermittently in animals. Ziya (S) the carpenter occasionally went off on a village trip to buy sheep and cattle in small numbers and ship them by lorry to Kayseri for sale. Another man in Süleymanli village told me of expeditions some years before by train to Istanbul with cattle he had bought up in the villages. Clearly, however, trade of this kind was a very minor part of the village economy.

The State

Although the village still produces much of what it consumes and officials appear to play only a small part in the lives of the people, in fact the village economy is dependent on the national economy and is largely shaped by government policy. The government decides taxes, cereal prices and credit policies, and directly or indirectly determines the prices of consumer goods.

Under the Ottoman Empire, tax collecting had been auctioned to contractors, who had been entitled to a fixed proportion of everyone's crop. The possibilities of extortion and of evasion under such a system are obvious, but what the villagers complained of most bitterly was the deterioration of the crops while waiting for the collector to arrive. The Republic finally abolished this system in 1925 (Lewis (1961) p. 461) and eventually replaced it by the collection by salaried officials of fixed cash sums. Land tax was paid on whatever land a villager had registered with the tax authorities, which was classified into grades and taxed accordingly. In 1949–55 the real value of this tax had declined since the last assessment in 1939, because of steep inflation, and was negligible. In any case, it did not correspond with the actual amounts of land to which villagers exercised *de facto* rights of ownership. Animals were also taxed per head, and in addition the village men paid a poll tax, the road tax, of T.L.12 (about £1 10s., or $4.20). This last tax was particularly unpopular, and fell very heavily on the poorest members of the community. I saw property seized by the tax collector from the homes of defaulters. The Democrat Party government in 1950 abolished the animal tax and the road tax, and left the economists to argue for the next decade that the agricultural section of the Turkish economy was grossly undertaxed.

State agricultural credit in Turkey has an old and honourable history. The Agricultural Bank was established in 1888 and survived as a semi-private Bank until 1936 when it became State-owned. Credit was steadily expanded, especially after the Second World War until, in 1950, T.L.400,000,000 (£50 million) credit was extended at a standard rate of six per cent (Robinson (1949) Letter 23).

When I arrived, Elbaşı was already the headquarters of a Credit Co-operative which served a number of villages. This was not in fact a co-operative in any normal sense, but a local branch of the Agricultural Bank with special rules, run by an official of the Bank who lived in Elbaşı. Members were compelled to offer mutual guarantees, and to contribute a small percentage of their loans, part to a fund to meet defaulting and part to establish their own share in the Co-operative. Members had the right to elect a committee, but all decisions lay in fact with the official. The villagers did not see the point of all this and regarded the small percentages as an imposition, tolerable because the Credit Co-operative, with its mutual guarantees, and its office in the village, was more generous than the old town branch of the Agricultural Bank had been. Yet in 1951–52, only 120 households took loans, and many of these did not take all they were entitled to borrow. Many of the remaining ninety households were entitled to loans but did not take them.

In Sakaltutan, in 1949–50, the villagers still drew their loans direct from the Agricultural Bank in Kayseri, though by 1955 they too were members of a Credit Co-operative. In 1950 I had the impression that most households which qualified had taken loans.

Normally, loans are collected by the Bank immediately after the harvest, and then within a short period fresh loans are made for the next season. The villagers in Sakaltutan told me that if any one villager defaulted the Bank would make no fresh loans to that village. In fact, it does seem that the debtors were grouped in mutually responsible groups, usually by villages.

The effect of the loans was not in any way to encourage capital improvements. Money from any source was used in any way the household needed to use it, and loans at low interest were naturally welcome. The first time a household received a loan it was thus a kind of shot in the arm for current expenses, but thereafter the year-to-year position was no different from what it had always been – the comparatively large sum from the harvest simply went into the bank and out again, and was then used for the usual purposes.

Nevertheless the system had advantages. The loan acted as a cushion. In good years, some households reduced their government loans, thus putting themselves in a position to borrow more than they had to pay back in a bad year or an expensive one.

The loans did not, however, help to meet the villagers' most serious problem: a year with no harvest. If the crops were below a certain percentage of average, the Bank declared a moratorium on all debts. The villager was then in the same position as he would have been without the Agricultural Bank. He had no crops to sell, no income to buy the annual necessities, and probably not even enough food to last until the next harvest. Because he owed the Bank one debt, he could not borrow again from this source. Some villagers have ways round this difficulty. The loans are personal, so that if a man's son or his wife can be declared a landowner, and if the headman will ratify the application, a fresh loan can be obtained. This kind of thing is more difficult once a Credit Co-operative has arrived in the village, because the local manager has local knowledge. But neighbours and kin may still be able to arrange to help each other out. In Elbaşı, I came across one case of a man who had not used his own rights to credit, borrowing on behalf of another; and there were probably similar instances.

The Bank also makes special loans, for example it helps with the purchase of machinery. One or two villagers in Elbaşı had used this service by 1955. In the summer of 1950, people in Sakaltutan received special supplementary loans, in bureaucratic theory to pay for the expense of harvesting, but in practice to buy food to last till the harvest came in.

Apart from the Bank, the Department of Agriculture made cleaned seed available on credit to the villagers each year. Not all villagers wanted the government type of seed, but most people accepted some of it. Once again, the rules for issuing were bureaucratically complex, but the requirements were easily met provided the headman was prepared to sign. At least one landless villager obtained and ate an allotment of seed.

In Elbaşı, the government veterinary service had introduced another form of government aid. Annually they brought two stallions, one of French farm stock and one Arab, to the village to serve the mares. The villagers appreciated this service. They did not keep the foals in the village but sold them for good prices (p. 83). In 1951, government officials also brought merino rams to cross with the *karamanli* village ewes. The villagers were dubious about the ability of the progeny to survive their winter, but said that in any case they had already put the rams to the flocks.

In a much more immediate sense, the government affects the village economy through its control of prices. The prices offered year to year by the Office of Soil Products (p. 73) is decided by the Cabinet itself. These have been above world price for every year except one since the Office was founded. The Democrat Party government made its decisions at least partly on political grounds. This guaranteed price is perhaps the greatest single benefit that the government has conferred on Turkish village agriculture. It destroyed the traditional situation in which prices drop to nothing in times and areas of glut, when the working household has a surplus, and rise to fantastic heights in times and areas of shortage, when the working household is hungry. The old system discourages production for market; the new system encourages it greatly.

Consumer prices are also determined, if less directly, by government policy. The government control of import duties and quotas largely decided the price of almost all manufactured goods. Through the State monopolies, the government decides the price of sugar, matches and cigarettes. The State-owned factories, held by the State Banks, decide the price of their products by bureaucratic expediency rather than by the economic pressures of the market. In particular, cloth and clothing were expensive during my stay. In 1950 and 1952, national shortages of petrol, tyres and spare parts limited lorry transport and put up village transport costs.

The villagers live only partly in the national money economy. In so far as they consume directly what they produce they are outside the effects of inflation and government price control. But a large and rapidly increasing part of their economy is within the national economy. In this sector, in general, they receive artificially high prices for their goods, but are forced to pay also artificially high prices for what they consume. This system has disadvantages both for them and for the national economy. But the guarantee of a stable and rewarding price for grain is an overwhelming advantage, and has provided the major stimulus to increased production.

The Economic System

Steady and striking economic changes had clearly been taking place in both these villages in the last ten or fifteen years before my field work. Traditionally, the economy of villages like Sakaltutan, and to a lesser degree Elbaşı also, was a near subsistence economy, (cf. Yasa (1957) pp. 26–28, 177). A high proportion of what the villages consumed they produced for themselves, and except for relatively few essentials, what the village did not produce it went without. For considerable periods, the villages could survive without the towns.

They still supply a large part of what they consume. All cereals, milk products, meat and eggs, and some at least of the fruit and vegetables consumed are produced in the village. The villages also supply their own fuel from straw, dung and scrub, build their own houses with local stone (though timber and other materials have to be imported), breed most of their own draught animals, and satisfy their own needs for *kilims*, bags and sacks. Some of these needs are met by a small amount of trade between villages, but in most of these items each village, and to some extent each household is self-sufficient. The villagers exaggerated this self-sufficiency, and liked to emphasise their independence; in their still traditional view of the world, the land gave an assurance of survival which such unreliable sources of income as a government salary did not.

The village also processes, through its own resident craftsmen, some imported raw materials to meet some of its needs for tools and utensils. These craftsmen are however far from able to supply all the needs, each serving not a single village but an area. Their services are supplemented by visiting craftsmen, and by the purchase of ready-made goods direct from the towns. Similarly, the village provides itself with shops for retail goods, but also purchases much of its needs direct from urban shops.

The factors which determine whether a consumer favours local shops or local craftsmen, or prefers to make use of outsiders, are complex, and special to each case. So too are those which determine what kind of enterprise a villager attempts, and at which he is successful. The purely economic factors are fairly obvious. A pedlar or itinerant craftsman, for example, has smaller overheads than a shopkeeper or resident craftsman, and a larger potential market. But he must transport his stock or the tools of his trade, and, seeking custom among strangers, he can rely less on kinship and neighbourhood ties. Again, the village consumer can buy village products more cheaply in the village, village imports more cheaply in the town. Personal services and crafts involving labour are cheaper in the village. But besides these economic factors, the network of social relationships plays an extremely important part in determining who uses whose services, and people may well prefer the use of familiar or friendly or traditional ways of satisfying their needs, even if these cost more.

Village imports nowadays are considerable. Essentials are all imported in increasing quantity – building for example has greatly expanded – and in addition, fruit and vegetables, especially cabbage and beet, which can be stored and eaten during the winter, tea and coffee, *helva* and sweets, some ready-made clothes, shoes and bedding, winter feed for animals to supplement village straw, paraffin (kerosene) for lighting, and such luxury as flash-lights, bicycles, radios, pressure lanterns, watches and fountain pens, fancy cups and glasses, mirrors, and so on; and very recently, and rarely, lorries, flour mill machinery, fuel and spare parts.

To pay for all this, the villages have been growing as much grain for market as possible, and also exporting their traditional products; cheese, milk, wool, livestock, *kilims* and woven bags. Elbaşı, by great expansion of the area under cultivation, has managed more or less to balance its trade, but like most villages, Sakaltutan has been forced to export labour on a large scale as well.

In spite of the rise in consumption and in earnings by both villages, there is little investment in agriculture. Very few of the village imports are directed to agricultural production, unless we count the materials for making the primitive tools. Recently, people have been buying steel ploughs, and one man in Elbaşı by 1955 had bought on credit a tractor and a set of agricultural equipment. But no one even thought about the means of raising the very low yields per *dönüm*.

The villages are homogeneous in production, and economic relations between them consist mainly of reciprocal exchanges and small loans, the use of craftsmen, advice on health and medicines for people and animals, religious and magical consultations, and sales of animals. The vast bulk of village buying and selling is with the towns. In spite of the village illusions that land makes a farmer independent in a way that mere earners of cash are not, the village is in fact directly and completely tied into the national economy.

In theory economic dependence is a two-way relationship. If the villages depend on the towns for their survival, so also do the towns depend on the villages for food and labour. But in fact even in purely economic terms, the townsmen with their greater concentration of wealth are always stronger in specific instances than the villagers, who are normally too near to serious want to take risks, and too numerous and divided to use the weapon of cutting off urban food supplies, or withholding labour.

It is a commonplace that the economic system of relatively

closed small-scale societies are part of the social system. Economic behaviour takes place between people who already have established social relations, in a social context where both parties are known and share the values and mutual expectations of the society to which they belong. In this situation economic behaviour often fails to respond to purely economic stimuli.

The village society is still a closed small-scale society but one with strong links and a growing intimacy with the more impersonal large-scale society of the nation and the cities. For example, the marketing of the main crop is conducted with officials, impersonally and impartially. On the other hand, other relations with town merchants, though they may also be purely economic, are usually more complex. A particular shopkeeper will be known to and trusted by men of a particular village or lineage. This established relation gives the villager more confidence, since the merchant has now something to lose by cheating. A man of this kind may act not only as a retailer but as a postal service, money-lender and general friend and adviser to his clients. The villagers, though often forced into relations with complete strangers, do not like such relations and constantly seek to turn the impersonal single-stranded tie into a multiple personal loyalty.

Membership of a relatively closed society affects economic behaviour in another and even more important way. For most villagers, what primarily concerns them is their place, not in the nation, but in their village. They are concerned with improving or at least maintaining their standing among the neighbours and kin where they were born and grew up. A few leave altogether, accepting a new scale of social importance in a new environment; and a larger minority live in two scales, an urban, migrant worker's world, and the village. But for most, the village is the only social arena that really matters. Hence economic activities are subordinate to this end. So long as the household can fulfil honourably enough its obligations and needs, that is, so long as it can marry off its children decently and house its married sons, then there is no pressing need to accumulate further wealth. Except for some of the very young men, people prefer to stay in the village if no urgent need drives them away. Hence the common phenomenom of the unreliability of migrant workers, and the oft-reported tendency for people to work less if they are paid more. Moreover, behaviour which is likely to arouse criticism or ridicule is not safe. Unless one is absolutely sure of success, innovation is to be avoided.

If village social organisation inhibits experiment, so does village culture, — 'culture' in the sense of a stock of inherited and acquired knowledge and experience. In 1955, there were still only two forms of new enterprise established. One, motor transport – obvious, profitable (at least at first), and a development of a traditional activity; the other, flour milling – even closer to traditional rural business enterprise. Neither required much specialist knowledge. But talk of poultry farms and small textile mills or workshops remained talk, because people lacked the knowledge and experience to be sure of success. It is lack of a tradition and of experience rather than of capital that inhibits spontaneous enterprise.

The strength of village society, and the fact that villagers see their personal future in terms of the village and not of the nation, accounts for the strong attachment to farming, and the almost unanimous dislike which migrant labourers, even the most highly skilled, expressed for their occupation. Prestige and power in the village were tied with landowning and with permanent residence, not with wandering about the country, however profitable this might be.

If village social organisation limits and shapes economic behaviour, the changing economy has great effects on traditional social organisation. Some details of these changes will form part of later chapters. But in general, the main change is the multiplication, for most adult male villagers, of a new private set of more or less impersonal social relations with employers, fellow-workers, officials, and buyers and sellers, different for each individual, all leading out of the village into the national society. A generation ago, such external relations were the prerogative of village leaders, and even for them were far fewer and less impersonal. This change inevitably opens the structure of village society, and lessens the authority of its leaders.

CHAPTER FIVE

THE HOUSEHOLD ECONOMY

Household Resources

The main resources of a household are threefold: land, animals, and able-bodied ploughmen. The essential equipment for living – the house and its contents – and the farming – tools, ox-cart, wooden plough, drag, – are still relatively cheap and easy to come by. In a traditional more or less self-sufficient household, production depends on a correct balance between these resources. Very roughly one working man, and one team of oxen can plough from fifteen to twenty or so *dönüm*, (eight to ten acres, thirty to forty decares) a year. By using three oxen, one resting while two worked, a man could improve on his output a little. Water buffalo are more efficient, and a pair of horses can plough about thirty *dönüm* a year. Most households kept a cow – prosperous ones up to four – a donkey or perhaps two, and some chickens. The number of sheep also is roughly tied to the scale of the household's farming operations, by the need to feed them during the winter, and to a lesser extent by the need for female labour to milk them in spring.

The economic balance in a farming household economy is illustrated by the horses in Elbaşı. The increase of area under cultivation which has taken place in recent years was partly made possible, and at the same time rendered economical, by the use of teams of horses for ploughing. But horses are much more difficult to feed in the winter, and unless a man has enough land to make full use of the extra work a horse can do in the brief ploughing and harvesting seasons, the cost of feeding it for the many months of enforced idleness is not repaid. The superior foals sired by government stallions (p. 77) were not retained to improve the village breed as the government in-

4

tended, because, even for the better off, the extra work they could do did not compensate for the extra food they ate.

Nowadays for many, indeed for most, village households the resources are out of balance. Some have too little man- and animal-power for their land and so let it out to share-croppers, or (as in Elbaşı), hire men to cultivate it, or even leave it uncultivated. More households are in the reverse situation. They have more man-power than their land will absorb. Some go as migrants, others acquire animal-power and take on share-cropping. But the fragmentation of holdings forces many men to remain in the village and maintain oxen and equipment when their land is insufficient to make full use of their own and their animals' labour.

Income and Outgo

Households range from those which have neither land nor animals, to those with two hundred *dönüm* or so, three or four teams of draught animals, and a sizeable flock; personal earned incomes range from casual unskilled village labourers, the shepherds for example, earning T.L.500 (£62 or $179) or less a year, to established skilled migrant labourers earning perhaps T.L.2,000 a year. Household incomes – farming income plus contributions from earning members – therefore vary enormously.

The accurate determination of these incomes would be possible only after long and careful interviewing and checking. I found villagers vague and inconsistent about income, partly because no one is willing to disclose details of resources to anyone else, partly because most of them do not think in terms of a recurrent income at all. They certainly budget to meet particular expenses from particular resources. But there is no occasion in village life when a man adds up all that comes in, and sets it off against all that goes out. Moreover, both farming and non-farming incomes are liable to fluctuate wildly from year to year, so that no one has an 'average annual income'.

The unit of land, the fertility, the crop, all vary according to plot, to year, and to informant. Not only does the land cropped alternate from year to year with the village fallow system; but because of shortages of seed and animals, sickness, death and inheritance, changes in share-cropping arrangements, and land disputes, a man rarely sows the same area two alternate years running.

According to informants' statements, I calculated normal yields in Sakaltutan at about fifteen bushels to the acre. 1949 – a year of national disaster – 1950 and 1951 were all years of poor yield, so I may have underestimated. In Elbaşı, equally rough calculations gave a figure nearer twenty bushels, but the difference may be illusory.

Taking the lower figure, a man with about ten acres (forty decares to work each year, twenty acres in all) would get about 150 bushels in a normal year. Of this, he would need to keep about fifty bushels to feed his household, and about twenty-five bushels for seed and a further twenty-five for animals, village dues and so forth. The balance of about fifty bushels would be sold, and in the years 1949–52, would have realised about T.L.300.

In Table 6, I give estimates, made during threshing, before the final count, of expected total yields of four households. The yields per acre were lower than usual, and the discrepancies in the rate are due partly to variations in optimism, partly to the general vagueness of informants about areas and quantities, and perhaps to actual difference in yields of different farmers and different pieces of land.

Table 6

EXPECTED CEREAL HARVESTS: SAKALTUTAN 1950

House-hold	Total land holding claimed village dönüm*	Bushels	Yield Bushels per Acre	Surplus for sale	Cash T.L.
1	150 (largest in Sakaltutan)	500	13·3	250	1500
2	60	150	10	60	375
3	75 (15 share cropped)	138	8	60	375
4	30	88	12	12	75

* Only half is worked each year

Actual yields were even lower than this. I found the last house-hold weeping together because the yield was only fifty bushels, barely enough for the household needs for food, fodder and seed, with nothing towards clothes, house repairs, a wedding due, and very considerable debts.

In Elbaşı, the poor households were in much the same position as corresponding households in Sakaltutan. At the other end of the scale the richer households provided a marked contrast. In 1951 and 1952, several households farming something like sixty acres each year harvested about one thousand bushels, and were able to sell, after allowing for their larger populations of both humans and animals, six hundred to seven hundred bushels, thus making a profit of about T.L.4,000. I happened to see an official receipt for one such household for roughly this sum.

Sheep can also provide a considerable cash income, besides providing milk, fat, meat and wool for the household. One informant in Elbaşı claimed that each ewe produces each spring a lamb worth T.L.25, cheese worth T.L.20 p.a., and two kilos of wool which pay all the expenses of its care and fodder, giving a net profit of T.L.45 p.a. This was unduly optimistic. It is true that costs are low, since the sheep live on free pasture most of the year, and on straw for the winter months. But not every ewe lambs successfully, disease is common, and insurance unheard of. This informant on the same occasion gave a not entirely logical estimate of about T.L.2,000 income from eighty-five ewes.

Cattle, buffaloes and horses are mainly kept for work, although the cows produce milk which is not marketed, and calves which are. Buffaloes produce more and better milk, and more valuable calves – a mature draught buffalo will fetch T.L.500, but for this a man must face the expense and risk of keeping it for three years or so. Horses are bred and sold in Elbaşı; even the family donkey may produce foals. Chickens and eggs are often sold, though chicken rearing is extremely casual; a few households breed pigeons.

To put a figure to the cash surplus from these sources is almost impossible. In general and with marked exceptions, I would guess that the total cash income from farming is between one-and-a-half and two times the cash income from grain.

To make any kind of estimate of total incomes by households is even more difficult. For Sakaltutan I was able to divide

86

roughly each household by its main source of income (p. 69). Forty-nine relied wholly or largely on agriculture, sixteen largely on migrant labour, twenty on a mixture of these, and thirteen on work inside the village. For Elbaşı, a much smaller proportion, indeed a smaller absolute number, derived income from outside, and probably a larger proportion earned their keep largely by work in the village. More than half of the households lived largely or wholly by agriculture.

The wealthiest of those in Elbaşı who lived by farming alone had considerable incomes. If my guess for global cash income is correct, then one purely agricultural household of six people had a total income in 1952 of about T.L.6,000 (£750, or $2,100), after having provided directly for much of their household and farming needs in kind. Another household head, with seven in his household, gave me an estimate of about T.L.3,000 cash income. 1951 and 1952 were good years, and of the twenty-six households assessed in the top class for village contributions (p. 53), quite a number must have had incomes comparable with these.

Even in Sakaltutan, the wealthiest household (Table 6, No. 1) would on a rough estimate have in a good year enjoyed an income not far less, about T.L.2,500, but this with a total population of thirteen, including two middle-aged heads of growing families. Another villager who had enough land claimed that in a good year, on the side of the village on which more than half his land lay, he would make T.L.3,000, though he was immediately contradicted. In answer to direct questions several people in Sakaltutan said that in a normal year, an average household would make between T.L.500 and T.L.1,000, and this seems to be about right for the majority of ordinary middling households.

We may compare these figures with the earnings of skilled craftsmen. The most successful and regular migrants made somewhere about T.L.2,000 a year. On the other hand, finding work is chancy, many did not stay the full nine months, and all admitted spending on frivolities in town. Perhaps T.L.600 to 900 for the actual annual contribution to the household budget would be right in most cases.

Where personal incomes of this order came into a farming household they brought reasonable comfort. One household head in Elbaşı, with five adult sons, had sixteen members un-questionably in his own household, and liked to include also a schoolmaster son with his wife and two children, and a widowed daughter and her three little girls. In fact both these house-holds were separate but the father farmed their land. In 1951, he sold at least T.L.3,000 worth of grain, so T.L.4,500 is a modest estimate of his gross income from farming. Two of his five sons were plasterers, but not regular migrants; perhaps they contributed T.L.800. Another son was Village Secretary to the *Nahiye*, in which capacity he was supposed to be paid T.L.150 a month, T.L.1,800 a year. In addition, he ran a coffee shop. Without including the teacher's salary, the total income from all sources cannot have been far short of T.L.8,000 (£1,000 or $2,800). True he had many people to care for, but most of the household food supplies and farming expenses were met directly out of household produce.

Similarly, a senior man in Sakaltutan had five sons. In 1950, three were migrant craftsmen and were already married. The households kept two teams of oxen, so could in a normal year expect at least T.L.1,000 from farming, and somewhere be-tween T.L.1,500 and 3,000 from earnings, if all three sons went away to work for longish periods. This household had fourteen people to feed and support.

In the rare case of a craftsman relying solely on his earnings to support his wife and young children, without an income from land, these would be no more than sufficient to meet his house-hold needs. In such a case, his wife and his older children, by working for neighbours at the harvest, would normally earn part of the family food supply. Still it is clear that the craftsmen, shopkeepers and others have to be highly successful to compare favourably with a moderate farming household.

The real poor in the village are those who have little or no land or cannot work their land, and who make all or most of their living by unskilled labour. These include the watchmen, the shepherds and several other households. The Sakaltutan watchman was paid in kind, thirty-seven bushels of grain, not much more than enough to feed himself, his wife and his child. He was probably able to make something by doing odd jobs and running errands – he earned in this way from me in 1949–50 – but a total income of T.L.500 (£125, or $350) in a year would be a generous estimate. There were in Sakaltutan some ten households whose standard of living was about the same as this, and another half-dozen who were little better off. In Elbaşı, perhaps twenty households would fall into the same category. Households at this level, who have no harvest of their own, often work for others at the harvest and earn grain to store for their staple for the year. The watchman in Elbaşı had a slightly higher wage than that of Sakaltutan, but he gambled with what money he got, and his wife and three sons were miserably poor. His wife and eldest son each worked under contract at the harvest for fifteen bushels of grain of mixed types, worth perhaps T.L.100. Two brothers in Sakaltutan, included in the ten poorest households above, worked as operators in the mill; they began at T.L.50 a month, but this was soon raised to T.L.75 and this regular income soon made a conspicuous difference to their homes and families.

Expenditure is as difficult to estimate as income. Farming households still provide themselves with most of their own food, most if not all their own winter feed, most of their own seed, such fertiliser as they use, all their own fuel for heating, and their own wool. All households own their house and carry out their own maintenance. Non-farming households either enjoy an income in food from share-cropped land, or earn some of their own food in return for services.

Nevertheless, all households must spend some cash, and many households spend a great deal. The head of household 3 in Table 6 (p. 85) gave me the following estimate of his cash expenses, for a household of three adults and three children:

Food:

fat	T.L.10	bones	T.L.15		
cabbage	T.L.5	sugar	T.L.15		
rice	T.L.5			T.L. 50	
Clothes and shoes				T.L. 80	
Cooking utensils				T.L. 30	
Taxes				T.L. 40	
Animal feed (waste from oil presses)				T.L.100	
Total				T.L.300	

This estimate is a little less than his estimated cash income of T.L.375 from grain, but it is extremely modest. The item for winter feed is arbitrary, since this would depend directly on the number of animals and the amount of the village harvest. On domestic items, he makes no mention of paraffin, tea and coffee, which in fact he did without, fruit in season which he would probably buy on the spur of the moment, and luxuries such as *helva*, the Turkish sweet made from nuts and honey which most village households do occasionally eat. More important, he makes no provision for medical expenses, often a very large item, sometimes ruinous. Landless households would obviously need to spend much more on food, but practically nothing on taxes and animal feed.

This estimate takes no account of the large irregular expenses, for instance replacing oxen or weddings. Most households would be facing at least one demand of this type most of the time. On the marriage of a daughter, the father usually breaks even, if he does not reap an immediate cash benefit. But the marriage of a son is an expensive business, involving, in 1950, a bride price of up to T.L.500 and perhaps as much again for food, entertainers, presents and new clothes. A new house people reckoned at about T.L.1,000 or more, according to size and style. Timber and hewn stone were expensive items, and the services of a mason and a carpenter, even in the village, cost a good deal. Many households were actually engaged in building. Each new married couple requires a new room, and moreover, many villagers were dissatisfied with the old windowless houses, often shared with the animals, and often using the natural rock for at least one wall. Between 1949 and 1955 the housing standard in Sakaltutan rose strikingly.

Even the wealthier households in Elbaşı had basically the same items of expenditure, though with larger numbers and higher standards they consumed far more. They were better dressed, built larger houses, gave more lavish weddings, paid higher bride prices, and used far more luxuries – paraffin, pressure lamps to impress guests, fancy coffee cups and drinking glasses, and so forth.

All these figures ignore another important factor – they are based on normal yields. A partial crop failure immediately reduces the poor to near starvation, the moderate to poverty, and even the comfortable to stringent economy. For one year, or even two, housing, weddings, clothing replacements, tool and utensil repairs and so on, can be curtailed or postponed, and at a pinch animals and equipment sold. Almost every villager is in debt, and debts can be allowed to remain, or even be increased. But after a run of poor harvests urgent needs accumulate, and credit becomes exhausted; serious hardship may turn to disaster.

Debt

People remarked to me more than once that no villager ever has ready cash. Urgent cash needs constantly run ahead of current income, and people borrow to meet the immediate situation. Debts are of four main kinds – loans from the Agricultural Bank or Credit Co-operative, loans from money-lenders at illegal and exorbitant rates of interest, casual borrowings among neighbours and kin, and outstanding credit for purchases. Debts of this last kind are mainly owed to village shops, but also less frequently to itinerant vendors of oxen, to kin for land, and occasionally to affines for the balance of a bride price. Accurate information on this topic is almost unobtainable. Even when precise and plausible answers were given to questions one had no means of checking them.

In both villages, a large proportion of households had loans from the Agricultural Bank (p. 75). Although the loans were not large or numerous enough to meet all credit needs, neither village as a whole used the service fully. A few men said that fear of what the government might do if they failed to pay kept them from accepting.

On illegal and commercial debts I was able to gather only superficial information. The technique in practice for usury is the familiar one of obtaining a signature for the receipt of a larger sum than the actual sum advanced so that the interest is concealed and the creditor can enforce collection in a court, if necessary. An illiterate peasant is easily tricked. One such case came to my notice in Sakaltutan, and I heard of two other cases of private debts of this kind, carrying about 100 per cent interest per annum. Such loans are for a fixed period, and the interest is predetermined. It does not grow automatically with the passing of time, but the debt is stepped up if the date of repayment is not kept.

Commercial debts are even harder to check. People often

4*

spoke of outstanding debts. Several owed hundreds of lire for oxen. In one case the ox was already dead. Another owed T.L.1,600 to his sister in another village for land which he had taken over from her share of the inheritance. When I, somewhat naïvely, pointed out that the existence of this debt was inconsistent with the taking on of other heavy expenses – weddings and new houses for his sons – he said quite cheerfully 'Kinsfolk can wait'. In Elbaşı, on the day in which the Agricultural Bank Credit Co-operative Officer paid out the annual loans, the village shopkeepers and the headman were waiting on the spot to catch each villager as he left the room with money in his hand. All creditors press for payment at this season.

The network of small personal loans is intricate and far reaching. By the end of my year in Sakaltutan, I had many small loans out in the village, all of which were honourably settled. When a special need arises, a man meets it by calling in loans or by contracting a number of new ones, or both. Borrowing from Peter to pay Paul is common. These loans are personal favours, and do not carry interest. But they do of course count as services rendered in the network of village reciprocity. Often such loans are contracted with kin or friends in other villages, since this arrangement limits communication between creditors, and also general gossip.

The incurring of debt is a privilege of wealth. Those who have no visible resources cannot borrow, either from the State or from their neighbours. It is the haves, not the have-nots, who borrow. The largest loan from the Credit Co-operative in Elbaşı was taken by one of the most prosperous men in the village. A man in Sakaltutan who announced publicly and unprompted that he had a T.L.1,000 of debts was boasting, like the man in England who talks about his overdraft. All households can make use of credit. Even if they have no desperate needs in the way of houses, animals or wives, they can always, for example, buy animals to sell at a later date at a higher price. Debt carries no stigma. Most people are or have been in debt, and it is nothing to be ashamed of.

Yet, as I have said, many people do not take up all the credit they can get, and I had the decided impression that most of the households in Elbaşı were less in debt than those of Sakaltutan because it is a more prosperous village, and therefore the urgent needs are fewer. If this is true, then in spite of the profit to be made by using credit wisely, people prefer not to have debts, and most of them are unwilling to risk raising a loan for speculative enterprises.

In many peasant populations, dealers and money-lenders are said to dominate the village economy. Constant relationships to their clients enable them to exercise political as well as economic influence. In the Turkish villages, since government agencies buy the grain and provide credit, there is no class of merchants or money-lenders who have permanent relations of this kind with particular villagers. Possibly such a system existed in the past. The tax farmers may well have exercised some such hold over some villagers. But most large private debts of which I knew were borrowed from men in other villages, and it may well be that for villages as remote and independent as Sakaltutan, the risks were, for political reasons, too high to tempt urban money-lenders into becoming their patrons.

Except when they become involved in illegal and usurious loans from professional money-lenders – and these cases now seem to be rare and becoming rarer, owing to government credit – the chronic indebtedness of the villager is not a social evil. Generally, those who are heavily in debt are those whose assets in land and animals give them both an overall solvent position, and great hope that they will be able to recover. Most villagers accept a certain degree of indebtedness, to neighbours and to the Agricultural Bank, as an ordinary and permanent part of their lives.

The Economic Organisation of Households

The household, as I have said, is a group of people who produce and consume in common (p. 35). It shares all resources belonging to members, it shares out the work according to sex, seniority and convenience, and it distributes the total income among its members according to need and social position.

The household is practically the only organised economic unit in rural society. Each household is in fact a firm engaged in agricultural production, and, excluding one or two newfangled enterprises, such as diesel mills, no other comparable economic unit exists. All agricultural production is organised through these 'firms'. In other areas, modern farms exist and are increasing, but there were none near my two villages.

This economic unity excludes the exercise of the rights of individual members against the group, represented by the household head. We do not, for example, find women exercising rights to specific pieces of land; nor, if a young kinsman is brought up in a household, are any rights which he may have to his own land acknowledged until he leaves the household.

Even when members of a household are quarrelling more or less openly, they do not seem to think of dividing the produce between them. Haci Ismet (T), head of the richest household in Sakaltutan, was more or less senile, and the household was run by his eldest son. The second son – both were middle-aged men – was not on good terms with his father and brother, and in anticipation of trouble over the division of the land, rights to certain pieces had been established in advance. But even so the household was still run as an economic unit at least as far as farming was concerned, if not personal earnings. On the other hand, the younger son's first wife and her grown son, who had left altogether and set up a separate household, took with them the land owned by her in her own right.

The village is an economic unit only in the sense that it imposes the alternations of crop land and pasture, and in the sense that it provides essential communal services. But it is in no sense a unit for production. Moreover, organised and traditional co-operation between the households of a village do not seem to exist. Households in trouble may be helped by their neighbours and kin, but normally each household arranges its own work entirely on its own.

This household unit, provided its resources are more or less in balance, is a relatively tough and flexible concern. When times are good, it can build up resources in animals, by buying or by keeping more of the natural increase than usual. In satisfactory years, it has money to spend on clothes, replacement of equipment, even weddings and housing. In less fortunate times, through illness of humans or working animals, or poor harvests, it can easily postpone heavy expenditure, and if necessary sell animals to meet a crisis. Because the techniques are so simple, and the village relies so little on the outside world for productive resources, recovery from misfortune can be rapid, so long as the household has enough land to employ and support its members.

As I have said, many households do not have a proper balance of resources between land, people and animals. But the household is flexible enough to meet this too. Labour that is redundant can be sent away to work, if only for the seasons of agricultural lull, from April to June, and from late August to the first snow. In a family, one brother usually remains a farmer, often the eldest who was called upon to help his father as he grew up, and the others become regular migrant craftsmen. In a few cases, brothers maintain a joint household on this basis after their father's death; there was one such household in Sakaltutan, and I came across several in other villages. In other cases, brothers may separate, but maintain special collabora-tion, often through share-cropping arrangements. Two men who were at the same time father's brothers' sons and brothers-in-law, and were both migrant plasterers, took it in turn to stay at home and look after each others' household and to do each others' farm work, while dividing both the crop and their cash earnings between their separate households.

Unless well provided with land, small and especially defective households are much less resilient and flexible. A man with young children and barely enough land to work single-handed has no margin for misfortunes. If he goes away to work, his wife and children are likely to suffer in his absence, since his wife alone cannot cope with both her own work and with the care of the land, let alone with crises such as children's illnesses—one man who had been away for two years returned to find his eldest son had been drowned in the village well. Yet if he stays in the village, he has nothing for medical and other special expenses, and no resources against the inevitable years of famine which will leave his household hungry. A widow with young children may be in an even more difficult position.

Planning ahead for a household economy is not a matter of setting a more or less predictable income against more or less regular outgoings. Most households have capital resources; ex-pendable resources in the form of animals, non-expendable in the form of land. Against these they have to set debts. Income arrives not in small weekly amounts but in windfalls. Villagers who cannot raise a few lire for a bottle of medicine may nevertheless be accustomed to thinking in terms of quite large sums – on which of course a household may have to survive until the next windfall, generally the next harvest. When they discuss wage-earning they talk about rates per day, or how much they can save in a month away, never about weekly and rarely about monthly wages. Most migrant labourers regard wage-earning not as a provision for daily needs, but as a way of raising lump sums when need presses, to clear a debt, to meet famine, or to finance a wedding, a house or an ox. In most cases, in the rare intervals when no such special need hangs over a household, men much prefer to stay at home.

This thinking in lump sums is precisely opposite to that of western urban workers, who prefer to have their lump-sum purchases converted to weekly outgo by hire-purchase and mortgage arrangements. This difference in outlook is surely related to levels of saving. In the village economy the notion of regular accumulation of cash or bank balance is largely absent. Saving normally takes the form of increasing the household stock of animals. Beyond a certain point, the accumulation of animals increases problems of feeding and looking after them so much that loss by illness becomes likely. This point is not often reached, largely because special demands face most households fairly frequently and use up spare resources.

Formally, the direction of economic activities in any village household lies with the household head. In a small household, the head will normally himself perform most of the major farming tasks and leave his wife to her recognised duties in the home. In larger households, the father directs his sons, and although exceptions came to my notice, in the majority of cases the authority of the head is unquestioned. Even adult sons are directly dependent on their father for cash – no one ever suggested making a son an allowance. So long as the household owns sufficient resources to be able to maintain itself by farming, the undisputed control of resources by the head makes it very difficult to challenge him, short of splitting the land. The cash which junior members earn by their efforts outside the household and often outside the village is a very different matter.

A priori, the solidarity of the household as a 'firm', and the authority of the head as dispenser of all income is threatened by the existence of direct private sources of income for members of his household. Independent incomes may lead to friction over the disposal of them, and in a few cases make it possible for a recalcitrant son to survive independently, without his share of the household food supply (p. 103). Nevertheless, what is remarkable is not the division and disputes, but the fact that normally sons and younger brothers hand over to their fathers or elder brothers a large share of their earnings and both sides are apparently content. The tradition that the household shares its resources seems so far to survive in the new and less appropriate situation.

In another way, new economic factors have altered the traditional picture of the household economy. The regular market for grain, and the possibility of earning reasonable wages have combined to give the wealthiest village households incomes in good years well beyond normal expenses. In 1952, much of this was going into housing and into more splendid weddings. By 1955, it was said in Sakaltutan that villagers had opened bank accounts. Two young migrants had houses of unprecedented luxury for the village, and one of them had invested in a lorry. But the problem remained unsolved. If in a modern economic and political context a villager achieves wealth beyond his immediate needs, what can he do with it? Village society and the village heritage of knowledge and experience offer no solution.

CHAPTER SIX

HOUSEHOLD AND FAMILY STRUCTURE

Introduction

The household is much more than an economic 'firm'. Within it, the main human physiological needs are met – shelter, rest, food and legitimate sex – and the most intimate and emotionally important social relations played out. If this appears a truism that applies to most human societies, it applies more to Turkish villages than to many. One reason for this is the very economic unity, which until recently tied the main occupation of men as well as women closely to the household group. A second reason is the strict segregation of the sexes and the fierce attitudes to feminine honour, which render it impossible for men and women to meet and co-operate except in and through their own households, or those of very close kin.

What goes on within the households is then a major part of village social life. An account of it involves both an account of the specific paired relationships that occur within it, and an account of the overall pattern these normally make. Such an account is not easy to give in a brief general form.

In my year's field work, the births, deaths, and marriages which involved changes and adjustments in my census, somehow impressed me at the time as exceptions in a stable pattern. Perhaps this attitude is allied to the surprise most people feel at the size of other people's children when they have not seen them for a long time. But this tendency to see the social world as something fixed is entirely misleading. Every household and every relationship within it is changing all the time. As people grow older they move from one socially defined group to another, and the circumstances in which they have to play their rôles change constantly.

Change of this kind does not of course imply an impermanent social order. The rôle of father is the same regardless of changes in the holders of the rôle; and in so far as young and old fathers or rich and poor fathers behave and are expected to behave differently, these differences are also a permanent part of the social order. Nevertheless any general description of, say, father-son relationships or mother-daughter-in-law is inadequate, because it cannot allow for all the special cases that from time to time arise. And there is a further source of error. Though rôles are relatively permanent, the overall structure of the society is changing, and the observer may well confuse in a single description customary behaviours which are on their way out and customary behaviours which are on their way in.

These difficulties are increased in the case of Turkish villages by the high wall which quite literally surrounds every household. Unrelated men do not enter the households of other families, private personal feelings are not publicly discussed, sex and anything to do with it is taboo in many social contexts, and this flavour of impropriety, as in many western contexts, makes straightforward information difficult to obtain. In only a limited number of households were we able to observe closely the way people treated each other, and even then our very presence had clearly some effect on the situation. Moreover, some interesting and important types of relationship – those between women of the same generation marrying into the same household, for example – only occur in a small number of households at any one time, so that few cases are available for observation.

Although the quality alters, family and kinship relationships continue for life. But people constantly leave their households and join or set up new ones, and any discussion of the close kin relationships automatically leads one out of a single household. Brothers, for example, begin as children in their father's house, but end as heads of neighbouring households in their own right. At the cost of some overlap with the discussion of kinship (Chapter 8), I shall follow this lead when it is appropriate to do so. Very rarely a household may contain non-kin servants, but I knew none among my acquaintances and ignore these cases in my discussion.

Mathematically, the number of possible pairs of kin relationships in a joint household is large. I shall deal only with the more common and important ones. Because the most striking structural feature of the household is the division between the sexes, I classify them by this criterion – relations between men, relations between women, and relations between men and women.

Men in the Household

Men form the permanent core of any normal household. The senior man, father or father's father of the other male members, owns the fabric of the house, and usually owns most or all of the land. His sons and grandsons are born into and remain in the household until his death, when one of his sons, usually the eldest, remains in this house as head, and the younger sons, sooner or later, set up their own independent households. The lifelong relation between male agnates of this minute lineage is the basis of the household as a continuing group.

Yet the men have normally much less to do with the actual life inside the household than the women. Men farm in household groups, and they eat and sleep in their households. But most of them spend as much of their time as possible away from the actual house. In the summer they are often working in the fields, or perhaps away from the village altogether as migrant labourers. When they are at leisure, they will prefer to talk in groups out of doors, or to foregather in guest rooms. I have seen men standing out in a snowstorm under a sheltered wall rather than go to join their wives in the house. Of course, the few richer villagers who own and preside over guest rooms stay at home, but normally the guest room is strictly segregated from the rest of the household. In winter, when no male guests except for very close neighbours and kin were present, I have come across women sitting in the guest room with their men, presumably solely for warmth. On one occasion, an unrelated but intimate neighbour entered and on his own initiative ordered the women out. The younger ones went, but two old women stood their ground. On other occasions, women and girls entered guest rooms on some pretext – for example, to see a kinsman who had just returned to the village – and stayed as long as possible, but the men were plainly anxious to be rid of them. The old mother of Haci Osman (H) of Sakaltutan, himself an old man, was permitted to sit silently in his often well-filled guest room evening after evening in the winter – a tribute to her old age and infirmity. Very occasionally then, women, mostly those who are past the menopause, penetrate to the male domain. On the other hand, one or two men shun the guest rooms and spend a good deal of time in their own homes. These are regarded as odd, and such conduct is due rather to unsatisfactory relations with other men rather than to love for or interest in the family.

The men's avoidance of the house, except for the specific purposes of eating and sleeping, reflects their wider social relationships. It is a simple if sometimes neglected fact that a higher position in any system of social relations involves a wider range of social ties outside it. The men's network and the women's touch at many points, but they are separate. The men's is wider, related to political power both in the village and in the wider society. One effect of the guest room and the informal open air groups of men is to maintain these wider relationships, and thus their clear superiority in village society.

Fathers and sons. The father's authority is strongly emphasised. Sons are expected to obey their fathers, and on the whole they do. Respect is based on a series of formal rules. One does not answer back, one does not speak in public in one's father's presence without specific invitation, and under no circumstances do fathers and sons refer to sexual matters in each other's presence, nor manifest any sexual behaviour. Sons do not smoke in their father's presence. Schooling apart, fathers are almost entirely responsible for educating and training their sons in socially acceptable behaviour, and in the essential farming skills. Sons are expected from about the age of eight to watch, water and feed the household animals, and at about twelve they learn to handle a plough.

No father normally hands over any land to his sons, nor makes any kind of will or testament (see pp. 94 and 107 for exceptions). The allocation of the estate is left until after his death. He is unlikely to disinherit formally, but for a man to leave the ancestral home is to forfeit his immediate rights to a livelihood from the land, and to imperil his hopes of inheritance, since his brothers remaining at home may well take the opportunity to

share the land between them and are likely to prove very
difficult to dispossess. Moreover, marriage is a vital and essential
step to adulthood, and it is always arranged and financed by
the father, if he is alive. Serious quarrels between father and
son never to my knowledge preceded the son's marriage.

Such quarrels certainly occurred. Hüsnü of Sakaltutan
wanted his married son to go away to learn a plasterer's trade
and earn money – the household was by no means a wealthy
one. The son did not want to go. This matter came up several
times in the headman's guest room – the current headman was a
kinsman, whose guest room this family normally used (p. 243) –
but people seemed to make a joke of it. The son complained
that the father did none of the household farm work, but kept
all the proceeds. One day he helped himself to money from his
father's money box. His father upbraided him, and the son
drew a knife. He was not bluffing. Earlier that spring a man
had been carried through the village over the snow to die in
hospital in Kayseri from a bullet wound inflicted during a
quarrel with his father – accidentally, according to the version
of the incident that reached me. Hüsnü was separated from his
son by the timely intervention of his own brother. I chanced to
call the next day, when the headman (in the rôle of a kinsman,
not of the headman), was presiding over a family conference to
reconcile the pair. Round the *tandır* were sitting Hüsnü, the
headman, another close neighbour and kinsman, the headman's
mother, and the children. My entry produced silence, then
suddenly Hüsnü, ignoring me, burst into an unrestrained tirade
against the vile inhuman ingratitude of such a son. The son
was crouching against the wall of the room with his back to the
others. Embarrassed, I did not stay long. The quarrel was
settled, and in the spring the young man with other young men
from the village went off to work, and came back by the harvest
already a plasterer, with money in his pocket.

Ömer, blessed with six sons, had trouble with his second.
This young man had become a plasterer young, and had enjoyed his taste of town life with money to spend in his pocket.
His father, by Sakaltutan standards, was well off for land, but
very much a villager, who went to town as little as possible. He
married this son to a daughter of the Hüsnü mentioned above,
in January, with due ceremony. Only a fortnight later, in spite

of strong pressure and against direct orders from the father, the son was off again to Adana, leaving his new bride in his father's house. Soon we heard that he had been involved in an unsuccessful elopement in Adana. He failed to appear at the *Şeker Bayramı* at the end of Ramazan, which in 1950 fell in June and July. He turned up soon after, ill, with very little left of his substantial earnings, and did nothing to help during the harvest. His father was very angry. 'I cannot make him work' he said to me. The son was unrepentant, and announced to me his secret intention of abandoning his village wife and marrying in Adana. But five years later he had not done so.

In both these cases the joint household survived acute tension, although in the short run, the sons could have supported themselves adequately without their fathers. In Sakaltutan, in two other cases, sons were apart from their fathers and on bad terms with them. The fathers had little or no land, and in one case the quarrel was said plausibly to be due to the bad relations between the son's stepmother and his wife. The other quarrel was more fundamental – the parents did not even visit or help their son when he had pneumonia. In another case, three brothers had set up independent households next to their father's house, because once again their wives and their stepmother could not work together. But they had remained on good terms with their father, and co-operation between stepmother and wives had survived the separation.

As a son approaches middle age and his father falls into dotage, control of household affairs may pass to the son. But formal respect for the father is never relaxed and he remains nominally head of the household. For example the village headman was about 35 years of age, and his official position and his self-importance gave the impression that he was in charge of his household. In fact, his old but still vigorous father was the real head, and had great influence on his son's public conduct as well. Old Ismet (T), much less vigorous, was treated with great deference and attention by his elder son – though not by his younger — but in this case the direction of household affairs was in the sons' hands.

Fathers and adopted and stepsons. Men seldom bring up boys whom they have not begotten, except explicitly as foster sons. Occasionally, a man who has no sons will take on a son of his brother or sister, or a son of his wife's brother or sister, and bring him up as his own son, and heir to his land. I knew of only one case of this kind in Sakaltutan. Haci Osman (H) had taken on an orphan child of his sister, who was also his father's brother's son's son (agnatic second cousin once removed). The villagers did not regard this young man as Haci Osman's heir, but he himself told me that contrary to village custom and Islamic law, he had formally adopted the boy under the Turkish Civil Code; the young man died while we were in the village, but he left a little son, who was, according to Haci Osman, heir to his not inconsiderable estate.

In Elbaşı, a fairly well landed man had adopted a brother's son as his heir, and married him to his only daughter. I gathered that this young man had, in village eyes, lost his rights in his own father's home, although according to the Şeriat, he had not, and although no modern legal arrangements had been made. In another case, a young man had been adopted by his father's brother, and had actually inherited his adopting father's house and fields and set up his own family there.

Where a man voluntarily takes a boy to be his heir, the relationship will plainly be as like a full father-son relationship as the two can make it. But the society does not recognise social as distinct from physiological fatherhood, and the equivalence would never therefore be complete. They would not use the terms 'father' and 'son' to each other.

Orphan children are common in this as in any society with a high death rate. Men often therefore have children in their household who are not their own. In the past, dead brothers' children seem normally to have been treated as servants and to have lost their share of their grandfather's estate, which was divided between their fathers' brothers, in accordance with the Şeriat (Vesey-Fitzgerald (1931) p. 121). Now their right to their dead fathers' land is generally admitted. Stepchildren and other orphans normally separate from their foster father's home as early as possible, and claim their father's land. Such separations are not a sign of strained relations. In Elbaşı, two households had taken in refugees who came to the village from the east of Turkey, as husbands to their daughters. In no other cases did I hear of a man actually living under the authority of his father-in-law, but these two men came to the village with no status and no kin of their own. In both cases, the couple had separated again by the time we reached the village, but were on good terms with the affinal foster home.

Brothers. More than any other kin, brothers are thrown together by the social system. If they are fairly close in age, they are likely to be lifelong neighbours, and the intimacy of a childhood under a common roof is likely to continue throughout life as neighbourly co-operation and mutual dependence (Chapter 8). Bound by common interests in inheritance and common duties to their parents and to their close agnates, they very often maintain a flow of daily contact and mutual services throughout life.

Seniority among brothers confers authority. The standard Turkish address to an elder brother is *ağabey*, a compound formed of two words of social respect, *ağa* and *bey*. In the village this is often abbreviated to *ağam*, 'my *ağa*', thus coinciding, significantly, with one possible and common address to a father. *Ağa* and *ağabey* are often used informally to refer to an elder brother.

Sets of brothers are numerous, and most of them seemed to conform more or less to the ideal. They normally shared or attended the same guest room, helped each other in the harvest, minded each other's families during absences from the village, stood by each other in sickness, and supported each other in fights and feuds. Many men probably spent more of their waking hours in the company of their brothers than in the company of their wives. When Musa (K) lost his wife, his elder brother conducted the negotiations for a new wife, although both were middle-aged men with adult children. In Elbaşı, I was discussing household fission with the second of four adult brothers, when he remarked, although they were separate, 'Yet we are still together. We are under the orders of my elder brother'.

In a few cases the relationship may be even closer. Brothers are normally expected to separate from their father's household fairly soon after his death. The period that in fact elapses varies from days to years, so that at any given time one may expect to find one or two households that have not yet separated following on the death of their father. In a very few cases separation may be indefinitely postponed. Sakaltutan contained one such household. The elder brother, a regular migrant and a vigorous personality, had clear authority over the other, who farmed their joint inheritance. In this case a third younger brother had separated from them. I heard of several similar joint fraternal households in other villages.

Of course, exceptions occur. Hayip (B) of Elbaşı was the youngest of three surviving brothers, but by far the most wealthy and successful. His elder brothers used his guest room frequently – by grace, not by right. Of three Sakaltutan brothers, the eldest had married into their mother's village, two hours away. The youngest made a reasonably comfortable income for his small family as a permanent worker in the Kayseri textile mill. Bekteş, the second, was for years allowed to work the whole of their joint small patrimony, from which he made a precarious and inadequate living. When a quarrel with his eldest brother over marriage arrangements precipitated a division of the land, he complained that his younger brother was 'cold', and did nothing to help. Yet they remained on speaking terms.

More serious quarrels between brothers are not uncommon, usually over the division of the patrimony. I did not actually hear of any cases of fratricide, though in two cases to my knowledge brother fired at brother, once in Sakaltutan (p. 125), and once, in another village, on the very day on which I made a visit. The expected intimacy and the habitual physical proximity of brothers make these fraternal quarrels bitter and violent.

Half-brothers are fairly common in a society where polygamy is still possible, and where premature death and remarriage are common events. Yet no word exists to distinguish half- from full brothers. When the fact is relevant, a specific statement is necessary – 'his mother was separate' or 'his father was separate'.

Paternal half-brothers grow up in the same household, and in terms of enforced intimacy their relationship is little different from that of full brothers. In fact, they are less close. I knew no case of half-brothers growing up in a polygamous household with living mothers still the current wives of their fathers. Rather one finds elder brothers who are stepsons of the new wife, while the younger brothers are her full sons. Often the elder stepsons leave the household before their father's death.

In Sakaltutan, Hasan (V) the plasterer and his two full brothers had left their father's household, leaving their half-brother behind. In Elbaşı, a pair of full brothers had left their father's household and their stepmother and set up a joint household together, while another pair of younger full brothers, half-brothers of the first pair, remained and shared the paternal household after the father's death. In each pair, one brother went away to work as a migrant, while the other worked the land. By 1951, both pairs had split, but all seemed on good terms. In both these cases, the father, exceptionally, allowed the separating sons to take a share of the land, which I understood to be a final settlement.

People are equally emphatic about the mutual love and co-operation due between maternal half-brothers. But in fact the circumstances are much more variable (pp. 196-7). The common interests and intense intimacy which bind paternal brothers are lacking. Maternal half-brothers are often not members of a single household, and even if they are, their interests in inheritance are different. Although they are spoken of as brothers, in fact the relationship is more like that of specially close non-agnatic cousins.

Relations among Women

The men are the owners and the core of the household, yet they work and talk and amuse themselves as far as possible outside it. The grown women of a household are strangers brought in as wives from some other household, except, rarely, for daughters or sisters due to marry out, or to return to their husbands. They are all, in one way or another, appendages of the core of male agnates. Adult women have rights and interests in more than one household, yet they belong unequivocally to none. In spite of this marginal position, they work and talk and amuse themselves largely within the household in which they reside, and their presence is indispensable to its daily routine.

Because it is the women who come to their husbands, the types of relationship between the women which are commonly found within households are more numerous than those among the men. For men we had only to consider father-son, and brother-brother relations. But among women there are at least four common types of relationship.

In simple households only mothers and daughters are present, but in large joint households, a number of women from diverse origins may live and work together. Relationships between them are not easy to observe, and the number of joint households on which we were able to collect evidence was small.

Mothers and daughters. Women want sons, but this does not mean that they do not love daughters. Girls grow up with the women of the household, and learn their most important lessons from their mother, helping her in all the household tasks. This intimacy, greater than that between any other pair of different generations, is violently interrupted by the girl's marriage, which normally takes place about puberty or soon after. Marriage is a time of acute grief to the bride's mother. One woman, on the marriage of her third daughter, told us that she had been seriously ill after each wedding, so painful was the parting. After marriage, a girl still looks to her own mother for help, advice and comfort. She visits regularly; if the distance is great, then for a month or so once a year; if her mother is in the same village, then frequently and casually. If she is ill, everyone expects her to be sent home to be nursed by her own mother.

Sisters. Before marriage, sisters are as close to each other as brothers; how this initial intimacy develops in later life depends on the physical distance and social relations between the households into which they marry. If they marry into the same household, or two very closely related households, or even if they are in the same village, they will normally maintain close co-operation throughout life.

Mother-in-law and daughter-in-law. The most critical relationships among the women within the household are between the incoming strangers. A girl starts as a new bride, and slowly increases her stake in her husband's household until she becomes in her turn mother-in-law.

In other studies of joint patrilineal households, it has been plausibly argued that the relationship between a bride and her mother-in-law is far more important for the stability and success of her marriage than her relationship to her husband. Fei, for example, draws a gloomy picture of the lot of a Chinese bride in her husband's household (Fei (1939) pp. 45 ff.). I therefore went to the field expecting to find this relationship one of 'tension' and 'hostility'. After field work I am surprised not at the tension, but at the comparatively smooth accomplishment of this violent change in her social environment which every young woman in turn must face. Certainly quarrels are fairly frequent, and the marked subordination and isolation of the new bride is itself a sign of 'tension'; another observer might have described this same data in much sharper terms.

A bride and a daughter-in-law are both in the village called *gelin*, clearly by etymology 'the one who comes'. She is expected to do all the more menial tasks in the household, and to wait on her mother-in-law. No sign of mutual affection is permitted her and her new husband, except in complete privacy, and like all young persons, she is not expected to initiate conversation with elders, or to argue with her husband or his senior kin. But she is under no formal restrictions or taboos, and informants invariably stated firmly that the bride must be treated like one's own daughter. Menial tasks and respectful silence before elders are no less expected of daughters than of brides, so the lowly status of the girl and her nominal daughterhood are not inconsistent.

On the whole, as I have said, it was the close co-operation between mother-in-law and her *gelin* which surprised us. In cases which we knew intimately, jobs and baby minding were shared with apparent amity. One girl expressed great affection for her husband's mother, saying that she got on better with her than with her own mother. In another instance in a fairly well-to-do household, a girl was left by the death of her mother-in-law to keep house single-handed for three small boys, her husband and her father-in-law. She said how much she missed her mother-in-law, who alone had defended her against the men, and dated her own miseries from her death.

At the other extreme, we heard of cases where girls deserted their husbands because they could not stand their mothers-in-law. One girl who had eloped from her father's home because, so we were told, her stepmother beat her, found her mother-in-law much worse. She was found ostensibly trying to drown herself in the pool above the village. In Sakaltutan, one woman turned her husband's old mother out of the house. But this was an exceptional case (p. 115).

When people who have had little or nothing to do with each other beforehand are pitchforked into extreme intimacy within a single household, such contingent factors as personality, the relative standing of natal and marital households, and the degree of difference of custom of the two households are bound to affect the development of relationships. On the other hand, every girl knows that this is her inevitable fate and is well drilled in respect for her mother-in-law. The body of domestic customs and skills within village society is highly uniform, so that she is bound to find a great deal that is familiar. She has no alternative to submission except the scandal and disgrace associated with divorce, and then to repeat her experience elsewhere under less favourable circumstances. If she stays on she has hopes of a son, who will immediately improve her position in her marital home, and eventually make it possible for her to be mistress in her own household. Her mother-in-law also wants a grandson, and has no wish to endanger the son's marriage, which has usually been a costly investment, nor to strain her son's relationship to herself. On both sides, therefore, the system provides rewards for success, and penalties for failure. Both sides know what is expected of them. If most daughters-in-law find it possible to co-operate with their mothers-in-law under these circumstances, it is not after all surprising. Tensions exist, but they should not be overt; and normally, they are not.

Co-Wives. In some of the rare cases of polygamy, co-wives live under one roof. The villagers did not have a common term for co-wives, but they had, and used frequently, a term for a second wife, a word which carried decidedly derogatory overtones, *kuma*. Only two men in Sakaltutan actually had two wives of approximately the same age co-resident with them. In one case their co-operation in caring for an old and ailing husband was apparently exemplary. The other two were said to quarrel, and certainly their husband, who in any case was away from the village a great deal as a skilled plumber, kept away from his house, living mostly in the patrimonial guest room which he shared with his brothers. In both the other cases of bigamy in Sakaltutan, one wife was much older than her husband, and the other much younger. The elder in each case was in effect discarded, and relations were accordingly bad.

People pity a woman whose husband takes another wife. Yet

a wife gains companionship, and help with household chores. The villagers say firmly that a man must provide equally for both wives. In one of the four cases, the explicit point of taking a second wife was to provide a son, and the first wife, who was incapable of bearing children, actually co-operated in procuring her. In another, the aim was also to produce more sons, because the first wife failed to bear more than one. Co-wives are expected to quarrel, but they do not always do so.

Sometimes co-wives do not share a household. One man in Elbaşı had married his brother's widow, and visited her on alternate nights, but did not shift his residence. In another case, a man of Sakaltutan had taken two widows in addition to his first wife who lived in his own household; the others both lived in their own households. His three widows were all still alive at the time of our stay. This type of case seems to be a sort of business arrangement to the benefit of all parties. Marriage to a brother's widow has obvious advantages in preventing any outsider getting his hands on the patrimonial land and house. Marriage to a widow with her own household is less easy to interpret because no case was current during my field work. A widow's life is hard – in the past it was even harder – and even a share of a husband to protect and advise on practical matters is a great advantage, especially if she is able to retain her independence through control of her former husband's house and land. The new husband gains some additional income from the land he helps to work, and the prospect of more sons, with little additional responsibility.

Brothers' wives. Turkish has a standard word for husband's brother's wife, *elti*. Brothers' wives normally begin married life by sharing a household. Even when the husband's father is dead, brothers often remain together until after they are all married. Nevertheless, in fact, very few households at any given time contain married brothers. In one household of this type where we were welcome, the mother-in-law had died. The two elder brothers had established families, and the third married while we were in the village. Two younger brothers were due to marry. Relations seemed reasonably amicable, and three years later the household had not yet split up, although another brother had by then married. In this case, each of the younger wives had their own room, and the senior couple used the main living room. The old father slept in the guest room.

Examples of dissension between women are not of course difficult to find. Women are normally said to be the cause of the splitting of households, and in fact this is generally true. How far this dissension is itself the reflection of the structural cleavage already existing between the husbands, I am not sure (p. 133). One split at least appeared to be due to personal rather than structural factors. Two brothers married two sisters, and all four lived together for a long time. One of the women, however, lost all her babies and eventually her husband divorced her, reluctantly, it seems, and took another wife. Now, instead of being sisters, the two wives were strangers to each other. Within a year the household had split. Nevertheless, tensions between brothers and between their growing families must add to the difficulties of amicable co-operation between women in a large joint household.

Men and women.—Men and women live in different social worlds. Only within the household do the two worlds touch closely, and even here the separateness of the sexes in the society at large affects individual relations between them.

Husband and wife. The basis of the household is the relationship of a husband and wife for the procreation of children. Marriage is a sharply defined status, with a clear-cut ceremonial beginning, and only a married woman is permitted to have sexual relations.—Pre-marital and extra-marital relations are punished by violence or serious disgrace.

Men wield authority. No woman was head of a household with a grown man in it, and where a husband chooses to be unreasonable and selfish, the only recourse of a woman is flight. Wives are occasionally beaten by their husbands; open references to such beatings always arouse much mirth.—Men decide all matters concerning the farming routine, all major sales and purchases, the marriage of children, visits to the doctor, in fact, everything of importance.

Women do of course influence their husbands in all these decisions. They can remind, argue, wheedle, scold, and their views on some matters may carry the day. But almost invariably it is the man who actually makes the decision. One man in Sakaltutan reversed a decision to sell a plough, and people laughed and said he was under his wife's thumb. In this household the land belonged largely to the wife. In one or two other cases, a man of weak character or intellect was dominated by a wife of determination and ability, but his submissiveness cost him his neighbours' respect.

Women do not look to their husbands for companionship; still less do men look to their wives. It is taken for granted that there is no common ground for conversation. A man must never show affection for his wife in front of anyone else. When a soldier returned to the village after years of absence, his kin and neighbours gathered round to welcome and embrace him. The ceremony lasted for hours, as one person after another heard the news and hastened to the guest room. His greeting for his wife was left over till bedtime – she could not even see him until all the others had finished with him. When men left Elbaşı on their way to Mecca, their sisters and mothers embraced them publicly and histrionically at the boarding of the lorry – but not their wives. Within the household, before close kin, the taboo on public affection is even stronger. Nobody talks about 'love' except occasionally in cases of adultery and elopement. The relationship is limited to economic co-operation and to sexual intimacy. Women frequently said to my wife that they did not love their husbands – not only in specific cases, but as a general description of village life. Men spoke very little of their relationship to their wives, and when they did, it was of the common bed, of their prowess therein, and of their large families that they boasted. More than once, men remarked to me in jest: 'We love our wives at night.'

Such a relationship between wife and husband permits a viable household to be built on any pair of the opposite sex who are each of them economically and physiologically efficient, and who can achieve a fairly low level of co-operation in the face of misfortune, interfering kin, and personal misunderstandings. Not all marriages are of this minimal type. In some cases a very real degree of mutual concern and affection may develop. One man who had left his father and was extremely poor had remained in the village as a herdsman instead of going off with the labour migrants because even after three children he did not wish to leave his wife. (It was she who told my wife of their unwillingness to part – I did not discuss the matter with him.) Eventually he did join the labour migrants and achieved a much greater prosperity.

The notion of 'successful' marriage in terms of personal relations does not exist in the village. The main criterion of success is the existence of healthy sons. Success is inconspicuous. If a wife is driven out or runs away, or dies, her husband normally loses no time in replacing her; a new wife may be installed in no more than a week (p. 195). Every household needs an efficient woman to cook its daily bread, and care for the small children. A woman who is chronically ill may well be replaced, or may find a new wife brought in to share her husband. If she fails within a reasonable number of years to produce sons, she is also likely to be replaced, or added to.

Mother-son. Every woman desires above all things the birth of a son. The new bride's position in her husband's household depends on this. Everyone will be pleased. Her son, moreover, is a permanent acquisition. As he grows, her position in her husband's household becomes increasingly assured; when he is adult he will marry and provide her with a daughter-in-law to wait upon her. A woman with sons will never be in want or homeless.

A mother is thought of as protective and indulgent to her small sons, in contrast to father who is stern and exacting. Of course, mothers discipline their sons, and are often driven to temporary distraction by their small children. But in general the good mother is comforter and defender against paternal wrath.

Adult men treat mothers with respect, and have an unshakeable duty to care for them. But they and not their mothers are in charge of the household. Men are automatically superior, and sons will give orders to their mothers when necessary.

The tie between mother and son holds the household together under the strain of the arrival of a daughter-in-law. Only one full son had left his father's house prematurely, whereas all other cases in both villages of premature separation were cases of stepsons removing their new wife from the stepmother-in-law (p. 132). Where the mother-son tie is weak, the new bride is able to persuade her husband to set up an independent household, where it is strong, she has to submit. Widows are sure of a place in their son's household until death. In only one case did a woman, after protracted quarrels, manage to drive her old

1 Horsemanship and a well-to-do house in a small town. (p.83)

2 Snow often lies for three months. In 1950 it was exceptionally deep. (p.23)

3 Household head and grand-daughter at the steps of the guest room. (p.22)

4 Harvesting. The scythe is a recent innovation. (p.46)

mother-in-law out of the house – and this husband was one of the feeblest men in the village. All other old widows living alone were childless, or at least sonless.

The mother-son relationship is probably more important to a woman than any other personal relationship. It is in itself of very great emotional importance, and it is also the key to satisfactory relations with other members of the household. The mother of sons will almost certainly be a confident and respected member of the household, or of one of the households, in which her sons live. Without sons, an old woman may if lucky be tolerated in her husband's household; otherwise she may have nowhere to go at all.

By contrast, the most important relationship of a man is not to women at all, but to his agnates – to his father and his brothers, if any. This lack of symmetry is both an example and a consequence of the sharp inferiority of women.

The fact that a woman's relation with her son is more important to her than that with her husband, and that a man's relation with his mother is more important, as a rule, than that with his wife reflects the stress in the society on procreation as the end of relations between the sexes, rather than sexual attraction and satisfaction.

A Woman and her Male Affines. Girls are deferential and distant with their husband's fathers. In two cases, neither of them in the villages in which we worked, we heard of specific complaints about the unreasonable demands of a father-in-law in expecting work, and in Elbaşı a scandal resulted from an old man making advances, firmly (and plausibly) stated to have been unsuccessful, to his son's wife. To her husband's brothers, who may at the beginning be part of the same household, respect is due, and from them, if need be, help is expected. Adultery with them seems generally to be considered unthinkable. One young man slept for a year or so in a single-roomed house with his brother's wife, while his brother was away, but the circumstances aroused no scandal or adverse comment that reached my ears, and all informants whom I questioned insisted that they had no suspicions. Brothers frequently took charge of each other's families in each other's absence, and a brother would be a perfectly respectable person to take a man's wife to town to the doctor or on some other long journey. Each would carry out their duties to the other, but in general the relation seemed to be one of friendly restraint.

Father-daughter. A girl only lives in her natal home for the first thirteen to seventeen years of her life. Her relations with the male members of her own household are therefore not only attenuated by the segregation of the sexes, but cut short early in her life.

Fathers are disappointed in the birth of a daughter. A man, asked how many children he has, will normally omit his daughters altogether from the count. People often bemoan the trouble of bringing up daughters only to see them pass to someone else just as soon as they become useful, at the point at which a son not only remains to help his household himself but provides the occasion for recruiting a further worker. Moreover, daughters are not a man's business. All small children belong to the province of women, and growing girls remain so.

Nevertheless, most fathers are affectionate towards their daughters. Little girls sometimes come into the men's sitting rooms with their brothers. I have seen men cuddle and kiss their little daughters in public, and I have also seen them taking very firm action against disobedience. Later, a father watches over the propriety of his daughter's behaviour, and is the main party, through intermediaries, to the negotiations for her marriage. He should spend at least the equivalent of the marriage payment on her trousseau, and people almost invariably insisted that they were out of pocket after the marriage of their daughters (p. 186).

After marriage, a girl returns home at intervals, and a good and comfortably placed father will make her annually a gift of clothes. I was told that a husband may leave the entire provision of his wife's clothes to her family, though clearly this is not invariably the case. If she is wronged by her husband's household her father will receive her. If she is ill, she returns to his house for care. A stern father may refuse to let his daughter use his house as a refuge from her husband. Two cases of this kind in Elbaşı were said in the recent past to have led to suicides, though in both the history was a complicated one. But whether affectionate or not, a father and daughter are not intimate in the way a father and son can be intimate, because their socially prescribed fields of interest and activity are wide apart.

Brother-sister. Small siblings play together, and small girls
act as nursemaids to the young of both sexes. The sexes tend to
separate for play quite young, and little boys tend to go with
their fathers and little girls with their mothers. The respectful
terms of address for elder siblings, *ağabey* for brother, and *abla*
for sister are invariably used, never personal names. Yet
younger brothers as they grow up begin to assert their male
prerogatives. I saw an eight-year-old boy giving peremptory
orders to a fourteen-year-old sister, which she carried out,
without his parents intervening or correcting him.

Once a girl has left her natal household, her brother's contact
with her diminishes sharply. Her welfare and that of her children is very much his concern, but there is no intimacy, no
grounds for conversation, no seeking each other's company. If a
woman is ill, a brother will be troubled. Bekteş (V) suddenly
disappeared from Sakaltutan late one evening, and I dis-
covered that word had come that his sister, who was married
in another village four hours away, and whom he had not seen
for years, was seriously ill. He had set out immediately. On the
other hand, he seldom spoke to another sister who lived quite
close to him in Sakaltutan. From the sister's point of view, her
brothers succeed her father as the point of refuge and defence
against her husband and his kin. If this need does not arise she
will have little or nothing to do with them.

Household Structure

The household is not simply a number of people tied to each
other in pairs, but a group, with its own internal structure.
Divisions within it rest mainly on the three obvious principles,
sex, age or generation, and family.

The contrast between men and women is sharply emphasised
in every way. They are separate in work and leisure. The
division of labour is clear, and in full households is strictly
observed. Men do the heavy work in the fields, control all
transport, and conduct all relations with the outside world,
including almost all buying and selling. They make all major
decisions, at least ostensibly, and defend the household and its
honour.

Women carry out all domestic tasks, manure fields near the

village, prepare fuel, and submit to the will of their men, at least outwardly. The women of a large household may in extreme cases be a heterogeneous collection of imported wives. In theory, their very presence is at their husband's pleasure, and they have no formal security of tenure.

Yet in another sense they are the indispensable fabric of the household, indeed they are the household. A large area of activity within the household is beneath the notice of the men, and this guarantees to the women an autonomy to manage their own affairs without interference. They accept the fact of their own overall inferiority as part of the metaphysical order, but their immersion in a world of their own greatly mitigates this inferiority. They see and understand the indispensability of their own activities, but they know of the world of men in the guest room only at second hand.

The major household resources are in the hands of the household head. Though the women have no generally acknowledged rights to minor domestic products as they have, for example, in rural Ireland, (Arensberg and Kimball (1940) p. 48). Some of them sold us, or tried to sell us, donkey bags which they had made, and in at least one case, kept the money. Women will trade eggs, chickens and grain with pedlars on their own initiative. But many women had obvious difficulties when coping with money, and their use of these resources was at their husband's pleasure. They do not trade outside the village; they go to towns very rarely – many of them never.

In a straightforward sense the mutual separateness and dependence of men and women holds the household together. Neither men nor women can live outside a household. They are also held together by the direct ties between them. But less obviously women are bound to each other by their relationships to men, and men by their relationships to women. It is the husband/son who unites mother-in-law and daughter-in-law, and the brothers that bring the wives together. Conversely, it follows from the fact that sons leave the paternal home to escape a stepmother, that the mother/son tie is one factor which binds the son to the father. Finally, one of the main responsibilities that unite the agnate male core of a household as a group is their joint duty to safeguard the honour of their women.

Between parents and children, the gulf of generation is wide and clear. The social distinctness and the enforced deference are thought of as due to generation differences. Outside the simple family, the generation differences and the age differences may not coincide. For example, if a man takes a young wife as a replacement, half-brothers may differ by twenty, even forty years in extreme cases, and nephews may be older than their uncles. In these cases it is seniority by age rather than formal seniority by generation that counts.

Both among men and women, seniority of generation and age confers authority and privilege, and divides, or in large households ranks, the household population. Girls are expected to be deferential to older women, to wait upon them, and to speak only when spoken to. Equally, boys and young men defer to and obey their male seniors. But there is no uniting of the sexes along the generation lines. Brothers do not group themselves with their sisters against their parents, nor husbands with wives against their children. Men are superior – adult sons command their mothers, and adult brothers their elder sisters.

Only about one village household in four contained more than one married couple, and even fewer two or more established families (see Table 2, p. 38). Each young couple is expected to have a room of their own; and once they have their own children, each couple becomes a separate family unit with interests to some extent in conflict with the interests of others in the household. People often spoke of the desire of the young family for independence, and a tug of war always takes place between the pressure of the young family to escape and the pressure of the rest of the household, especially the household head, to keep them loyally attached.

The paired relationships which I discussed above operate within a group organised on these three different and not entirely consistent principles. The way they work out in any given case depends largely on the overall structural pattern of the particular household. Of course, personal idiosyncracies and likes and dislikes play a great part, but they do so within a traditional household structure, and not in an arbitrary way. Indeed, this particular society, by the strength of its rules of conduct, and especially by the social segregation of the sexes and of young and old, minimises the potential disruption caused by personal dislike.

CHAPTER SEVEN

THE DOMESTIC CYCLE

The Transmission of Rights and Duties

All households aim to grow and proliferate. The ideal cycle is already clear: the large, patrilineal joint household which on the death of its head splits into a number of simple households, each headed by one of his sons, and each seeking in turn to grow again into a large joint household.

Anthropologists have traditionally distinguished between inheritance, the transmission of rights to property, and succession, the transmission of offices or rôles. In these villages this distinction is particularly clear and striking. The successful man with more than one married son transmits all his property but he cannot pass on his social position as a senior elder and head of a large and wealthy household. Thus, although his material wealth is passed on, his power and prestige are dissolved by his death.

The villagers acknowledged three sets of rules governing inheritance: the Turkish Civil Code, the Şeriat, and custom. These sets of rules are not mutually consistent, but they do have some resemblance to each other on general points. The only rules which can be legally enforced are those which are least followed, the Turkish Civil Code.

No single consistent body of rules then governs inheritance. Which rules are followed, and how they are applied, depends on the state of family affairs, that is, the relative strength and the interests of the close kin involved. The allocation carried out at the time of the division into new junior households is usually, in fact if not in theory, definitive, and although disputes may drag on for years afterwards it is extremely difficult in practice to upset a settlement once it has been carried out.

Both the Şeriat and the Turkish Civil Code recognise limited rights of testamentary disposition. No villager ever referred to these, and I was repeatedly told that men never concerned themselves with the division of their property after their death. What happened to their descendants was a matter for God, not for them.

In no specific case in the villages is one of the three sets of rules deliberately and consistently applied. Cases which are referred to the courts are obviously an exception, but in my experience very few village cases are so referred, and I cannot quote one instance. Moreover, to go to court is not to apply the state rules but to employ others to do so. To set forth the formal rules of one or all of these systems would not tell us what in fact happens. Indeed it is difficult to find out what does happen.

People may assert claims under any rules, and every settlement therefore involves ignoring or adjusting somebody's claims. Discussions are not normally public and open, and people avoid questions about specific examples, answering in general terms. Since I did not witness an actual division, and since some of the implications and problems did not strike me until I came to write, I have had to depend to some extent on reconstruction and guesswork. But my guesses are founded on a general knowledge of village society.

The transmission of power and prestige is more complex, and more fundamental for village social structure. The system worked to prevent a stable hereditary hierarchy. I shall deal first with inheritance, a key element in the argument, and then move on to the wider question of long-term mobility in village society.

Inheritance: Sons and Widows

General questions about division of the land are always answered very simply. Villagers will draw a quadrangle in the dust, and divide it by lines down the middle. Each plot they insist is thus separately divided between the sons, in strict equality; because no two plots are equal in value, every plot must be separately divided. Questions about the rights of daughters are not so easily or consistently answered. They are entitled to an equal share but 'sometimes they do not take'.

The general claim of the villagers to live by the Şeriat does not affect their conduct of inheritance. They know that a daughter's share is in Islamic law half a son's. I never heard of this provision having being applied nor even seriously suggested. They could give no reason for its neglect; and no one ever argued, which they could correctly have done, that the land had never been *mulk* (freehold) but *miri* (State land) and therefore not subject directly to Şeriat rules. Sometimes they will refer to the current State law, but again, though some of them know some of its provisions, they do not normally claim to be applying it. Its provisions are no more than a convenient argument in certain cases.

A simple division of land between sons seems to have been the normal customary procedure, and is still common in straightforward cases. One result of this is that the layout of fields becomes a kind of genealogical map; although the land is individually owned the holdings tend to lie in agnatic blocks. My questions about the past agnatic connections of village lineages sometimes provoked the villagers themselves into conjectural history based on the relative position of their fields.

Such a simple division is usually achieved by a direct understanding between the brothers. They are left *de facto* in joint control of the household lands, and if they are not at loggerheads it is relatively simple to present the world with a *fait accompli*. In the past a deceased brother's sons were sometimes excluded (p. 104). This practice is now regarded as inequitable, and is also illegal.

Though I never discussed in detail such a division, I did come across brothers' quarrels over the spoils. On one visit to another village, I arrived by chance on a day on which an armed man was in homicidal pursuit of his brother. The version I was given attributed the quarrel to his suddenly advancing, years after the original amicable division, a claim that he had in fact been given less than half; undoubtedly he himself would have given a more plausible account of his case. On the whole, however, relations between adult brothers who had already separated varied from mutual tolerance to intimate co-operation. I was told that in fact divisions are conducted by the arbitration of elders. Fields can be measured and divided into strictly equal shares. Movable property is valued in cash. If one of the heirs claims that the valuation of an article is too low, then he is asked to value it himself and accept it as part of his share at the higher valuation. The effect of this rule is that goods go to whomever is prepared to value them most highly, giving the division something of the nature of an auction sale, and ensuring, so I was told, that everyone is satisfied, or at least can only blame himself if he is not. Small differences between the final total value of the shares are adjusted by cash.

The division between brothers may be complicated by the need to provide for a widow, or even two. The villagers say that the Şeriat provides for an eighth-share for a widow and the Turkish Civil Code for a quarter-share, in which they are roughly correct.[1] But neither of these rules seems to be applied. Occasionally, the division is postponed until after the mother's death. Otherwise the widow simply lives with one son without taking a definite share – she may of course own land in her own right which passes to the household in which she lives – or in other cases a widow appears to have accepted a non-legal compromise arrangement for her own lifetime. Such a peaceful settlement of the family affairs without a public quarrel carries considerable prestige.

Inheritance: Daughters

The real complications and many of the disputes about inheritance arise out of the claims of daughters. These claims are generally admitted to be formally valid, but they are by no means always accepted or enforced.

Daughters have often married to other villages, or have a sufficiency in their marital households. Time and again, men said that to interfere on behalf of one's wife's claims was mean and undignified, and that it was entirely up to the wife herself what she did about it. 'What my father left me is enough for me', as one man remarked, is clearly the socially approved attitude, even if its expression is at times disingenuous. The fact

[1] The Şeriat allocates a one-eighth share to a spouse of the deceased if children survive, otherwise, one-quarter. The Turkish Civil Code gives a choice of half the estate in trust or one-quarter in full possession if children survive, otherwise, both these rights. (S. Vesey-Fitzgerald (1931) p. 121; Turkish Civil Code, Article 444.)

5*

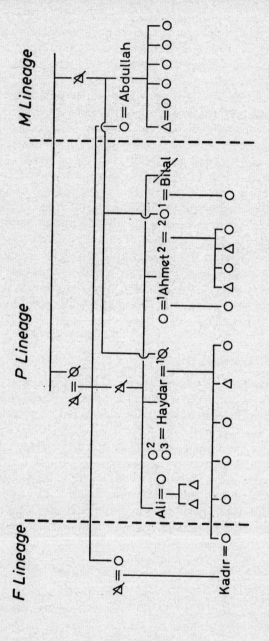

5 Genealogy: Abdullah and the four brothers

that their sisters are either married and out of the household, or else very young, puts the adult brothers in a strong position. They can and do frequently ignore their sisters' rights. I suspect that at least in part the expressed sentiment about the impropriety of taking up women's claims simply reflects the very great difficulty in forcing the brothers to disgorge what they have already taken over. Nevertheless, unenforced claims are not always allowed to die, and may be revived when a death, a quarrel, or some other change in the situation presents a favourable opportunity.

A number of land disputes from Sakaltutan illustrate my point that brothers divide the land between them, and then are almost immovable. Two old men had survived their third brother and his adult son. Their brother's son's widow and her two boys formed one of the poorest households in the village. The widow rightly claimed a third of the patrimonial land for her sons. This had been divided off once, and then taken over again by the elder brother, who thus worked two-thirds of his father's land. The dispute rankled, and once flared up into an open quarrel at my very door. But the widow could do nothing. No one would support her to the point of violence against her husband's father's brother, and her sex, her poverty and her total lack of sophistication made it practically impossible for her to enlist official or legal support.

In another case, two of the better off lineages of Sakaltutan had intermarried. Abdullah (M), an elderly man in 1950, with a married adult son and several daughters, had married his father's sister's daughter; she was also father's sister to the four brothers of P lineage – Ali, Haydar, Ahmet and Bilal.

Abdullah had given no land to his sisters. The four brothers of P lineage had divided between them all the land of their father's father. Bilal (P) died, and his share, together with his wife and daughter, went to his brother, Ahmet. As I understood it, it was proposed by both sides to redivide the land, so that Abdullah's wife would receive a share of P land, and Haydar and Ahmet would receive for their wives a share of M land. Ali was expected to give up his father's sister's share of the land without getting any compensation, while Kadır of F lineage would benefit through his mother. Ali and Ahmet quarrelled when Ahmet attempted to move boundary marks. In the heat of this quarrel Ali shot, missed Ahmet, but hit his foster daughter, Bilal's daughter, in the hand; Ali duly went to prison, for a year. This was a serious attempt to upset a settlement once reached, but in spite of the willingness of most of the parties in this case, the attempt foundered on the usual rock. No one with insufficient land is willing to see any of it go to anyone else so long as he is able to use a gun.

A third case puzzled me a good deal at first. Haci Osman (H) of Sakaltutan had failed to produce children of his own in spite of trying four different wives. Finally he had adopted a sister's orphan son, who was also his agnate (a second-cousin's son). He had given no share of his father's land to his sisters, two of whom had surviving sons in the village. Two sons of one sister had spent much time in Izmir, leaving their young wives to share a household, and to work their father's land. Three sons of the other sister had derived very little from their father. One, the eldest, had acquired a sufficiency of land for his household from his wife's father, who was also his father's brother, but the other two were very poor. These three brothers were close neighbours of mine, and I discussed this matter with them. They were positive that they had rights to a share of Haci Osman's land, but they made no attempt to relieve their obvious poverty by taking action to establish them. When one of them lost his wife, Haci Osman helped with advice, influence, and a loan in a negotiations for a new one; and later, when he built and ran a mill in co-operation with other villagers, they became his employees.

The explanation that eluded me at the time was not in fact difficult. As I have said, inheritance is not so much a matter of rights under a definite set of rules, as of relative power. If the two poor brothers had pressed their claims, they would have alienated a useful, important and generally respected kinsman, and probably have turned other villagers against them. They would, even if successful, only have been entitled to one-ninth each of the land which Haci Osman had inherited from his father – and I suspect that he would have argued, probably correctly, that much of his land had come from other sources, for example, purchase, or simply seizure of land not in cultivation. This ninth then would have been very little, and would not have made any great difference to their poverty. Moreover, they would have been opposed to an intelligent and sophistic-ated man who had the ear of the local officials, and the moral prestige of having made the pilgrimage to Mecca. Their chance of success was negligible, and the value of their gains if success-ful would scarcely outweigh the permanent enmity of their influential mother's brother.

On a later visit, I was told that Haci Osman had registered all the land of his household in his own name when he was headman of the village at some point in the past, and he him-self said that he had formally adopted his informally adopted dead son's son as his heir under the Turkish Civil Code. But neither of these facts seemed to be generally known in the village.

Ironically, the wife of the younger of these two brothers is also formally entitled to land, through her mother, from the comparatively well-to-do family of Haci Ömer (D). Her mother's father is said, plausibly, to have been in his day one of the wealthiest and most important men in the village. His three sons divided the land between them and are still comparatively influential and comfortable. Their sisters got nothing. Since there are four surviving sisters, any rearrangement would be disastrous for the three brothers. Yet whenever I asked about this, those who were in a position to make formally justifiable claims would say 'of course they will give – it is the law.'

Brothers divided their land in this way in many cases, indeed in most, unless there were more complicated factors. Neverthe-less, the right of daughters to inherit equally with their brothers was publicly acknowledged, and in some cases they do so in-herit. Ömer (G), for example, told me that he had a large outstanding debt to his sister, who had married to another village, for her share of the land.

Where women inherit, they often do so because they have no brothers. In most cases, where a girl has left her natal village, she sells any land to which she is entitled to her closest kin, but if the land is near the village boundary with the village to which she has married, she may keep it. Enough cases of this type existed for much land close to but within the village boundary to belong to households of other villages. Very rarely, rights to more central plots will be retained, and worked on a share-cropping basis, or rental for cash.

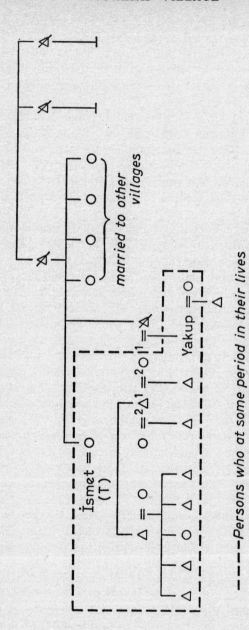

married to other villages

İsmet = ○
(T)

Yakup = ○

– – – – Persons who at some period in their lives
were members of İsmet's household

6 Genealogy: İsmet

One striking but complicated case illustrates female inheritance, and at the same time the opportunism of village inheritance. Ismet (T) had come to the village as a boy with a widowed mother. He had thus no agnatic rights to land. He had married a daughter of a prolific lineage, all the men of which were victims of the wars from 1911 to 1922. Among them was her brother, who left an infant son Yakup, the only male survivor of the lineage. Ismet managed to arrange for the widow, Yakup's mother, to marry his second son, who was only a boy and very much her junior. Ismet was thus in a very strong position. His wife's rights to inherit her lineage lands were naturally recognised. Yakup, the only surviving male of the lineage, was a member of Ismet's household, being step grandson (son's wife's son) and nephew by marriage (wife's brother's son) at the same time. Four other women of the lineage appear either to have been ignored or bought out. In 1949, the immigrant Ismet was the largest landowner in the village, although Yakup was by then married with a reasonable sufficiency of land of his own, and his mother and another son also formed a separate household with a little land said to belong personally to her. How the details of what land passed to whom were worked out, and how customary rights, *de facto* possession and plain seizure were blended, I do not know and cannot reconstruct. But plainly Ismet took his opportunity with both hands.

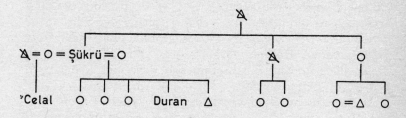

7 Genealogy: Şükrü

A case from Elbaşı illustrates a similar disregard for formal and complicated rules. Şükrü, a man with a sufficiency of land, died in the winter of 1952. During the summer, shortly before my departure, his heirs were disputing the division of inheritance.

Şükrü had kept together his father's land; neither his brother's daughters nor his sister's daughters had ever received a share. Moreover, his senior surviving wife had been separated from him for years, and was living with her son by a former marriage, Celal. This particular argument was complicated and rendered urgent by the fact that Şükrü had left a debt to the Agricultural Bank of T.L.400. I met his sons, Duran and Celal, and his sister's daughter's husband, when they were invited by the headman to his guest room to discuss the matter. The headman argued with them that the whole estate was not large enough for them to 'stuff lawyers', so they had better settle it between themselves. The discussion was complicated, involving short-term problems about the debt, the work of harvesting, and the division of the crops, as well as the long-term difficulties about the land. He suggested seven equal divisions – one each for the widows, and one each for Şükrü's children – not a legally correct decision, but at least equitable. I had the impression from a general interchange of cigarettes that this solution had been accepted by the three men, but I gathered subsequently that Şükrü's nieces were claiming shares and that even the main disputants were not satisfied. The case was not settled when I left, but clearly no one was going to take the matter to court. I am sure in fact that Şükrü's two sons would never agree, unless compelled, to a sevenfold division of the land, let alone to giving a share to female patrilateral cousins. No one even thought, as far as I know, of dividing the land according to the genealogy – that is, giving one-third to be divided between each of the groups of siblings descended from Şükrü's father. Duran's obvious course would be simply to divide the land with his brother and then stick it out until people got used to the idea.

All these examples point to the same conclusion. The distribution of any given estate is largely a matter of relative power and influence. Rules both customary and legal are used rather as weapons than as principles for right conduct.

Customary morality gives men a decided advantage in the struggle. Daughters may be theoretically entitled, but their rights are unimportant, and should never be allowed to prevent a man from possessing enough land to care for a family. A man ought properly to derive his wealth from his agnates, and not look to inherit through mother or wife.

Decreasing village autonomy, the decline in the power and importance of lineages, and the increase of administrative control and interference have increased the chances of establishing and enforcing a claim to female inheritance. At the same time, the universal recognition in the village that sisters ought to receive a share seems to reflect growing urban influence and perhaps the slow acceptance of the new Civil Code of the country. Moreover, the motives for claiming female inheritance grow stronger as land grows scarcer. While therefore female inheritance in special cases has always occurred, inheritance by daughters when there are living adult sons is probably fairly new, and increasing.

Household Fission

The rule is clear. On the death of a household head, his sons are expected within a reasonable period to divide up the property between them and establish separate independent households.

Separation is accepted rather than approved. It is a subject for comment and joking; it is as though people felt that families ought to be able to live together in peace, even though they do not expect them to do so. For those who stay together longer than usual, there is no adverse comment or joking.

In fact, the separation of brothers is sometimes delayed for long periods, even, in rare cases, for their lifetime. In such cases, the elder brother is usually a dominant personality. One household, in a neighbouring village which I visited early in my field work, was shared by two old brothers. In some of the rare apparently stable shared households of this type, one brother farmed, while the other worked as a craftsman, usually a migrant (p. 38, Table 2). In one village I was told of a stable household shared by three brothers – twenty souls in all.

If a father dies prematurely, leaving unmarried sons, all the sons normally remain together until all are married, the elder shouldering the father's responsibility. But they are apt to separate as soon as this operation is complete. Haci Ömer and his two brothers told me that they had remained together eight years after their father's death, and had been separated sixteen. They must therefore have separated when the youngest brother was nineteen, that is, as soon as possible after his marriage. Zübeyr and his three brothers (F) in Sakaltutan were in process of making their marriage arrangements. The second already had a wife, the eldest married during our stay, and marriages were being arranged for the two younger brothers. They declared their firm intention of remaining together until all were married, and had completed military service. In fact, of course, a young unmarried man cannot live alone, so that they are normally bound to live with and marry in the house of their closest kin. One young widower had returned to the household of a married brother, pending remarriage. Households of orphaned siblings cannot therefore very well split until all are married.

Occasionally, a son will set up an independent household while his father is still alive. I came across only one case, in a neighbouring village, where the separation of a married son was said to have been arranged completely amicably, because the household had become too large. This family boasted to me of their co-operation and intimacy, claiming that they had no quarrels.

Most cases of sons leaving the paternal household prematurely were due to quarrels. People were never willing to discuss details of these quarrels in cold blood afterwards – they were always rather ashamed of them. The separating sons were stepsons of their father's current wife; I only knew one who had left his own mother. His quarrel was so serious that, when he was dangerously ill with pneumonia, his parents took no notice, and it was his father-in-law who took him in, to give him the warmth and shelter that his own hovel could not provide. In one other case a son had accompanied his mother when she left because his father, her husband (T), who was her junior, took a younger wife (p. 196). In all the other three cases, relations with the parental household continued, warm in two cases, and slight in one. One father, still vigorous, was helping his three adult married sons to build houses alongside his own, and the whole family was still co-operating closely.

In Elbaşı there were only two cases; one was the school headmaster, whose separate house was provided in the school building, and whose father included him in the total population of his own large household. The other was the usual case of a stepmother. Father and son were neighbours and on good terms.

The accepted rule that brothers divide the household after their father's death avoids the need for a build up of pressures to explosion point as, for example, Srinivas describes for joint households in an Indian village (Srinivas (1952)). The great insistence on absolute equality between recognised heirs prevents very much jockeying for advantage among brothers, unless exceptional circumstances give one brother an opportunity. Nevertheless, as households grow, the pressure to fission increases. Where a father lives to an old age and leaves more than one mature family of grandchildren in his house, division is likely to be much more rapid than with a less mature family, and in a few rare cases fission may begin before the old man has passed on. Men blame quarrels of this kind on the women. Srinivas's arguments (1952, p. 30) could be applied here. The tensions between one elementary family and another inside the households probably reflect as much the rivalry of the brothers as the incompatibility of the women. Disputes are very often at basis disagreements about relative rank; not so much about the pecking order – seniority settles this – as about how hard the pecking should be. Relative rank among the household women turns very largely on the relative rank of the brothers. The closeness of brothers, their mutual dependence and their opportunities for avoiding each other socially when angry, may enable them to avoid among themselves the open quarrels of which they are the underlying cause among their wives.

Srinivas's analysis is so plausible that it cannot be altogether untrue. Yet it is also plausible to argue that the tension between the women of a joint household, often born strangers to each other and brought together by chance, must be in some cases the result of their personal incompatibilities. It would be impossible to prove either explanation false; and it is also impossible to state in general any precise weighting of the two factors.

The Cycle of Wealth

This cycle of domestic growth and fission is at the same time an economic cycle. The resources under the control of the household head grow with the growing population of the household, and then on his death are divided among the independent households of his heirs.

I shall turn later to a more detailed account of village rank. As I have already said, there is considerable mobility from generation to generation. This social mobility between households and lineages is clearly systematically connected with the domestic cycle I have outlined. Exactly how the cycle works out will vary with the type of social situation, and especially with the resources available, the possible uses of spare labour, and the control of the household head over married sons. To analyse this adequately would require detailed histories of a number of villages. Instead, since written records for villages barely exist, and since I devoted too little of my time in the field to reconstructing in detail the history of the two villages, I must rely on argument based on the material available to me.

I distinguished two types of land situation: two models. Real village situations were obviously always far more complicated than the models indicate; yet these models correspond approximately to two stages in the social history of a large number of Anatolian villages; and they make possible illuminating deductions about the changes which have taken place.

In the first situation, land is freely available. Any household is able to take over land so long as it has the manpower and the draught animals to work it. Land not worked reverts to pasture. In the second situation, all cultivable land that can be spared from the village pasture is owned and cultivated. Households can only increase their holdings by taking land from other households.

The First Model: Land in Plenty

Wherever the village is small in relation to the territory available, land for cultivation is freely available. Such was the situation in Elbaşı until 1946 or so, and such it must have been in Sakaltutan up to the early nineteen-twenties, as I shall shortly show. Plainly such a situation existed in most, if not all, villages in the area in the recent past, and indeed in many other parts of Anatolia.

Other evidence supports this view. Reports from Alişar, a

village between Kayseri and Yozgat, in 1932 state that un-
irrigated and uncultivated land bore signs of previous cultivation.

'The considerable area of land no longer cultivated suggests
that the peasants of Alişar are unable with their present equipment to utilise all the arable land within the village limits.'
(Morrison (1938) Chap. II.)

The Village Law of 1924 (p. 271) contained provisions for the
fixing and registering of the boundaries of village territories.
Before this date, and even after it, boundaries were vague,
depending on general features of the landscape (p. 49). Even
if, in some cases, villagers knew clearly the boundaries between
them, it is plausible that many, cultivating only the land near
the settlement, were not concerned with precise rights to the
extensive pastures which lay between them and their neighbours.

The situation I have described is not inconsistent with the
existence of tax farmers or even of absentee landowners. So long
as the dues are paid on the crop produced and not on the extent
of land held, the rights of the urban landlords or tax collectors
are over villages as social groups, and not over specific pieces
of land. Each villager can therefore still be free *de facto* to take
on fresh land whenever he wishes to do so. His tax or rent is in
fact personal, a proportion of income due to a political superior.

I have already (p. 83) described the limits of cultivation per
ploughman imposed by the traditional techniques. Very
roughly, each extra adult man equipped with a plough, seed
and a team of oxen would add a possible twenty *dönüm* (about
ten to fifteen acres, four to six ha.) to the annual cultivated area
of a household.

Quite apart from these physical limitations, many villagers
did not in the past strive to increase their cultivations beyond a
certain point, because they had nothing to gain by so doing.
To market grain was not easy. Moreover, in years of surplus local
prices would be low, whereas in years of high prices the villager
was unlikely to have any surplus to market.

Transport was a major difficulty. Ox-carts carry comparatively small loads, and move more slowly than a man walking.
Thus even from Sakaltutan a journey to Kayseri would have
taken some ten hours or more. Moreover, many people told me

that in the days before and immediately after the establishment of the Republic highwaymen were common. Indeed, some villagers cheerfully told me of their own exploits. Grain for the local market presumably moved under convoy, which made it difficult for the small producer to sell except to dealers in the village. The tax farmers, for example, bought surplus grain from the villagers, a system which would hardly make for an advantageous deal for the villagers. Mümtaz Turhan reports from his own village in eastern Turkey (Turhan (1951) p. 95) that cash cropping of cereals was regarded as dishonourable. In my area it was not that marketing was dishonourable but that it was limited to the well-to-do with surpluses large enough to justify the trouble involved.

In general, therefore, no household could cultivate more than a certain amount, and only prosperous households tried to produce more than enough for their own needs.

As sons reached maturity the household was able to expand its land holding. This would make possible, and require, an increase in its animal population as well. Thus the wealth controlled by the head increased, the surpluses produced by each constituent element were pooled in his hands, and the whole unit benefited by efficiency in proportion. The head might well join the village leaders (_ağalar_) or even become the most influential among them. At this point the marketing of grain would be both possible and worthwhile. Yet on his death, each son would inherit only approximately as much land as he himself had been ploughing. Every new household, born out of the splitting of a large one, would thus start with roughly the same amount of land, whether it sprang from a household with only one male heir, or one with ten. Each young household head would depend on his own procreative prowess, skill, hard work and luck to build for himself a position of prominence in his later years. Even in cases where the son of an eminent father himself became eminent, the son did not succeed to his father's position, but built up a new one for himself, after an interregnum filled by households of other village lineages. Few could succeed completely in the face of illness, premature deaths, infertility, crop failures, animal diseases and other hazards. If this model had ever functioned uncomplicated by other factors, then it would have corresponded to the ideal society of some social moralists – perfect equality of opportunity, barring acts of God. But of course it did not.

Even if land is a free good, the means to work it are not. A man needs equipment and, more especially, draught animals. There is no doubt that in contrast to many primitive societies and to some other Middle Eastern areas, these villages contained landless men, or rather oxenless men. Even now, some richer households have servants – *çirak* – who live in their master's household. In the past such arrangements were quite common. One whole village, called, perhaps significantly, *Çiraz*, whose territory formed an enclave within that of a larger village, was said to have been founded entirely by freed servants of their richer neighbours. Presumably they had been rewarded by gifts of oxen and the right to plough in their masters' territory. Casual labour was also said to have been much commoner in the past. People in Elbaşı were quite explicit about this. Once the village was full of landless labourers, they said, but now they had all got their own oxen and started to plough for themselves. To judge from stories about people's ancestral origins, many of these oxenless servants in the past were vagrants, but some must have been settled villagers.

Just how difficult it was to move from oxenless labourer to landowner it is hard to guess. Oxen are costly in relation to a subsistence income, and a man also needs a homestead, a plough and seed. Possibly share-cropping in some form offered a way or the rewards of shepherds and servants occasionally provided the necessary capital. Obviously some people did succeed. But equally obviously it was not as simple a matter to set up initially as a landowner as it was for an established landowner to expand his operations as his household grew.

Practically all village households own sheep and goats. These constitute a form of inheritable wealth apart from land, and might therefore upset the rough equality of inheritance between the sons of different households. Villages varied and still vary sharply in the extent to which they depend on sheep and goats. Even within one area, as de Planhol (1958, pp. 234 ff.) makes clear, rights to summer or winter pasture away from the village were fairly common but highly variable. Wealth in animals tends to follow a similar pattern. Special winter pastures are not normally available on the plateau, and the flock must be fed during the winter from the straw of the cereal crops. The size of the flock is thus closely tied to the extent of the cultivated lands of its owner. It is also partly related to the size of the household, since the sheep must be milked in the spring and this is women's work among the villagers. Sheep, moreover, are easily stolen and a large flock needs a reasonably large defence, so that sons are as necessary to the security of the household flocks as are women to its productivity. In fact, large households probably gained proportionally more from sheep farming than did small households, thus reinforcing the swing from poverty to wealth and back as the household changed from small to large and split into small again.

More important, land varied sharply in value. Land near the village is manured and often irrigated. This more valuable land was never allowed to go out of cultivation and was always owned by someone, and moreover, the amounts of it held by different households would vary greatly according to the accidents of past history – how prolific they had been, how many brotherless heiresses their members had married, whether they had been strong enough to appropriate land by arbitrary means. But here again the effect is to reinforce the levelling process of the cycle. The single heir of a less successful father is on balance likely to inherit more of the most valuable category of land than the co-heirs of a more prolific and powerful father.

I have been arguing that, so long as land was freely available, no household was likely to retain a position of eminence in the village beyond the death of the household head, and that therefore there was a continual rise and fall in the relative position of households, and groups of fraternal households. Certain disturbing factors, such as the existence of a lower stratum which had difficulty in getting started on the ladder, and the difference in holdings of sheep and in fertility of land gave some people an advantage over others but did not cancel out the general mobility of the society.

One other factor of disturbance remains – a much more damaging one to my model. I have already said that the village contained landless people who often acted as servants (çirak), either long-term or casual, to their more wealthy neighbours. In theory, this practice would make possible an expansion of farming limited only by the availability of labour, and by the possibility of making some use of the extra crops and herds acquired, either by marketing them or by feeding a political or perhaps an armed following.

It is highly probable that on analogies from other parts of the Middle East (Barth (1959) p. 89) the successful did in fact use retainers in this way. The odds against a high degree of success were great. No village is a power vacuum, and once a man's power began to grow, he would face rivals prepared to use violence. Only he himself personally would be able to hold his supporters together, so he would need vigour and good health over a fairly long period. Successful contacts with the leaders of other villages, and – more important – with merchants, officials and powerful people in the towns, would reinforce his control over his own village, and he might even expand his empire over other villages. A man with this degree of success would have several wives and many sons; he would need sons in order to get started and he would achieve more by his success.

No one son would inherit both the wealth and the unique position in the network of contacts and patronage that gave his father power. Of course, the sons of an eminent and wealthy father would start with advantages, and one lineage might be able to claim a number of successful men over the generations. But these would not form a continuous dynasty, but a haphazard series, interrupted by periods when men of other village lineages dominated or at least divided the village. Most villages appear to have contained at least two potentially powerful lineages of this type. *A priori* then, the possibility of employing labour and even retainers, if it introduced a greater social distance between the top of village society and the bottom, did not prevent a high rate of social mobility between households and lineages. In spite of complications and occasional conspicuous exceptions, the main features of the model seem to hold. As long as land was a free good, a man with a minimum of capital with which to start cultivating, good health and many sons could establish a high ranking position in village society, but without giving any one son more than a slight lead over his neighbours in the new race for wealth and power.

The maintenance of this situation depends on the population of any given village remaining small enough to allow more cultivable land than the village needs. I have no accurate and detailed information on the population of villages prior to 1925, but it seems likely that the population, subject to disease, famine and conscription, was growing only slowly if at all, and may well have fallen during the wars from 1911 to 1922. Thus, while many households were able to expand their cultivations, others were forced by loss of manpower or ox-power to abandon land, leaving it free for others ultimately to take over.

One clear example of this from Sakaltutan has already been given, and to my knowledge at least three patrilineal groups had died out or left the village within recent memory. Morrison (1938, Chap. II) reports that about nine per cent of the whole village territory of Alişar was abandoned fields. He also says, it is true, that some ninety per cent of this abandoned land was still claimed, but by 1932, the end of free land was already in sight; and a claim to abandoned land is easily made but much more difficult to establish unless one is able to work it. Neighbours, he tells us, were liable to filch unworked land.

So long then as the population is kept stable by a high death rate, this type of domestic cycle, with its implications of a high degree of social mobility up and down over the generations, can revolve indefinitely.

The Second Model: Land Shortage

But once Republican peace and order were established in Turkey, the population was anything but stable. With rapid and steady population growth the supply of spare cultivable land is bound to be exhausted sooner or later. This supply has been drying up in Turkey over the last half-century, and little if any now remains; certainly not in the area in which I was working.

In the new situation, sons are still as much desired as ever. They are still a source of prestige, religious as well as secular; they form an armed guard for the defence of the household, and they enable father to take his ease. Even in the past sons who could not be absorbed as extra labour on the household lands could increase household income as labourers, servants, shepherds or migrants. But when household land does not expand in proportion to the male labour force, fission leaves each son with less land than he is capable of working. One or two may succeed in acquiring extra by inheritance through women, by purchase, or by simple appropriation. But over the whole village, in two or three generations, many households will be reduced to poverty.

In the first model, the balance between man- and animal-power and land was assured by more or less freely adjusting the amount of land. Now the attitude to land rights changes, and land becomes important even if it cannot be worked. Hence share-cropping sharply increases. Anyone who is unable to work part or all of his land will be keen to lease it, while many neighbours, having insufficient of their own, will be anxious to share-crop for others.

Some Cases

I have presented this argument so far as a pair of models. These are, of course, designed to make sense of the material from the two villages. This material does not constitute proof. But proof is not the point, since a model is not true or false but more or less useful and appropriate. The cases that follow conform in general to the model, but in some details diverge from it. They are in part reconstructions based on statements of informants, on landholdings, and on the assumption of a basically agnatic system of inheritance.

Table 3 (p. 53) shows the large number of small and very small holdings of land in Sakaltutan. In every case, the small size of these holdings was said to be due directly to the division of paternal holdings among heirs. The process of division seems to have been under way for roughly two generations. Heads of large joint households in the period 1900 to 1910, that is, the fathers of the oldest living generation in the village in 1950, seem to have had as much land as they needed. As late as the early nineteen-twenties households with adequate manpower seem still to have been able to expand their holdings as need arose.

Hamit (V) (Fig. 8) was about eighty years of age in 1950; the only survivor of five brothers who had grown up, only one of whom had no living descendants. He said he had inherited thirty dönüm (fifteen acres, six ha.) from his father, and fifteen from his mother, making forty-five in all. His father presumably then held about 150 dönüm; much more than he

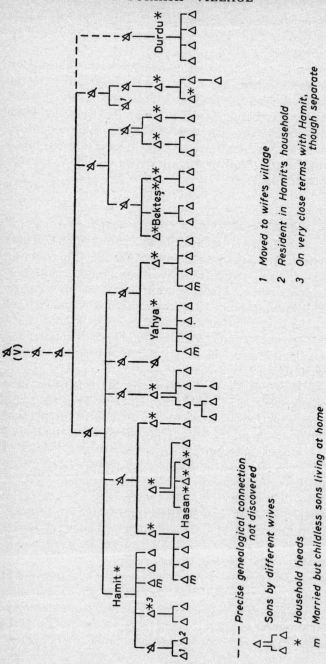

8 Genealogy: V lineage

- - - Precise genealogical connection
        not discovered

△┐△ Sons by different wives
 └△

* Household heads

m Married but childless sons living at home

◁ Deceased

1 Moved to wife's village

2 Resident in Hamit's household

3 On very close terms with Hamit,
    though separate

Names given only when mentioned in the text

is likely to have inherited. It is likely he was able to increase his holding as Hamit and his brothers grew up, probably somewhere between 1890 and 1910.

Hamit himself was less fortunate. His eldest son, born about 1895, died about 1940; but his second and third sons' official years of birth were about 1916 and 1921 respectively. His eldest grandson was born about 1925. Hence at no point before the late nineteen-twenties did he have much help with farming, and it is not surprising that he did not succeed in expanding his own holdings.

Two of his brothers had fared likewise. They had both passed on to their heirs about the same quantity of land as Hamit had inherited from his father. One had had two sons, born 1905 and 1910, the other only one. But a third brother had passed on about one hundred *dönüm* at least, and perhaps more. He had been the most successful begetter of sons. Their official dates of birth were 1900, 1908 and 1918. Thus in the immediate post war period (1922–25) he would have had at least two sons old enough to plough, and it seems reasonable to assume that it was then that he was able to expand his holdings.

One such example may seem a little thin; in fact similar evidence from other lineages leads to similar conclusions, putting the matter beyond reasonable doubt.

The closing down of the right to plough village pasture must have been gradual. Even now people are accused of surreptitious encroachment on village meadow land, and plainly public opinion in the village against such ploughing would form slowly, and become really effective only when the situation began to look serious. The absence of men in the armies between 1911 and 1923 and the loss of many of them, may actually have reversed the process for a time.

Elbaşı had a very much larger territory, said to have been fixed by one of its sons who became the local Land Registration Officer (*tapu memürü*) under the Ottoman Empire. Only after the Second World War was free ploughing of village pasture stopped, and the conflicts generated thereby were still acute in 1951. More and more of the villagers realised that land was too valuable an asset to be left unoccupied, and as the supply diminished the end came with a land rush. People, I was told, left their undisputed and more fertile plots near the village uncultivated in order to use their ploughing resources to stake claims at the margins. The threat to the village pasture led to organised opposition in the village to this movement. When a man set out to stake a claim, neighbours would follow him, and sit in rows staking claims to the strips immediately alongside the furrow he was ploughing, rendering his claim useless and absurd. These situations naturally led to violence. The administration intervened and ruled that no more land should be ploughed up. In 1951 surreptitious ploughing of pasture by those whose land was adjacent to it was still said to be going on, but not on a great scale, and not without the danger of rousing both neighbours and authorities to intervene.

The effects of the previous régime when marginal land was a free good were still plainly to be seen in the social structure. Well-to-do families often had extremely poor affines, and even extremely poor agnates. One family in particular illustrates my point.

Haci Bayram (B) had been a great man, and had served as District Officer under the imperial administration. He had had at least five sons on whom presumably his eminence was built. He had crowned it all by making the pilgrimage to Mecca, in those days a costly trip. Spent up, he had returned to the village a *Haci*, to die in modest circumstances. His five sons had inherited a modicum of land and one beast each. They began their independence poor.

Of these five, three younger full brothers were still alive in 1951. The eldest survivor had had four daughters, all by this time married. His land was worked by a stepson, who, I was assured, had no right to inherit it. The old man was poor and insignificant. The second of the three had had three sons of his own; his first wife had died after a long illness, and this, he said, had ruined him. Yet his household had a comfortable sufficiency.

The youngest brother, Hayip (B), had five sons, all adult and all but one, the village headmaster, still living in his household. The eldest, who had a son already old enough to work, had been headman about the time of the land rush. Hayip had not been slow to seize the opportunity, and his was one of the wealthiest households in the village. He had an imposing guest room, and was having a new dwelling house for the family built during our stay. But his existing family house betrayed his recent poverty, and his lowliness was too well remembered for his wealth to earn him much respect. His sons in turn will inherit only modest-sized holdings, which they will have no possibility of expanding except by direct purchase.

Haci Bayram's two elder sons had been by a different mother, and were a great deal older. One had left in the village another set of four brothers with sharply different degrees of wealth. The eldest, Mahsud, a man of about fifty, had about as much land as Hayip; the others barely enough to keep the household going. I failed to check on the history of this disparity, but as Mahsud had only three sons, the eldest of whom was only twenty, this case does not fit my model. Possibly it was Mahsud's father who had taken the initiative, and somehow, as elder brother, he had retained the extra land which his father had acquired, and restricted the division to the patrimonial estate.

Elbaşı also provided one example of a personal rise to real pre-eminence, and the corresponding extinction of this power with the death of the holder. Kara Osman (Ax) it was said, had 'held the whole district in his hand', and had been a friend of Ataturk. Quite what this meant I am not sure; but plainly during the War of Independence and in the early days of the Republic he must have had great political influence in the area. He had had one successful son who must have been born early in his married life, for he had married and left a grandson senior to Kara Osman's other sons, two more of whom must have been adolescent in the mid nineteen-twenties. Thus he had at least four descendants to work for him. He may have had others who died without issue.

In 1923 Turkey agreed with Greece to transfer to Greece all Christians of the Greek Orthodox Church. A large village standing below Elbaşı, on the stream which irrigated a wide belt of meadow and crop land, was emptied of its population. Kara Osman moved in, and took over a large area of land, said to be a thousand *dönüm*. This might mean anything from 100 ha. (250 acres) to 250 ha. (over 600 acres). He was in any case very much wealthier than anyone else in the village. 'At his gate,' they said, 'there were ten labourers.' He was one of the first in this part of Turkey to own a tractor and a combine harvester, before these became familiar sights in the Turkish countryside.

I was told that twelve people claimed shares in his estate and that they had taken the case to the courts. I have records only of eleven, one grandson, five sons, (two of them still children), two daughters and three widows, who were certainly not all married to him under State law. By 1955, four years after his death, the matter was still unsettled though the brothers claimed to be reconciled. I suspect that in the end the four household heads, the grandson and the three adult sons, reached agreement which the rest were unable to upset. But whatever the outcome no single heir could in any way rival his father's pre-eminence.

Conclusion

In general then, over much of Anatolia, the village social system worked against the maintenance of wealth in any one household or line of households through more than one generation. Broad was the way and easy the path to mediocrity or poverty, through the division of the land, illness, premature deaths, the birth of too many daughters, the barrenness of wives or the death of oxen. But strait as it was, the gate to prosperity was open, through the successful rearing of many sons to provide economic resources and fighting men for the expansion of household power and wealth. Land shortage closes this gate; the downward path is now even easier to tread but there is no way up again. Fathers still profit from large families of sons but the more successful they are in breeding them, the smaller their sons' holdings, and the more hopeless their sons' prospects of attaining importance in the village.

The second model with its prospects of hopelessness applies to the present situation in Turkey only in so far as the villages are forced to solve their problems within themselves. But already the villages are part of the national economy, and from the outside there is hope, at a price. To feed a family, many men must go away to work. Even the better off can only hope to acquire the extra resources to establish importance in the village by going outside. But the very need to move out for long periods into a different world makes the achievement more difficult, and, at the same time, as the contestants become aware of

5 A village blacksmith. (p.60)

6 Water arriving. Most villages have more than one fountain. (p.18)

7 A village mill making cracked wheat (bulgar). (p.46)

other social arenas, less desirable. The successful migrant spends on material prestige symbols of a more urban kind, and not on traditional generosity, on building loyalty and dependence in the village itself. The two most stylish guest rooms in Sakaltutan in 1955 belonged to young migrant craftsmen. But neither were men of importance in village affairs. In the next generation, the father with little land and an earned income from his own migration will surely be less able to hold his sons, and even if he can hold their loyalty, he will be unable to use them in the traditional way.

CHAPTER EIGHT

KINSHIP

Kinship Rôles

All societies attach rights and duties to kinship relationships outside the family or domestic group. At one extreme are those societies in which a very large part of social intercourse and a large number of technical, economic, and political activities are carried on within acknowledged kinship relations, and in which accordingly the rights and duties of kin to each other are various, numerous and in some matters highly specific and heavily sanctioned. At the other extreme are those societies like industrial Europe and America in which these rights and duties are relatively unimportant in many political and economic matters, seldom distinct or precise, and sanctioned mainly by reciprocity – that is, people are free to contract out of their duties to their kin, on pain only of losing their rights to claim reciprocal friendly support and help.

Within these Turkish villages, that is, excluding the political and economic dependence of the rural area on the wider society, kinship relations are the single most important set of relationships outside the domestic group, and a very high proportion of activity is kinship activity. Yet with some minor exceptions, and one major one, which I shall discuss below, different kinship rôles do not carry specific and distinct rights and duties, but rather a general duty of affection, help and support.

Kin visit each others' houses, spend their leisure time together, co-operate in work, help each other in small crises, such as temporary shortages or the arrival of the unexpected guest, and in major crises such as sickness, food shortages, sickness of animals, and the ceremonies of birth, circumcision, marriage and death. The degree of intimacy of relationship of this kind must obviously vary greatly. It depends partly on the closeness of the kinship link, with a noticeable tendency for agnatic links to be stronger than others. But it also varies with other factors. Even the boundary between kin and non-kin is not clearly marked. Obviously, as the social distance increases, the scale and frequency of the exchange of mutual services and friendly intercourse diminishes, but no hard line exists between kinship – *akrabalık* – and neighbourliness – *komşuluk*. More than once, people said to me that they were kin, *akraba*, then when pressed for details corrected themselves; 'Not exactly kin, neighbours. But it's all the same really.'

Hüseyn (F) and Yahya (V) lived side by side in Sakaltutan, at one edge of the village. Though they recognised no kin tie, they were constantly together. Hüseyn's orphaned agnatic cousin was married to Yahya's daughter, and Hüseyn's guest room was used for the meal given by Yahya to the boy's side when they came to fetch the bride. This case was perhaps exceptional, but it illustrates a perfectly acceptable type of relationship.

The Nuer, a patrilineal people of the southern Sudan, cannot imagine a confusion of distinct kinship rôles. In particular, the distinction between agnates and other consanguineal kin and affines is sharp. No one can give and receive cattle for the marriage of the same girl (Evans-Pritchard (1951) pp. 152 ff.). Most unilineal societies have such sharp distinctions. In these villages, on the contrary, again with one major exception, father's sister's daughter, different kinds of uncles and aunts are not theoretically sharply distinct. A man may through the practice of marriage, be mother's brother and classificatory father's brother to the same child. Some informants even denied, incorrectly, that the rôles of mother's brother and father's brother differ at all.

The lack of specificity in kinship rôles goes with an absence of formal or organised sanctions. No public authority, for example, admonishes those who fail in their duties, as the Lozi are lectured in their courts of law (Gluckman (1955) p. 358 and *passim*). Those who feel that they have been let down have no sanctions to apply except to withdraw from social relations with the offenders – unless the matter is serious enough to call for violence. Reciprocity is the main sanction. But the very lack of specificity and formality weakens this sanction also, because the loss of support from one kinsman or set of kin can often be made good by close ties with another. Indeed, where the network of recognised kin ties is of close mesh, most people have far more kinship relations than they keep up with, and are forced to choose which of these relationships they will pursue, and which they will allow to remain more or less inoperative. Their choice is governed not only by genealogical closeness, but also by physical distance, temperament, convenience, relative rank and wealth, current village hostilities and so on.

Kinship is not only a matter of relations between households. Each adult member of a household has his or her personal links and preferences. Between the men of a single household, who share their agnatic ties, the differences are not usually conspicuous, but adult women, who have been imported as adult strangers with ready-made fields of relationships, normally differ sharply from their husbands and from each other in their choice of intimacies. The more or less universal tendency for husband and wife to draw each other into their own fields of social intimacy is less marked here than in many societies because of the social segregation between the sexes. Of course, where a woman marries a close kinsman, the divergence is less; and also where she marries at a great distance from home, it may again be less, because she makes her new relationships with her husband's female kin.

To contract out of some of one's kinship duties does not normally disturb other people in the community, and leads at the very worst to criticism and gossip. The one major exception to this lack of specificity is the duty of agnates to defend each other in quarrels, and to avenge homicide. But even this duty, as I shall explain, is in practice optional – people can and do contract out of it.

The general lack of specificity and the optional and variable character of kinship ties make the kinship system amorphous, without making it unimportant. The amorphousness renders description difficult, and my statements about rights and duties of kin in this chapter and the next may at times be misleadingly definite. I am well aware that not only people's behaviour, but their statements about what behaviour ought to be, will vary from situation to situation, from individual to individual and even from hour to hour.

Terminology

The close connection the world over between the structure of kinship relations and the terminology has been amply demonstrated. Striking instances are found in almost every society that has been studied. Significantly different rôles normally carry different names. But in spite of this demonstration, we still lack a study of negative instances; indeed we do not have a criterion of what is and what is not a negative instance.

Turkish kinship terminology does not correspond consistently to the structure of kinship rôles. The situation is complicated by the use, in the villages, of the standard Turkish terms current in Istanbul, with only relatively minor variations of dialect and usage, although the two societies are very different.

I have listed in the accompanying chart (p. 152) the village terms, with the corresponding standard Turkish terms, translation and some comments. These lists are not strictly comparable, since the standard list is based on general, educated usage and on dictionaries, and not, like the village list, on observation.

Standard Turkish distinguishes parents and children by descriptive terms, (*baba, anne, oğul, kız*); also parents' siblings by similar descriptive terms, father's brother (*amca*), father's sister (*hala*), mother's brother (*dayı*), mother's sister (*teyze*). Their children (cousins) are similarly distinguished. Siblings' children (nephews and nieces) are on the other hand all covered by a single term (*vigen*). A single term each also covers grandfather, grandmother and grandchildren. Close affines are distinguished by a fairly full set of terms.

This system differs markedly from most Western European systems only in distinguishing between parents' siblings (uncles and aunts), parents' siblings' children (cousins), and different types of affines. It has no classificatory terms in the accepted sense, though some terms are used loosely – parents' friends may be classed as parents' siblings for the benefit of small children, for example. *Kız*, the word for daughter, is also the normal word for girl. Agnates are not stressed, nor does the system in any way reflect a lineage structure. The distinction, for example, between parents' siblings seems now to correspond to nothing structural.

CHART OF KINSHIP TERMS

For the sake of completeness, I give a full list of the kinship terms in use in the villages of the area. Except as indicated, these correspond to standard Turkish (abbreviated below as S.T.). See Chapter Eight for discussion.

baba, peder	father
ağa (used by son or younger brother) (title of respect to an older man)	father, elder brother (not S.T.)
anne, valide	mother
ebeveyn	parents
oğul	son
kız	daughter
uşak	child (S.T. boy)
döl (used mainly by women)	child (S.T. foetus)
evlat	child or children
kardeş, birader	brother
kız kardeş, hemşire, bacı (bacı is also a title of respect to an older woman)	sister
ağabey (used mainly by younger siblings)	elder brother
abla (used mainly by younger siblings) (also a title of respect to an older woman)	elder sister
dede, büyük baba	grandfather
ebbe	grandmother (not S.T.)
büyük anne	grandmother
emme	father's brother (used in a classificatory sense)
dayı	mother's brother
amme	father's sister (not S.T.)
hala	mother's sister (father's sister in S.T.)
yiğen	nephew or niece
emmem oğlu	father's brother's son, used in a classificatory sense (the final *m* is a possessive suffix, meaning *my*)
emmem kızı	father's brother's daughter
emm' uşağı	father's brother's child
dayım oğlu	mother's brother's son
dayım kızı	mother's brother's daughter
day' uşağı	mother's brother's child
halam oğlu	mother's sister's son
halam kızı	mother's sister's daughter
hal' uşağı	mother's sister's child
ammem oğlu	father's sister's son
ammem kızı	father's sister's daughter

amm' uşağı	father's sister's child
emmeti	distant agnate
koca, herif	husband
aile	wife (S.T. family)
avrat, horanta	wife
kayın	spouse's kin, especially brother
kayınpeder, kayınata	father-in-law
kayınanne, kayınvalide	mother-in-law
guvah	bridegroom, son-in-law (S.T. *güvey*)
damat	bridegroom, son-in-law
gelin	bride, daughter-in-law
kayınbirader	spouse's brother
görümce	husband's sister
baldız	wife's sister
yenge (see pp. 182 ff.)	uncle's wife (in S.T. brother's wife; I did not hear it so used in the village)
enişte	sister's husband; aunt's husband
bacanak	wife's sister's husband
elti	husband's brother's wife
dünür	own child's parents-in-law
babalık	stepfather
annelik	stepmother
oğulluk	stepson (kızlık does not mean stepdaughter)
süt anneşi	foster mother (wet nurse)
süt kardeşi	foster brother

The system has some minor inconsistencies which seem to lack any obvious social explanation. *Yiğen*, nephew, niece, is the reciprocal of the four distinct terms for parents' siblings. Wife's sister is distinct from husband's sister, yet wife's brother and husband's brother are the same. Terms for grandparents' siblings are not clear, especially terms for mother's father's siblings and for father's mother's siblings.

Even in standard Turkish synonyms for many of the main terms have been borrowed from Persian and Arabic. These terms mostly correspond in meaning to the Turkish terms, and I have no observations on differences of contextual usage. Sometimes they have slightly different meanings. *Evlad*, for example, is used for child or children without specifying sex.

The village system in the main reflects the standard Turkish system, but differs not only in dialect but also significantly in usage. The number of synonyms in current use struck me as high, and terms are very often loosely used. Because people normally used standard Turkish when speaking to me my impression of dialect usage grew only slowly and may still be at fault.

Although the formal terminology does not show any stress of agnation, village usage does. The terms for father's brother (paternal uncle) and father's brother's son (agnatic first cousin) are commonly used for all recognised agnates, as if they were classificatory terms, whereas the other terms for uncles and cousins are not so used, or at least to a much smaller degree. This classificatory looseness is never applied to the words for father and brother; even in what I have called adoption (pp. 41-2), the adopted child uses the term appropriate to the original kinship relation, and not the term for father. For example, Ahmet (K) always spoke of and addressed Mahmut (K) an agnatic second cousin (father's father's brother's son's son) as *emme*, because although equal in generation he was twenty years his senior. Mahmut responded by *emmem oğlu* thus treating Ahmet as an equal.

One curious and interesting feature of the village system is its lack of a straightforward word for wife. The word *avrat*, commonly heard, is indecent; the word *aile* is the standard Turkish word for family, though I am not sure how far it carries any implication that children are included. A third word, a local dialect word, *horanta*, is more commonly used for the population of a household and does imply children. My general impression from many conversations is that villagers do not speak of a man's wife without including children as part of the same concept. On the other hand the word normally translated as daughter-in-law or bride, *gelin*, is used in a very large number of contexts, even by a husband to refer to his wife.

The terms for affines are much the same as those in standard Turkish. *Kayın*, kin of spouse, is used by itself in a fairly general way, and also compounded with other kinship terms to indicate particular kin of spouse. Equally, *enişte*, strictly the sister's husband, is freely used of the husbands of close kin. *Görümce* and *baldız*, though they are known, I seldom heard in the villages.

The villages also used three terms which do not have counterparts in standard Turkish: *bacanak*, wife's sister's husband (i.e. a man who shares one's *kayın*); *elti*, husband's brother's wife, a

woman who is likely to share a household with one at some
point and remain a neighbour throughout married life, and
dünür, child's spouse's parents. All three terms are in common
use in the villages where they refer to relations important in
village society (p. 172).

Details apart, the kinship structure and the terminology are
not a close fit. The village is presented by a larger society with
ready-made kinship terminology, the main feature of which is
that it is readily adaptable to a wide range of possible social
systems, and has only a general negative relation to the social
structure. Some details have clearly been adapted to fit particular aspects of village society; others seem to have no explanation
of this sort. To put the matter another way: if we had nothing
but a record of the kinship terminology of this society, how
much could we safely deduce about the kinship system? Very
little.

Rights and Duties of Agnates

Agnates have a duty which separates them sharply from all
other kin. They must stand together in disputes. If a man
quarrels, his agnates must support him. If he is attacked, they
must defend him. If he is killed, they must avenge him. By
defining loyalties in serious cases, this duty divides the villages
into fairly clear cut and potentially hostile agnatic groups.

These groups are fundamental to the village political structure, and are the basis of the feuding system. Both of these
topics will be treated more fully in chapter eleven.

Agnates of course share the general duties of kin to each
other; indeed these are normally stronger between agnates
than among others, and services rendered are less precisely
evaluated and less meticulously reciprocated.

In the winter, almost all village men meet together to gossip
in a number of guest rooms. In the summer more casual groups
form out of doors during the evenings. I shall analyse these
groups later (p. 240). Their core is usually agnatic, and
the guest rooms are often identified with a particular lineage.

In a crisis, it is the duty first and foremost of agnates to help
out. In Sakaltutan, one old man lived in the lower quarter in

his wife's house, among his affines, and in day to day converse maintained with them far more visible friendly contacts than with his agnates who lived on the patrimonial site in the centre of the village. At the harvest both he and his only grown son fell seriously ill. No one was left to reap and gather in the crops. In this emergency, it was his agnates, not his neighbours, who saved him from destitution. Of the six men who worked together to reap his fields, at a time when everybody is anxious to be about his own business, only one was an affine and neighbour. Two were brothers, one was second agnatic cousin (father's father's brother's son's son), and two were third agnatic cousins (father's father's father's brother's son's son's son). Two other older cousins failed to help, but no closer agnate was absent.

Musa (K) had recently lost a wife through sickness. In the absence of any other adult woman, this loss caused disastrous disorganisation to his household during the harvest. In this crisis, the group which I found harvesting his fields consisted mainly of agnates. All the acknowledged members of his lineage in the village were present, his two brothers, his two agnatic first cousins (father's brother's sons), and his only agnatic second cousin. In addition, the group contained his son-in-law from the next village, who came in duty bound, and two close neighbours to whom he automatically acquired a strict, if not urgent, duty to repay a day's labour. Among agnates also, a reciprocal duty was of course acknowledged, but within a much more constant and flexible flow of mutual services. They all stated firmly that they had formed the group to help Musa. But in fact the group went in turn round the fields of each member, spending one day on each, so that Musa's advantage was, it seemed to me, eventually eroded.

Agnates have special responsibilities to assist at marriages. If a boy's father is no longer alive, his close agnates are likely to bear the main burden of seeing him married. Zübeyr (F) who, when I reached the village, was away in town working, returned to the village in December, and was married in March (pp. 144–5). His senior agnatic first cousin (father's brother's son), Hüseyn (F), acted as host, made most of the arrangements, and helped financially. He was an older man, by village standards prosperous and honourable. It was to Hüseyn's neighbour and constant companion Yahya's daughter (p. 149) that Zübeyr was married. Another agnatic first cousin, somewhat younger, also assisted materially with the arrangements.

In normal weddings, the customs and rites express the opposition between groom's kin and bride's kin. People line up according to neighbourhoods and the closeness of the kin ties to each side, but the agnates are the core of committed people on both. The two sides meet when the boy's side come to fetch the bride, and the tension between them is plain. At this particular wedding, a young man who was the bride's father's first agnatic cousin (father's father's brother's son) was also a friend and migrant workmate of the groom. He came with his neighbours and other comrades at the head of the procession to fetch her to her new home. This defection from lineage loyalty was remarked upon, and he was picked for especially unpleasant treatment in the horseplay to which the groom's party are by custom required to submit during the ceremonies.

On the day which marks the end of Ramazan, called in Turkey *Şeker Bayramı*, the villagers visit each other in peace, and all should shake hands and wish each other a blessed feast day. In Sakaltutan, where I witnessed this ceremony, numbers are small enough for this to be possible. All households who own guest rooms of any kind open them, and one senior man sits there to welcome visitors, while parties of younger men tour the village calling at each guest room. These parties consisted mainly of agnates; even those normally on rather cool terms were to be seen together on this day. Similarly, at the Feast of Sacrifice, the *Kurban Bayramı*, which follows twelve weeks later, people share animals for sacrifice. Once again, many of the groups had an agnatic core; but since seven householders share an ox or cow, and a sheep serves for one household only, strictly agnatic groups are arithmetically impossible.

All these co-operative activities then have an agnatic bias; but it is only a bias. None of them are in theory or practice tied to particular rôles, and they are conspicuous among agnates solely because agnates are in general closer to each other than to anyone else.

The Lineages

The lineages are small groups of shallow depth, reckoning common agnatic descent from the grandfather or great-grandfather of the senior living generation. For example, the largest group in Sakaltutan, reckoning genealogically, contained twenty households (p. 162). Sakaltutan contained ten such groups, the others ranging from three or four to ten households, and Elbaşı a correspondingly larger number. In some cases, distinct groups were vaguely said to have had common agnatic ancestry, but no one knew or cared very much. One or two lineages in each village had traditions about the arrival of their founding father in the village.

Shallow patrilineal groups of this kind are found in many peasant societies – in Arab countries and in Asia (Granquist (1931), Peters (1964), Embree (1946). Srinivas (1952) etc., etc.) Since the non-overlapping groups defined by descent from a common ancestor through one sex only, it seems pointless to refuse them the name 'lineage'. But it is true that this is no complex large-scale segmentary system such as is found in Middle East tribal society, and in other parts of the world (Peters (1960), Evans-Pritchard (1940), Freedman (1958) etc.). These lineages are in many ways strikingly unlike the lineages of these larger scale systems both in form and function.

They can hardly be called corporate. (cf. Fortes (1953) p. 25, Evans-Pritchard (1940) p. 203.) They are not legal or jural persons in custom or in law. They own nothing in common (for one exception, see p. 242), they have no common ritual symbols, their leaders are not often clearly and formally recognised, and they are neither exogamous nor endogamous. More importantly, though it is impossible to belong to two lineages, it is possible for some households tacitly to contract out of lineage activities, and a few households with no close agnates have no lineage affiliation at all.

Their existence and persistence does not rely on the part they play as units in a larger system, but on the recognition and fulfilling of the special personal rights and duties of agnates to each other. It is the fact that the men of a number of households recognise both close relations of a general kind and the specific duty to defend each other that constitutes the group.

This group is much more obvious in a crisis when faced with an active quarrel and the possibility of violence.

Yet their existence is clearly recognised in the villages. They are in this area called *kabile*, a word of Arabic origin, which in Istanbul means tribe. One man in Elbaşı, urging me to write letters to the village, said I could write to each of the five *kabile*, and the letters could be read out in the guest rooms. Here *kabile* corresponded rather to the village quarters than to the actual lineage, which numbered more than five. But he thought in terms of agnatic groups.

Moreover, each lineage has its own name. These are almost always based on the name or nickname of a founding ancestor, for example, Köse Aliler (the Bald Alis), Hamuslılar (those from Damascus), Sarılar (the Blondes), Şeyhuşağı (offspring of the Şeyh). Before 1935, these names were apparently one recognised way of distinguishing people in the villages. In 1935, everyone was compelled by law to adopt a surname of the normal European type based on linguistically pure Turkish roots. The new names were in most cases quite independent and unlike existing village names, and most people seem to have been allocated names from an official list. Certainly the villages are now full of Truebloods, Trueturks, Whitesouls, Brights, Strongs, Sturdies, Lions and so forth (Özkan, Öztürk, Akcan, Aydın, Gürbüz, Aslan).

Neither the old lineage names nor the modern names are universally used. Sometimes women and children do not know even their own official surnames, and only those responsible for official village business will know all the village surnames. I used official surnames to keep my records for the same reason that officials do so – convenience of identification. In most cases the older names are known and still used, but in a few they were disputed, or simply not known. First names and current nicknames normally suffice for the villagers' own purposes.

I made several attempts to collect complete lists of the traditional lineage names in both villages, but in spite of prompting, the lists never came out the same, because people always disagreed about the details. Some names, they said, were not fully fledged *kabile*, but only branches (*şübe*), or arms (*kol*) of other lineages, and in a few cases they even differed on which lineage certain village households belonged to. In all, I recorded eleven such names in Sakaltutan and nineteen in Elbaşı.

In Sakaltutan, the division of the village into agnatic groups was recognised in another way. People talked of the great ones, *büyükler*, the senior members of the village. Once or twice, a group of great ones met *ad hoc* when some important village business came up – a self-selecting group. But it was also custo-mary after a full wedding ceremony for the groom's side to feast the *büyükler*. I witnessed such a gathering three times, and once was party to drawing up the list of guests. This was done casually at the last moment, with the implicit assumption that everyone knew in any case what would happen and who would be invited. On each occasion about forty of the hundred village household heads were invited. Each time, a few people not entitled as 'great ones' were invited, either to help with serving and hospitality, or because of a special tie to the host.

The *büyükler* are not heads of lineages, nor are they simply village elders. They are the senior members of segments of lineages. Whether or not a man would receive an invitation in-dependently of a senior and important father's brother's son would depend less on the solidarity of the lineage to which they both belonged, than on his own personal seniority and im-portance. The invitation goes to the senior man, but he may delegate it to an agnate if he wishes. Household heads who have no agnates were invited in person, with the exception of one or two very poor and junior men. Thus, practically speaking, the guests at the feast represented agnatically the whole village.

In Elbaşı a similar informal self-selected body of elders for important deliberations certainly exists. But in a larger less homogeneous community they do not constitute a more or less stable group of wedding guests.

Village lineages often inhabit clusters of houses. A successful household normally expands by building on rooms for married sons, and in due course the old house is divided by partitions; in the next generation the new households will seek to expand again. When the population is growing, this system leads to congestion, and people move away from the centre, sometimes breaking away from their close agnates. Sometimes the whole agnatic group will move to a new site, leaving more space between their houses, and the whole process starts again. The village thinks of lineages as belonging to certain parts of the village, and in Elbaşı some of the village quarters were named after their main lineages, in spite of the numerous anomalies which existed in fact.

The lineage is an affair of men. Women belong to at least two households. By the same token three-quarters of them, except, that is, for those who marry within the lineage (pp. 202-3), belong to at least two lineages. As members of their husband's household they co-operate as he does with the households of his close agnates, but they also have a range of close kin ties of their own, the more so the closer to home they marry. When it comes to quarrels and fights women often side fiercely with their men, not out of lineage loyalty but out of direct personal loyalty. Where a woman's natal lineage clashes with her husband's lineage, behaviour is difficult to predict. Young women are in any case likely to avoid public participation out of shame; older women are perhaps more likely to side with husbands and sons against fathers and brothers.

Effective Lineages

In one sense, a lineage only exists at a time of hostility, and consists only of those agnates who support their group in quarrels. Alternatively, lineage membership may be assessed from the general degree of intimacy and co-operation. Thirdly, and simplest, one may reckon genealogically. In most cases these three criteria would produce different results.

In theory, mutual defence is a duty binding on close agnates. In practice, either through active quarrels or through indifference, people contract out of this duty as out of the more general neighbourly services, on the same penalty – loss of reciprocal rights. To forego this protection is clearly dangerous; but on occasion, it is also dangerous to retain it, and some men declare themselves peace lovers and uninterested in their kinsmen's quarrels. Some of the poorer and more lowly lineages in Elbaşı have no visible unity at all. Even in the more prominent ones it is often difficult to know who would in fact fight if the need arose. Where agnates are in close daily contact, lineage solidarity may be assumed, but apparent indifference in day to day life by no means implies that people are not still lineage members in the important sense.

Lineage membership finishes at the village boundary. Where for some reason an agnatic branch of a lineage exists in another village the special duties of agnates lapse.[1] Migrants from one village to another are thus left without agnatic defence in their new village. In practice, in all cases I knew of, a man setting up house in another village went to the village of his mother, and married a girl of her natal lineage. He would then normally become *de facto* a member of his mother's lineage, which was also his wife's lineage. Since lineages had no formal structure, it was impossible to know how far active support would in fact be carried.

In one or two other cases, genealogical ties were not precisely known, and the actual affiliation of people was not clear. These may have resulted from immigration along an affinal link, or from the attempt to compensate for a loss of agnatic kin by shadowy affiliation to another group. Even fairly definite groups of agnates often had one or two peripheral households associated with them. For lineages consisting of a core of loyal households I shall use the word 'effective'. In the next two sections, I analyse briefly the lineage composition of the two villages.

Sakaltutan Lineages

Of the ten recognisable lineages listed, only seven are without any shadow of doubt worthy to be called effective. Of these, one might well be described as two effective lineages. Fourteen other households belong to none of the ten named lineages. (See Fig. 3, p. 19.)

V Lineage, Twenty Households.

Thirteen of these households were directly descended from the father of old Hamit, still alive at about eighty, through him or three of his brothers. Three other segments, one of four households, one of two and one of one household, were descended from Hamit's father's brothers. Some, including one or two of the thirteen gave the impression of taking little interest in their affiliations. The head of one of these, Durdu, was later shot dead in a lineage quarrel, proving that im-

---

[1] There may be a time-lag. I observed no very recent cases.

pressions can be misleading (p. 250). Most of the households were explicit about their lineage affiliations, associated with each other a great deal, and were loyal to the lineage in its quarrels. One other household claimed to belong; the head, a poor, old, and sick man, was an immigrant, married to a woman of the lineage, but did not join in lineage activities.

D Lineage, Ten Households.

Three brothers, including Haci Ömer, dominated this group, and were very influential in the village. The heads of another group of four households were sons and grandsons of a man brought to the village by his widowed mother, and brought up as the son of a close agnate of the father of the first three. Two other households claimed definitely to be of common descent with this group, but did not know how, and one other belonged, but its young head was on military service. The lineage claimed descent from one of four brothers said to have founded the village.

G Lineage, Six Households.

All were descended from the grandfather of the oldest living generation, but showed no conspicuous solidarity. They claimed descent from the village founders.

S Lineage, Six Households.

Five of these, including Ziya, were brothers or brother's son to each other, and one young man was attached through a brother of their common ancestor. A very self-conscious and slightly belligerent group, but with its own sharp internal rift. All were close neighbours. They claimed descent from the village founders.

F Lineage, Nine Households.

Divided into two sharply distinct groups, in each of which were brothers and brothers' sons, apparently connected through a common great-grandfather. One segment (five households) was much poorer than the other. Neither was belligerent. Probably also descended from the village founders.

H Lineage.

Haci Osman, a well-to-do man who had been to Mecca in 1949, was the head of one of four agnatically related households (H). The head of one of these was his old, sick, ineffectual father's

brother's son, and the two other household heads were descended from his great-grandfather. Some said these belonged
to S Lineage, but Haci Osman said he thought he was agnatically related to G. In his case, there was little emphasis on the
lineage, which was weak in manpower; but a less precisely
defined group of people, mainly his sister's sons, frequented his
guest room and depended on his patronage. Through these
followers he was a man of great influence.

Two other effective lineages were explicitly descended from
immigrants.

K Lineage, Eight Households.
All great-grandchildren of one man, divided into a group of
three and a group of five. Close ties were recognised; they
shared a common guest room, and were close neighbours. One
other household head, an orphaned son, brought up in his
mother's father's household, was sister's son to one of the households, but kept himself apart. Though socially close to each
other, this lineage did not, while I was in the village, have any
enemies.

M Lineage, Four Households.
This, another immigrant lineage, was by contrast militant. All
were descended from the grandfather of the senior living member, an old man. The lineage contained two large and prosperous households, and was at feud with V Lineage.

Two other groups in the village acknowledge some common
agnatic ancestry, but showed no sign of mutual interest.

R Lineage, Nine Households.
Three separate groups of households, whose heads in each case
were close agnates, one of four, one of three and one of two
households, all gave one particular name four or five generations back in their genealogies. They took no special interest
in each other at all.

P Lineage, Ten Households.
One group of three households and another of five claimed a
common link, and two other men, brothers, were said also to
spring from the same agnatic origin. They none of them showed
interest in each other, beyond their own immediate agnates.

The remaining fourteen households were isolated agnatically; they included three brothers claiming agnatic connection to G Lineage, another agnatic set of three landless households, Ismet (T)'s large and rich immigrant household plus a small offshoot (pp. 127-8), one moderate household which was the last of a once large lineage, and one or two poor households isolated or paired with brothers.

Elbaşı Lineages

The arrangement of lineages in Elbaşı was even less tidy than in Sakaltutan. A high proportion of households seemed uninterested in agnatic connections. The village contained eighteen households which were fairly recent immigrants from the east of Turkey, who had failed to return to their homes after the Russian invasion of 1877 and 1915, and eight immigrant households of local origin. In a few cases agnatic connections were known on a wider range than any in Sakaltutan, but the effective lineages were no larger.

A Lineage was by far the largest agnatic stock I came across. One man put its strength at one hundred households, another at sixty. In fact, about fifty households claimed or were said to be agnates of this stock – most of them on reliable grounds. In this lineage, unlike others, the main segments had not acquired names of their own. But the leading households in the stock were split into two hostile groups, one (Ax) containing ten and the other (Ay) eighteen households. This second larger wing was itself genealogically segmented into two. In one of these, all eight households, who were close agnates of the four brothers who lead it, were effective members, but in the other segment only some of the households seemed to take much interest. Another group of four households, brothers or brothers' sons to each other, acknowledged agnatic connection to this main stock, but seemed uncommitted if not unfriendly. A fourth group of six agnatically related households had a separate lineage name, and one of its wealthy members denied any connection with A. But the evidence including some of his own, was against him. The remaining households of the fifty were divided into small groups of close agnates, ranging from two to five households, not too sure of their agnatic connections, and not particularly interested.

B Lineage numbered fifteen households, including one immigrant attached through his mother and his wife, and one widow
with three daughters, whose father and late husband were both
members of the lineage. In this case, all households, even the
poorest, seemed to acknowledge loyalty to the group.

Another genealogically large lineage – about twenty households in all – was also amorphous. One branch of six, C
Lineage, had a separate name and a reputation for solidarity
and aloofness. A man of this group was shot dead during our
stay, (p. 261). In the ensuing quarrel, they received no support
from members of the larger lineage. Among the twenty was
another set of seven households descended from a common
grandfather, but I do not know how much internal solidarity
they possessed.

Z Lineage claimed a long and distinguished history, and
gave its name to a village quarter. A central core of about eight
households made regular and fairly exclusive use of one guest
room. Two other senior acknowledged members kept apart
because of a quarrel, and other households admitted agnatic
connection but showed no interest. Two refugee households had
married into the group and behaved as members.

Another genealogically large lineage, sixteen households in
all, was divided into two groups, which barely acknowledged the
link between them – one informant again denied it in the face
of the evidence. Another lineage numbered nine related households, including some influential ones, but I cannot say how
effective relationships were. Two smaller lineages consisted
entirely of poorer households, one of five and one of six.

Together with the refugee households, these lineages cover
about 150 households, just over two-thirds of the village. Besides these, I heard of another nine named lineage groups, most
of which contained from one or two to five current households,
and one of which was extinct. Of the rest of the households, I
assume that they did not know or were not interested in anyone
except the close circle of kin, among whom in most cases close
agnates would have a special place. Most of them were grouped
in sets of brothers or brothers' sons, very often with the same
adopted official surname. In some of these cases my impression
that people have little or no interest in their lineages may
simply be due to my ignorance.

In Elbaşı then, there were in all some nine groups which qualify, some more, some less definitely as what I have called effective lineages, all of which contained some fairly influential and well-to-do households. In addition, there were other named lineage groups either small in numbers, or poor, or both. Of the eighteen refugee households, some were themselves developing small lineages of their own, and others had merged in existing lineages. The remainder, about one-quarter of the village households, seemed to have little interest in lineages beyond regarding their brothers and agnatic first cousins as rather special kin.

Defence and Prestige

If the primary duty of agnates is defence, why do so many people in the village take so little interest in lineage membership? And, if so many people can manage without, why do some find their lineage membership so important?

Soon after I settled in Sakaltutan, I was discussing land shortage in the village, and was told of villages not so very far away where there was land to be had for the ploughing. In more distant parts there were said to be empty lands. Why then, I asked, did the villagers not go to these well landed parts? 'Who,' they replied, 'would come to our side in quarrels?' At the time the implications of this reply surprised me. Later I realised that fear of aggression and violence within the village was genuine and well-founded.

Property rights, especially land rights, could not be taken for granted. Neighbours might at any time encroach on one's boundaries, or seek to establish some kind of claim. Security lay not in legality, but in strength. As I have argued, although a functioning system for State protection of individual rights existed even in 1950, the situation did not encourage villagers to call in outsiders or refer disputes to officials or lawyers. Membership of a group strong enough to retaliate is a much more effective insurance against trouble. But trouble is not something to be expected by everyone every day, and the dependence of people on their lineages is related largely to the current quarrels and fears. At the same time, insurance involves premiums, in the shape in this case of commitment to defend others, and those confident in their own ability to avoid trouble, or with very little to lose, sometimes prefer to avoid lineage responsibilities. Others, of course, had no choice because they did not possess sufficient agnates to form effective lineages. In a few cases, such men might rely on political skill and wealth to prevent any attack on their position or property.

In the larger lineages more was at stake than simple defence of rights. They had prestige and influence in the village to maintain. A large close-knit lineage with a goodly number of reliable knives and guns was clearly worth belonging to, and the restraints and demands of such a group on its members would not outweigh the advantages of membership.

Prestige was also dependent on honour, *namus*, and this was directly related to the women of lineage households. To show interest in a woman other than by formally seeking her hand in marriage was a deadly insult to her menfolk. Most killings, or attempted killings, while I was in touch with this area were directly or indirectly the result of the alleged 'insulting' of a woman.

The toughness with which a man chose in practice to defend his honour would clearly be highly variable. Those at the bottom of the village hierarchy were less concerned anyway with the honour of their women, particularly if these had already lost it. The better-off, by leading quiet and virtuous lives, marrying virtuous women, and not attending too closely to gossip and suspicion, might avoid quarrels; but others seemed to seek trouble and be ready at the slightest hint of dishonourable intentions to resort to violence. Clearly, the more sensitive a man is to his honour the more he needs lineage support.

I have already stressed the absence of any clear criterion for effective lineage membership, except at times of actual violence. I have also shown that only a proportion of households in each village belonged to effective lineages, most of which contained a core of better-off households, and a number of poorer ones. This arrangement is in a sense only a special case of the normal structure of village social relations. The richer and more influential men act as protectors and helpers for the poorer and weaker ones, so that the village consists of pyramid-like groups centred on the more powerful. The size of a man's following increases his importance, and his importance in turn brings in followers (p. 257). Success depends partly on conformity to accepted rules of conduct such as generosity and piety. But it will also depend on the number of established relationships he already has – mainly agnatic relationships. In other words, both for those in the village who wish to be leaders and equally for those who wish to be followers, the cultural emphasis on agnation provides one of the main grounds for recruitment of groups for mutual protection and the enhancement of prestige. But the villages also contain some who have no wish to belong to lineages, and some who have no lineage to belong to. Between them, these cover perhaps half the population of Elbaşı and rather less than half that of Sakaltutan.

Fission

No effective lineage numbered as much as twenty households – most of them very much less – and none had a genealogical depth of more than three generations above the senior living generation; five in all. Both the reason for this effective limit, and the way in which fission actually takes place, are implicit in the description I have just given.

The lineage has no clear-cut membership except at times of active hostility. It lacks any formal criterion of membership and any symbol of unity except its name. Even when a lineage has a leader he holds no formal position. When there are no active quarrels the lineage persists because members seek each others' company, meet together in guest rooms, help each other in various ways and publicly acknowledge their agnatic ties. Readiness to side actively with each other can only be observed when the need actually arises. Ties may therefore loosen slowly, with the growth of households and changes in the relation between them, without any sharp break being obvious unless and until the threat of danger makes it clear who is loyal to whom.

The lack of formal membership leaves only the vaguer criterion of relative friendliness. But the number of intimate ties one household can maintain, and the size of the group which can meet regularly for social intercourse, is limited. Above, say, a dozen households the maintenance of a loyalty which depends on personal intimacy becomes difficult. Larger groups break up into their constituent agnatic genealogical segments. Most people lose interest in their more remote agnates. They seldom know their patrilineal ancestors beyond their great-grandfather and the connections become forgotten altogether. Even in a large stock like A Lineage, who retain an awareness of agnatic connections over a much wider span, internal quarrels, or simply mutual indifference, take the place of forgetfulness in breaking the effective lineages down to the same size – something less than twenty households at the outside.

Mother's Close Kin

In many patrilineal societies the mother's brother has a sharply contrasting rôle to the father and the father's brother. So long as clear exogamous agnatic groups exist, this seems to be inevitable since the mother's brother must be the closest male kinsman of ego who is always outside ego's own group, and thus lies off ego's direct road to wealth and power. But in a society where a man's mother's brother may have been anyone from his father's father's brother's son to a complete stranger from a village five hours away, a sharp distinction between maternal and paternal uncles is not to be expected.[1] One or two informants insisted that there is no difference at all, but this is an overstatement

Distance permitting, a child has the free run of its mother's natal household. Both mother's parents and mother's brothers treat the child with affection and indulgence. One old man whose daughter's small son, also his own brother's son's son, lived next door to him, boasted that this child preferred his household to its own. A set of brothers in Elbaşı told me that they had been brought up in their mother's brother's household. Bekteş (V) of Sakaltutan, helped the brothers of his sister's deceased husband with the arrangements for his sister's orphaned son's wedding, although he was himself poor. Later, he built himself a small guest room and whitewashed the inside walls. A younger son of the same sister by her second husband

[1] The Tswana of Southern Africa are permitted to marry their father's brother's daughter yet distinguish the rôles of father's brother and mother's brother in the usual way. But actual cases are reported as only 1 · 1 per cent of the sample. (I. Schapera (1950) pp. 144, 156.)

painted aircraft and motor cars on the inviting new walls. Religious texts and symbols were acceptable as village murals, but this secular innovation made Bekteş very angry. Yet he took no action, and I am fairly sure neither a close agnate nor an unrelated neighbour would have dared to do such a thing, or would have got off so lightly. The sister of a fairly well-to-do man of Elbaşı, had married one of two fairly poor brothers by whom she had several children. He succeeded in forcing her husband into betrothing her eldest daughter against the girl's wishes, to a young widower kinsman of his own, in spite of the determined resistance by the girl's father's elder brother. When a girl *en route* to the doctor from a neighbouring village died and was buried in Sakaltutan, her mother's brother took second place only to her father in the funeral ceremonies.

All these examples show the importance that a mother's brother may play in the life of his nephew or niece. On the other hand, a great many men took very little day-to-day interest in their sisters' children. Apparent indifference is not inconsistent with the fulfilling of duties at a time of crisis. Yet the point remains that a large element of permissiveness and vagueness makes it impossible to describe even this rôle in precise terms.

Emme, father's brother, and *dayı*, mother's brother, may not be as sharply contrasted as they are in some societies. Yet they are distinct. The mother's brother represents the interest of the mother's kin in the child, and is usually more indulgent and more of a friend. The father's brother is perhaps felt to be closer, and to have more precise binding responsibilities, including that of defence. But no one sees any difficulty in combining the rôle of classificatory *emme* with *dayı* in those cases where a child's parents are agnatic cousins.

The terminology equally distinguishes between mother's sister and father's sister. I heard no formal statement of the difference between these rôles; the relationship in both cases should be one of affection and helpfulness, but what actually happens depends primarily on physical and social distance. Other things being equal, as a woman is closer to her sister than her brother, sharing with her the paramount woman's interest in children, so a mother's sister is perhaps likely to be closer and more motherly than a father's sister.

Affines

Affines comprise the kin of one's spouse, and the spouses of one's kin and their close kin. All consanguineal kinship relations begin inevitably at the birth of the younger partner. But most affines are added to one in later life, when one's primary loyalties are already formed. The greater social distance and the mutual suspicion which result call, as is commonly recognised, for special rules and more precisely defined rights and duties, at least in the beginning.

The relationship of a girl to her husband's household has already been described (p. 108). Beyond them, she will be referred to as *gelin* (bride, daughter-in-law), by all who identify with her husband's group. If she is strange to her husband's village then all his co-villagers may call her *gelin;* certainly his close kin, especially his agnates, will do so.

The corresponding male terms, *guvah* or *damat*, also mean equally bridegroom or son-in-law. The ties of a man to his wife's parents are more than friendliness. They have done him a great and never to be repaid favour by granting him their daughter, and he owes them respect and services. When Musa (K) needed help with his harvest (p. 156) his son-in-law left his own harvest in another village in order to help, and this with no expectation of return.

This subordinate relationship alters with time. As the wife's security, stake and power in her marital household increase, her parents' hold over her, and thus, indirectly, over her husband, decreases. His deference to them may change to personal warmth or to formal coolness. In time, of course, they will die, and the head of his wife's natal household will be her brother, a man of his own generation. At this stage, formal duties matter less, and actual relations vary from great warmth to active hostility.

Early in marriage, the groom's parents will normally be providing the young couple with a part of their own home, and the parents of the bride will be watching anxiously to see fair play for their daughter. Some marriages are deliberately arranged in order to provide or cement an alliance, giving the two sides reasons for ostensible friendliness. Very often they are already kin. The relationship between the two sets of parents is vital, and hence the existence of a special kin term to cover it.

Men finding themselves as sons-in-law to the same father-in-law recognise also a special link between themselves, with a special term. This link is even more permissive than most. A man may ignore his *bacanak* as far as possible, or may court him and use him. One man pompously remarked in public 'Among us, a *bacanak* is highly valued'.

Women

At marriage the men stay put, and the women move. All ties involving one or more women, that is, all but agnatic ties between men, are variable, since the way kin treat each other depends on both the physical and the current social distance between them, which in turn depend on the marriage of the women involved.

Kin ties between women are affected by another factor. Women do not in the day-to-day life move easily round the village, let alone between villages. They are tied by household duties, by small children or grandchildren, and by modesty, to their home. At the same time, they are extremely gregarious. No woman ever remains alone if she can manage to avoid it, and loneliness is constantly spoken of as a great evil. House doors are never shut to other women and children, who come and go without ceremony or greeting. Expeditions to fetch water, or to the fields to work, are normally undertaken in company.

For a girl set down by her marriage in a strange village, her new daily circle may include no previous kin at all. New intimacies must be forged among neighbours and affines. In practice, in almost any village close to her own a woman will have some kin; she is often marrying into an already allied household. But even then her new circle is still bound to include many strangers. Even a girl who marries her father's brother's son in the next house in her own village will find in her circle some strangers who have moved into it by their own marriage.

Thus any set of women who meet daily and share their tasks, their child-minding, and their gossip will include some who are neither kin nor childhood neighbours to each other. Such a set will change its composition fairly steadily over time, by marriages in and out, and divorces, as well as deaths and the growing up of daughters.

The women explicitly recognise this situation. One group told my wife that *akrabalık*, kinship, did not count for women as it did for men. What mattered to women was neighbourliness, *komşuluk*. They did not mean that kinship does not count at all. Ties with kin are kept up by occasional visits, by gossip and news, by children going back and forth. Where close kin are within reach, the relationship may be very close. Bekteş's wife had a sister a few doors away, and these two were constantly exchanging visits, bread and children more freely than either did with the households around them. Two young married women of lineage in Sakaltutan were both married to the other end of the village, yet they were very frequent visitors of their mothers and sisters.

The importance of kin ties to a woman vary not only with the accident of marriage, but also with the stage it has reached. In her early years, she is an inferior in her household, and still looks to her natal kin for love and support. As she establishes a growing family of her own, and close ties with her affines through the children, she becomes more centred on her marital home, her neighbours, and her grandchildren than on her natal kin. An old widowed mother normally remains with her sons, among the neighbours of her adult lifetime. Of course, childlessness, serious quarrels, a husband's death, or a divorce may make normality impossible. The worst that can befall a woman is an old age *kimsesiz*, without anyone, dependent on the charity of neighbours who have no obligation to help.

In Sakaltutan, the women's terms of address matched this lack of emphasis on particular kin ties. All women call their equals and juniors, whether kin or not, *kız*, girl, occasionally putting a personal name in front of it to avoid ambiguity. Older women, if addressed at all, are addressed by kinship terms, often by a term closer than the actual link. Non-kin equally are addressed as *abla*, elder sister; as *bacı*, a word also meaning sister, but commonly used as a respect title like *aga* or *efendi* for the men; or as *amme* (father's sister).

Inter-village Kinship

The half-hour to two hours' walking between villages is a physical barrier to frequent contact. The village boundary is also a social barrier. A man knows the men of his own village from his own childhood, or from theirs. Friends and enemies, they all belong as no outsider can. Women often straddle two villages. Yet women's daily contacts are more restricted than men's. They occasionally go from one village to another in pairs or groups, but normally, for any distance, a man is expected to escort them.

Although people are always to be seen passing back and forth between villages, for most individuals a visit to another village is a comparative rarity. Women visit their natal homes at least once a year; children go to see uncles and aunts; animals, food and utensils are borrowed and returned, or bought and sold; craftsman are hired; cures and charms and advice sought; marriages discussed and arranged; weddings and funerals attended; the sick visited; loans asked, given, and repaid; crops shared, grain milled, border land disputed; refreshment and shelter offered and accepted. Even when kinship is not directly the occasion for contact, it almost always provides a channel.

On one occasion, Bekteş was escorting me from the town out to Sakaltutan on foot in deep snow. We arrived at the village before Sakaltutan late in the day and near exhaustion. We stopped to rest at the house of his nearest kinsman, the husband of a second paternal cousin, (father's father's brother's son's daughter), whom he called sister's husband, (*enişte*), and were pressed to stay the night. Somewhat reluctantly, Bekteş agreed. On two occasions, to my knowledge, he went secretly to matrilateral kin in another village for a loan, once because his food supply was exhausted, and once because he needed treatment from a religious expert for a malady which he believed the doctor unable to cure. On another occasion, when two or three of us were setting out to negotiate for a bride from a somewhat distant village, we met a man of Sakaltutan, kin to our party, whose current wife – his second – was from the village we were to visit. He at once offered to come with us, partly to see his affines, partly to use his influence on our behalf – unsuccessfully as it transpired.

Over one-third of the marriages I recorded in Sakaltutan crossed village frontiers (p. 205). Each of these would create or renew a number of affinal and cognatic ties. Quite often ties between two lineages in different villages were maintained over a number of generations by cross-cousin marriage, full or classificatory. Thus G Lineage had exchanged women for at least three generations with a lineage in another village, with whom they had thus established a complex set of personal kin ties.

Agnatic kin ties between villages are rare. Men seem to move normally between villages in only three types of situation. The first, of which traces survive, was probably common in the past. A poor boy or young man may become a servant, (*çirak*, p. 56), and remain permanently in the village of his master. Secondly, if a widow marries to a new village or returns from her husband's to her own, she may take a small son with her, and he may then remain as a member of his mother's village of residence. Thirdly, an adult man may occasionally marry into and move to another village, if such a move offers better prospects than remaining in his father's house. In almost all cases of this type I came across, the man moved to his mother's village and married a close agnate of hers – very often a girl with no brothers. No adult man had moved into Sakaltutan for two or three generations, and only three had left as adults to settle permanently in other villages. Even Elbaşı, an administrative centre with land in plenty until the end of the Second World War, had had to my knowledge only eight immigrant households in two generations, apart from the wartime refugees from eastern Turkey. Most of these had married in or come in as stepsons. One was a stranger, and another was a Kurd who was married to a woman of the area, whose sister was also married in Elbaşı.

Even where agnatic ties do exist between villages, the primary duty of defence and revenge seems to lapse. No quarrel or feud between lineages ever crossed village frontiers, and while brothers might maintain very close ties, including an annual sharing of the produce of the patrimonial land, their rights and duties were not different in kind from inter-village ties of other kin.

A kinsman in another village is not, as in one's own village, a peak above a generally high level of intimacy, but an oasis in a desert of strangers. The visitor, instead of being dependent on the formal hospitality of the village headman, has people of his own in the village. Inter-village kinship thus functions very differently from kinship within the village, and this difference overrides distinctions between kinds of kinship relationship. The day-to-day petty help between close neighbours is replaced by a less intimate but equally important mutual dependence for protection in a strange environment. The villagers love to hear news, to visit and entertain their kin from other villages, and this constant coming and going provides the occasion for innumerable exchanges of political and economic importance.

CHAPTER NINE

MARRIAGE

Ceremony and Custom

Both as an event and as a relationship, marriage is at the centre of village society. The household is founded directly upon it, and its internal structure shaped by the marriages of its members. Almost all except agnatic relations between households result from marriages. From the moment when a couple are united, they direct their long-term plans to the marriages of their children. This central position of marriage is matched by the great ceremonial emphasis it receives. Weddings are the most conspicuous occasions in village life, and almost the only opportunity for organised merry-making. Their social and ritual importance is consistent with their cost – one wedding may cost almost the total annual income of a household.

No two weddings are arranged and celebrated in precisely the same way. They vary with social standing, with the social distance between the parties, and with area. Even within a single village, two normal weddings of similar scale may vary in a number of details. The season for proper weddings is the winter, preferably early, before the severe snow, or late – after the thaw has begun. The winter I passed in Sakaltutan was one of acute economic shortage and very severe weather; I witnessed only two full-scale weddings within the village, and the departure of two brides to other villages. In Elbasi, a homicide prevented any weddings at all in the autumn of 1951, though twenty were planned. Summer weddings are always limited affairs, and I only saw one of them in each village. I did, however, attend two full-scale weddings in other villages as a guest from Sakaltutan. The composite account which follows is based partly on observation

8 Father and bride: the last farewell. (p.183)

9 Travelling craftsmen are sometimes highly specialised. These men carry a large saw for making planks from baulks of timber: they are a kind of travelling saw mill. (p.64–70)

10 The trousseau on its way. (p.181)

11 Dancing at a wedding: notice the lady's masculine feet. Men never watch women dance. (p.182)

on these occasions, partly on the statements of informants.[1]

Initiative lies with the father of the groom. In theory, the young people themselves have no say at all, and the women can only suggest and advise. It is the household head who decides, and it is he who makes the formal approach. In fact, a boy's own wish may often influence his father's choice, and even a girl of strong character and skill may be able to exercise some influence. As for the women, marriage is their main interest, and their gossip and planning must be a major factor in the decision which is formally their husband's right.

A boy is normally married between the ages of sixteen and twenty-two or so, though there are always exceptions. Three or four men told me of marriage in their very early teens. 'My understanding did not suffice' (*aklım yetmedi*), one of them commented. In one of these cases, the household desperately needed more womanpower; in the others, a very poor boy or an orphan was married by his seniors to the widow of an older kinsman before the opportunity slipped away. At the other end, one or two men married late, either from poverty or from prolonged absence from the village. I knew no confirmed bachelors.

Girls are normally married at about fourteen to eighteen years of age. Orphans and the very poor are sometimes married even younger. One woman described her early marriage. Neither she nor her husband yet knew what to do – 'we were ashamed (*utandık*)' – and she found the work expected of her very hard. By contrast, the oldest normal unmarried girl of whom I heard was said to be twenty-three. No explanation was offered by people; but her father was very rich and important for a villager, and probably family prestige was a major factor.

Once a man has fixed his choice, he goes with, or sends, one or two close kin, and a respected senior man less close to him as negotiator, to pay a formal visit to the girl's home. They are received by a similarly constituted committee, and negotiations are conducted with great delicacy through the intermediaries. I was told in Sakaltutan that a bride price is agreed at this meeting, and a first instalment (*hecelik*) is expected either on

[1] For comparative data on Turkish weddings, see H. Z. Koşay (1941); also I. Yasa (1957), chapter VIII.

the spot or within a few days. In Elbaşı, to mention financial details at this point is shameful, though both sides will of course have a fair idea how much is likely to be asked and given.

The next step, betrothal (*nişan*), follows within a month or so. A group of women, four or five or more, including the groom's mother, and kin and non-kin neighbours, pay a formal visit to the girl's home, accompanied, if the journey requires it, by two or three men. They are given a large ceremonial meal, which they reciprocate the next morning from supplies which they have brought with them. The men leave the women to make the acquaintance of their future affines, returning to fetch them after a day or two. The two groups of women spend the evenings in dancing and singing – strictly without men. They bring presents – ideally including gold ornaments – for the bride, and throw her coins when she dances for them.

During the betrothal period which follows, the couple are not supposed to see each other, and people say that the father will use violence if he discovers that his daughter has broken this rule. Nevertheless, couples normally do meet, with the connivance of the women of the bride's household. All fathers in fact know the custom, and are presumably normally careful not to make embarrassing discoveries. The groom is expected to visit the household of his betrothed from time to time, bringing her gifts, and these visits provide the necessary opportunities. Betrothals may last anything from a week or two to several years. A respectable engagement lasts months at least, and if the young man is away working or doing military service, or either household runs into misfortune, the delay may be much longer. Long engagements, I was told, are punctuated by visits similar to the original betrothal visit.

The unofficial courting of the betrothal period comes out into the open if an engagement is broken. Then it is said that the girl's honour is blemished because she has been secretly embraced by her betrothed, and thus her chances of a good marriage have been lost.

Formal childhood betrothal appears to be unknown. In one case, a widow promised her son's baby daughter to her new husband as a bride for his infant son, her new stepson. This promise was kept, but I was told it did not count as a betrothal, the ceremonies for which took place at the usual time. Similar understandings are common among close kin.[1]

The girl's household are responsible for providing the trousseau (*ceğiz*). Preparations begin at a girl's birth, and as she grows up she must herself weave prayer mats (*kilim*) and saddlebags (*hebe*). Nevertheless, much has to be bought, and a special expedition is made to Kayseri just before the wedding. In Elbaşı, this expedition provides the cue for the father of the bride to send a message to the groom's father asking for money to buy the trousseau. I am told that this usually produces a crisis, and failure to agree on the sum is said sometimes to lead to the breaking off of negotiations. By this time both sides have invested time, money and honour in the marriage, and a rupture is therefore already a serious matter. In Sakaltutan, the payment of the balance of the bride price may lead to similar haggling, though the prior agreement and the fact that a large sum has already been paid makes a rupture even less likely.

The men of the groom's household also have some shopping to do. They must buy the cloth to make the wedding dress, a special wooden trunk that will be the bride's for her lifetime, and presents for members of her household and other kin. These are set out for inspection by the women of the groom's kin and neighbours, who pay a formal visit by invitation, pass frank comments, eat a special type of bread baked for the occasion, and leave a gift. The trunk with the gifts inside, (called *düzen*, that which makes smooth) is then taken by a small party of men to the bride's household. At this visit, at which once again a special meal may be eaten, final details of dates, numbers of guests and such like are fixed. Then the trunk is opened formally, and once again its contents are publicly inspected and criticised while the special bread is eaten, this time by the bride's womenfolk.

In Sakaltutan, the trousseau consisted normally of a complete set of mattresses and bedding, home-woven donkey bags and rugs, a supply of clothes for the bride, and presents of clothing for all the members of the groom's household and close kin, especially the groom himself. The same trunk in which the *düzen* arrives is used to pack the return gifts. The trousseau, like

[1] I. Yasa (1957) pp. 105–6 reports cases of child marriage, involving no more than the transferring of a child to its future spouse's household. I have no evidence against this having happened in the past in this area.

the *düzen*, is publicly inspected, first at a ceremony held in the bride's household, for her close kin and neighbours, and again three days after the consummation of the marriage, by the women of the groom's household and neighbourhood.

In Sakaltutan, the wedding begins four days or more before consummation, with the raising of a flag over the groom's house, the offering of hospitality in a large guest room – often borrowed from kin or neighbours – and the arrival of a drummer and piper. During the day, the men wrestle, dance, dress up as bandits, play soldiers, or watch professional male entertainers, sometimes dressed as dancing girls. In the evening the festivities continue in the guest room, with songs, stories, practical jokes and charades, often bawdy, and when the numbers drop, late at night, a game of 'find the ring' played with upturned coffee cups.

Women, during the day, watch from afar. But in the evenings they too forgather, to dance in strict privacy, in a large living room or guest room. By this stage, seven or eight women, (*yenge*) will have been chosen, whose task it is to fetch the bride. They consist of kin of the groom, including members of his household (but never his mother), and one or two from other villages, and also of one or two non-kin neighbours. These are expected to dress in their wedding clothes and dance every evening during the *dügün*. In Sakaltutan, the final day must always, they insisted, be a Thursday or a Sunday, though in Elbaşı the only days said to be barred were Tuesday and Friday. On the appropriate day, or the evening before if the distance is great, a party of men twenty to thirty strong, not including the groom, escort the *yenge* to the bride's home.

On the girl's side, far less public ceremony has taken place. A close circle of women kin and neighbours meet to dance for a few nights before the wedding. On the day before, the bride's right hand is ceremonially dyed with henna.

When the party arrives to fetch the bride, the men and women are entertained separately. The men may be allocated to different hosts in the girl's village, if the wedding is on a large scale. Dancing, foolery, coffee and cigarettes abound. The visitors are said to be 'under the orders' of their hosts. There is much talk of singing publicly for the company, with threats of beating with cushions for the defaulters, and the guests are made the butts for a variety of practical jokes.

At this point a form of dance practised in Sakaltutan and immediately neighbouring villages reaches its climax. A dozen or so men dance in a circle. One man goes into the circle and braces himself with his arms folded behind his back, and another jumps in and, with wild leaps and fierce shouts, punches him in the middle of the back. The puncher then takes the place of the victim, and another volunteer leaps into the ring, to deliver a punch and in his turn to become a victim. Mostly, the punching is moderate, and if anyone punches to hurt, he can expect the next man to do likewise. But, on one occasion, just before the bride left her home, the young men on the two sides were leaping into the ring alternately and punching as hard as they could. The village has stories of men's backs being broken at this game. In Elbaşı it was regarded as typically uncouth, and unsuitable for civilised villages.

Meanwhile, the women guests are entertained by the girl's close womenfolk. Four of the visiting *yenge*, and one woman of the girl's side, also called *yenge*, take the bride into an inner room or cave where, solemnly lamenting and weeping, they dress her for her new husband. From this moment until she is alone with him, she is not allowed to speak, but weeps constantly. When she is ready, they leave her alone and rejoin the company. Finally a large meal is served, separately to the men and the women, and the groom's party prepare to depart in procession, as they came, headed by pipe and drum. The *yengeler* bring up the rear, with the bride in their midst. With much weeping and kissing of hands, she takes her leave, and mounted if possible on a white horse – (in fact, the means of transport I came across included a donkey, a horsedrawn cart, a lorry, a taxi, and the bride's own two legs) – she sets off, alone among the people of her new environment.

Numerous rites at the threshold of the new house are reported from all parts of Turkey. In Sakaltutan, the bride entered her new home under the legs of the mother-in-law, who was held up for the purpose. In Elbaşı, she was showered with nuts and coins by the groom. Once arrived, often in the morning, she must wait alone and silent until evening for her groom to come to her.

On the return of the party bringing the bride, the festivities in general end, and the drummer and piper take their leave.

Some of the men forgather for a ceremonial meal as guests of the boy's household (p. 160). The groom has been solemnly shaved and dressed in ritual silence by two or three specially chosen age mates, and attends this last solemn meal. He must not speak until he is alone with his bride. Finally, the whole company escorts him to evening prayer in the mosque, and then with religious chanting to his house, where a senior kinswoman takes him by the hand and leads him to his bride.

Normally the balance of the bride price has either been paid, or is paid during these last ceremonies. Also, secretly, the two fathers or other representatives of the couple retire at some point with an imam and perform the *nikah*, the religious rite which validates the marriage. This is always done in secret because enemies can easily, by tying magic knots at this moment, render the groom impotent. In theory, this rite alone makes the marriage valid in village eyes. No other part of the ceremony is indispensable (Stirling (1957), p. 29).

Virginity is highly valued, and the bride is expected to bleed at her deflowering. Accounts varied, but some ceremonial inspection by the women belonging to the groom's household seems to be normal, and the absence of blood is taken as proof of unchastity. An unchaste girl should be sent home in disgrace, but no one seemed very sure what in fact happens in such a case, or would quote actual instances.

The new bride is treated as a special person. She wears her new clothes till they are no longer new. For a week or two she is not allowed out of the house, and is only slowly broken into her new duties. She is not allowed to return home for a period varying, according to the distance, from a few weeks to six months or even a year. After a few weeks her husband's parents 'open the road' between the households by a formal visit, after which her own people may visit her. A bride is said to remain a stranger in the new household for the first year.

When one or both of the pair has been married before – a class of marriage I call 'secondary' in this book – the scale of the ceremonies is greatly reduced; there is normally almost no wedding festivity – *dügün* – at all. On one occasion I was one of a small party who went by night to a neighbouring village to fetch a bride to a widower in Sakaltutan. (We had been told that only three weeks before she had left her first husband, her mother's brother's son, soon after marrying him, and that his family were likely to start shooting if they knew of the new marriage. The girl turned out to be practically blind, and incapable of work, and probably this whole story was poppycock.) We drank a brief coffee with her father and the go-between and set off on our return; as we entered our own village one or two of our company fired shots into the air, and the escort, which included only one woman (*yenge*), sang songs. We all, bar the bride and the *yenge*, went to a guest room, and I responded to a call for coffee and cigarettes. An elderly neighbour with a reputation for religious and magical knowledge was invited to pronounce the *nikah*. He offered us a range of qualities of *nikah* at various prices, and a price was chosen. We then all provided the groom with wedding clothes by a whip-round on the spot of the most respectable garments in the company – my trousers were a little small for him, but no one seemed worried – and off he went to his bride.

This example must represent the extreme of exiguity. Though no secondary marriage ever has public festivities, normally some gifts, formal visits and meals for kin are exchanged on a small scale.

Bride Price

The transfer of a woman from her natal to her marital household is accompanied here, as in many other societies, by exchanges of wealth. Among these is the cash payment which I have called bride price, known in these villages as 'head thing', *başlık*.

It has been argued, sometimes fiercely, that the payment of bride price, or marriage payment as it is often called, is not sale. It is therefore interesting that the villagers normally use the ordinary Turkish word for to sell, *satmak* (Koşay (1944) p. ix), in speaking of the marriage of a girl. Moreover, the ordinary words for give and take, *vermek* and *almak*, which are commonly used in Turkish for buy and sell, are also commonly used in the villages for giving and taking in marriage; in some contexts at least they seem to imply an idea of buying and selling.

Yet in fact the villagers themselves insist fiercely that this is no ordinary sale. 'Are our daughters cattle that we should sell them?' Nowadays, the bride price is often regarded, especially by educated observers, as a quid pro quo for the trousseau. The villagers themselves insisted time and again that every honourable father is out of pocket over his daughter's wedding, in spite of the bride price.

Certainly in Elbaşı at least, the trousseau was systematically evaluated item by item against the bride price, leaving entertainment and other expenses aside. Yet in immediate terms, the claim must be false. Part of the trousseau is collected at home over a long period, some of it actually made by the girl herself, and these items are said always to be priced artificaly high in the bride price negotiations. Part of the bride price must therefore represent a good recompense for work done in the past by the women of the household. On one occasion, a group of men admitted this in argument.

Bride price procedures varied within quite short distances. Not only did Sakaltutan differ in some details from Elbaşı, but the villages to the west, nearer Kayseri, like Kayseri itself, had altogether different customs. Here, in place of a bride price paid in cash to the father, the father of the groom supplies the girl with gold ornaments of an agreed value. But these remain the girl's property, and return with her to her new husband. It is even possible, I was told, to borrow these, to give them to the bride, to recover them from her after the wedding, and then to restore them to their owner. The cost of trousseau supplied by the bride's father is not in this system covered by payment made by the groom's kin, and I was told that the marriage of a number of daughters might well ruin a man.

The amount asked for a girl varies greatly from marriage to marriage and from village to village, and since 1949 it has been rising steadily. This rise is largely due to inflation, but the evidence I have suggests that the rise is steeper than the general rise in prices. The rise in real incomes has enabled the villagers to spend more on weddings, trousseau and bride price. In 1949-50 in Sakaltutan the normal amount for a respectable family to pay for a bride was about T.L.500. In one case, where a girl was sent an exceptionally long way to a more prosperous area, the price was T.L.750. In 1951 and 1952, in Elbaşı, I heard of bride prices of T.L.1,250. In 1954, this same price was given for a girl of Sakaltutan marrying to a village four hours from home, while in 1955, people in Elbaşı were talking of bride prices of T.L.2,000.[1]

Bride price is directly related to the value of the trousseau and the scale of the festivities. The public examination of the trousseau makes skimping readily detectable, and since the one major aim of the proceedings is prestige, meanness or deceit provide their own sanctions. The public festivities are even more plainly a matter of conspicuous consumption. People said – perhaps an exaggeration – that the bride price represented only one-third of the cost of marrying a son.

Not every one can find the resources for such a display. In fact, the scale of bride price and the scale of the wedding vary with the social rank of the parties and with the social distance between them. Any household which aspires to respectability will demand, and expect to give bride price, but if the household is poor, it may be a much reduced one. Thus, in 1950 a girl was married to a close-by village for only T.L.300. Her father was old and poor, and had not the resources to face large-scale ceremonies.

Between brothers, bride price is very much less, and a wedding between father's brother's children is always a small-scale affair, with little or no publicity. During my stay, a girl was married to the house next door to her father's brother's son for only T.L.200 and with so little fuss that I did not know of it till after it had happened. But between less close kin, kinship seems to affect the bride price proportionately less. One man, who told me how he had bargained the price for his son's bride down from T.L.700 to T.L.400 said that this was due to his not very close kinship with the bride's father. The stranger the environment to which a girl is to go, the higher the bride price and the greater the festivities. One nearby village had kin ties with a more prosperous village, Elmalı, some fifty miles away, through migration in the last generation. When a girl was married to this distant place, her whole native village combined to provide entertainment worthy of their more sophisticated affines.

When an unmarried girl marries a man who is already, or has been previously married, this relation between bride price and festivities no longer holds. The price is often much the same as would be asked from an unmarried young man's father, but the fes-

[1] Yasa states that in Hasanoğlan what he calls 'the father's portion', and the wedding expenses, were declining. (I. Yasa (1957) p. 122.)

tivities are minimal. A normal trousseau is not customary in such cases, and a father makes a larger profit in cash than in a normal marriage; though he makes a decidedly smaller one in prestige.

For a widow or divorcée, the price is always much lower – about T.L.200 in 1950 – and arranged *ad hoc*. A small trousseau may be sent, but in general, again, a father spends much less than he gets.

Bride price is sometimes said to be a symbol of the legal transfer of rights over a woman. But in these villages it certainly is not. A woman is no less a bride if a bride price has not been paid, so long as a *nikah* has been pronounced. On the other hand, payment of bride price without *nikah* is not a marriage. Moreover, if the marriage breaks up, the bride price is not re-payable to the husband or his father.

Rather, the cash payment appears as a material consideration to induce the holder of certain rights to part with them. It is in no sense a sale of the woman, but it is a kind of sale of the right to take her to wife. We cannot say that the money is direct compensation for the loss of a member of a household, because no one can hold on to his daughters as workers, and every father is anxious to marry them off as well as he can. What the father of the groom really buys is prestige for himself and his new affines. The owner of a modest, healthy, hardworking, unmarried girl drives as hard a bargain as he can in order to show the high standing of himself and his daughter in the community and to demonstrate his virtuous solicitude for her. If he did not do this, he would be shamed.

Basically, then, the bride price is conspicuous consumption. The less known the other party, the more the need to impress them; the more distant they are socially, the more outsiders will be involved in and know about the wedding. Thus there are two good reasons why the consumption tends to become more conspicuous the greater the social distance. The less honourable the girl, the less the distance between the households, the less the circle of people involved, the less the readiness of the parties for reason of poverty to spend on ceremonies, the smaller the bride price. Equally, a foster father will take less trouble over a girl who is not his daughter, because she reflects less on him and his household. Bride price, then, does not play an indispensable function in village society, but is simply a self-perpetuating

custom, a response to general public expectations, involving
that which touches a man most nearly – the honour of his
womenfolk. Mercenary motives are not of course absent, but
the aim is to appear magnanimous – without spending more
than need be. It follows also that the less a man's honour and
public face are involved, the more mercenary his behaviour.
Thus for dishonoured, divorced, or widowed daughters, a
father asks shamelessly what the market will bear, and gives as
little as possible in return.

The Choice of a Bride

No formal rules restrict the choice of marriage partners, save
only the limited incest rules of Islam. These bar to a man only
his lineal descendants and ascendants, his parents' sisters, his
own sisters, his siblings' daughters and grand-daughters, his
father's wives and widows, their stepdaughters, his wife's
mother and son's wife, and his current wife's sisters. The breast-
feeding of an infant by a foster mother – not uncommon in
village society, which knows no bottle-feeding – forms a link
equal to a biological one for the reckoning of incest. No endogamous or exogamous groups exist.

Parents choosing a bride for their son look for honour and
efficiency. At least in theory, honour is by far the most important. Any obvious interest in the opposite sex, let alone
contact with a boy or man, sullies a girl's reputation. Secondly,
she should be healthy and hardworking, thirdly she should be
skilful, and fourthly she should be good-tempered and submissive. That is, she should be likely to contribute economically,
and unlikely to cause trouble. Explicitly at least, sex appeal and
beauty are not considered important.

The finding of a bride for a son is regarded as an important
and difficult undertaking. Fathers of daughters are expected to
be unwilling to give their daughters away. How far affection
and a genuine concern for the daughter's welfare after marriage
is a real factor in a father's decision it is extremely difficult
to estimate. One man, for example, was reported to have refused his daughter to a widower on the grounds that her
children would be overshadowed by his existing male children,
and her position in his household therefore lower. Even here

the concern is with her status rather than her happiness. In some cases, fathers refuse to send their girls to strangers, or to distant villages, in case they be badly treated. But the more general attitude seemed to be that the girl must bear with whatever suits her father's convenience.

For both households, a marriage is an opportunity to establish new friendships or to strengthen old ones, and at the same time to build or maintain prestige. Household heads are therefore likely to choose new affines with care, a boy's father no less than a girl's. A boy's father can conceal his caution more easily because he holds the initiative, whereas a girl's father who is unwilling is placed in the position of refusing; though a refusal is normally expressed indirectly and tactfully, by making difficult conditions.

Normally, a man looking for a bride for his son moves outward through a series of concentric circles, beginning with his brothers' households, turning next to other close kin, then to neighbours and co-villagers and finally to strangers in other villages; or rather he moves along the chains of social relationships that happen to be open to him, choosing the closest girl who is both suitable and available. Women are more active than men in speculating and gossiping about marriages, and a wife's social net-work is as important as her husband's. The chain may well lead directly, through kinship, to another village. To give one example among many, a man gave his daughter to his sister's husband's sister's son. Both the linking marriages were between villages, so that Sakaltutan established a new link with one village through an old link with another.

In quite a number of cases, younger siblings had married into the families of their elders' affines. In two cases, three such marriages had taken place between two families. One man had exchanged a widowed younger sister for the widowed mother of a poor neighbour, and another had exchanged a daughter by his first marriage for a young second wife. Occasionally, a widow with a child marries a widower with a child. These children are expected to marry each other and remain in the parental household, and in several cases had actually done so.

A close kinswoman is not only easier to find; she may also be easier to fit into the household, since she will already have established relationships with the members, especially with her new mother-in-law.

The words 'suitable and available' of course cover a host of factors. Quarrels and personal dislike may prevent an obvious match; or a chance contact or strong personal preference may lead to a surprising one. Moreover, the opposite argument from the normal one is also heard: that a marriage between households on friendly terms may well lead to estrangement, while marriage with strangers will bring the household new friends and allies. Nevertheless most marriages follow the established lines of kinship and friendship as far as is reasonably possible.

One factor which does not enter openly into the choice is the hope of wealth through inheritance. I was repeatedly told that it was shameful to think of such things, and that in any case it was foolish, since only God knew who would inherit what. At first I found this attitude surprising. But women's inheritance is always uncertain – indeed, the accidents of birth, death and remarriage make all inheritance uncertain, the more so because all rights are dependent on possessing the strength to establish them. In any case, fathers seemed remarkably unconcerned about their sons' prosperity after their own deaths.

Power and prestige are much commoner considerations. Some village households undoubtedly seek to use marriage as a means for recruiting followers and allies, or for repairing bruised or broken relationships (p. 252). If some of the poorer households did not aspire to motives of this kind, they would still be concerned to choose affines who would bring them honour rather than disgrace. But to perceive and evaluate such motives accurately even in contemporary marriages is difficult, and for past marriages wellnigh impossible. The villagers themselves implicitly emphasise the complexity of, and apparent arbitrariness of the human element in marriage, by their attribution of all marriages to the Divine Will. God's command ('*Allahın emri*') is the standard answer to all questions about marriages, and the same phrase constantly enters into the negotiations. Like the two greater mysteries, birth and death, the allocation of spouses, even in a God-controlled world, is seen as pre-eminently a province of Divine intervention.

In most human societies, the choice of marriage partners depends to some degree on the mutual attraction of the young people themselves. In this society, desirability is not a private matter, but almost exclusively social. The bride price, negotiated *ad hoc* in each case, acts as a public measure of this social evaluation of the girl. It is one of the main pressures which keep bride price rising as incomes rise.

Pre-marital Sex and Elopement

The highly prized honour of a marriageable daughter is naturally well defended. Young women are seldom left alone, and older members of their households are constantly on the watch. Many of the girls undoubtedly share their elders' morality, and avoid opportunities. They are mostly married fairly soon after puberty – and people say explicitly that it is unwise to keep a mature girl unmarried lest she lose her honour.

The young men marry later, and for most of them adventure in the village must be difficult and dangerous. Open courtship is absolutely out of the question. It is impossible to know how much goes on in secrecy. Certainly the caves behind and below the houses, which are used for storing straw, have a reputation for illicit love, but I doubt if they are very often used by girls before betrothal, simply because they are so seldom allowed out of the sight of their elders. It was generally agreed by informants, whether they disapproved or not, that most young men solve the problem of physical satisfaction by paying for their pleasure in town.

Some men claimed that village women, particularly the young ones, are so unsophisticated that if a man can only engineer the opportunity, seduction is simple. Others said that even a betrothed girl will defend her virginity until after marriage, and *a priori* I find it difficult to believe that girls do not know a great deal about sexual matters very early in life. The village women are less prudish among themselves than the men, and sex and reproduction form a major interest in their conversation.

In any case, much less than a secret assignation is needed to rouse gossip and bring a girl's honour into question. One girl of rather poor family was married very suddenly to her fiancé in another village with no ceremonies at all. It turned out that one of the village young men had been making passes at her, and was said to have paid an old man in potatoes for charms to win her affections. Her father's reaction was to hurry her out of harm's way – and incidentally to exchange the prestige of a proper wedding for a cash advantage, for, though he forwent part of the bride price, he escaped with a much reduced trousseau, and no expensive entertaining. After I left the village, a young girl was kidnapped by village lads. People said that it was only a boyish prank, and that a Kayseri *hoca* had pronounced her quite unsullied. Nevertheless she was rapidly and unceremoniously married off to a distant village, though, perhaps because they did not know all the facts, perhaps because of her guardian's high standing, a large bride price was paid.

In spite of the strict rules and defences, boys and girls are bound to see each other in the ordinary daily round of work. Some at least manage to exchange messages and arrange secret meetings. Occasionally such an affair ends in elopement.

The Turkish *kız kaçırma*, to make a girl run away, is nearer in meaning to 'kidnapping' than 'elopement', and puts the responsibility firmly on the man. It is a recognised, although dangerous and disapproved, method of acquiring a wife. It not only provides for passion in a system in which it is formally ignored, it also provides a way of evading the heavy costs of normal marriage; and occasionally it can be a move in hostilities between lineages.

Five out of the 134 contemporary marriages in Sakaltutan were known to me to have begun with elopement and I am confident there were others about which I did not hear. Three cases were said to have taken place in a neighbouring village during our stay in Sakaltutan, and one actually occurred in Elbaşı during our stay there. Roughly I would estimate that about one marriage in twenty begins by elopement – more towards the lower end of the village hierarchy than at the top.

An elopement involves three parties, the families of the two young people, and the couple as a new unit. Normally, the young man takes his bride to his own household, who ought by rights to be ashamed, but in fact are usually not unduly distressed. The bride's family of the other household are expected to react strongly, to threaten violence, and to be difficult to reconcile. In practice, what happens depends on the situation. I was not able to gather full material on any one elopement, though I heard of a number both past and present.

One informant of Sakaltutan told me that his wife, who was a close neighbour, had been a childhood playmate. He and she had a secret understanding, and the marriage was apparently acceptable to both parties. But his father was poor, and put off the wedding. To save his father expense and trouble, he said, after six months of secret courting, he simply brought the girl home one night. Instead of being pleased, his father was very angry, and said he would far rather have contracted debts than faced such a disgrace. Nevertheless, since both fathers were on good terms, and neither too well off, the new marriage was accepted.

A case occurred in Elbaşı during our stay. A young man from a middle-range family, persuaded the daughter of a fairly poor man from the far end of the village to come home with him. She accepted largely because she could not abide her step-mother. Her father was very angry, and declared he would have no more to do with her, but no one talked of violence. After only a few days she found her mother-in-law, who was notorious for meanness and bad temper, to be a fire rather hotter than the frying pan of a stepmother she had left behind. She attempted, whether seriously or not I do not know, to drown herself in the village spring, but was rescued and dissuaded by a group of women and taken to the house of her mother's brother's son. She remained with him for a while, but eventually was reconciled to her father and married off to a distant village.

One of my best informants in Elbaşı had eloped with the sister of a neighbour. In spite of three formal reconciliations, one of which I effected, they were not on speaking terms. No money passed in this case. Another young man in a household in which we were accepted had obtained his wife by the same means. He was said to have been asked a bride price before the elopement of T.L.1,000, and to have settled the matter after the elopement for T.L.200, with no trousseau. Many of the stories of elopement fitted this pattern – a highly variable period of intransigent indignation, followed by a settlement for cash, and reconciliation. But people insisted that elopement was a serious matter, and liable to cause violence, and this is not pure talk. A man from a neighbouring village belonged to a lineage which had been involved in reciprocal elopement with a rival lineage. He met a member of this rival lineage casually in Kayseri. Words led to blows, and he was knifed to death.

Remarriage and Polygamy

During the early nineteen-fifties the death rate was still high enough to ensure a good number of widows and widowers, most of whom remarry. Add to these those who remarry following a divorce and the very few polygamous marriages, and the total is a sizeable proportion of all marriages. These are what I call secondary marriages. As I am treating remarriage after divorce here with remarriage after bereavement, where appropriate the word widow or widower includes also divorced persons.

The loss of a wife is a serious blow to a man. He cannot himself look after small children, or cook. He cannot even decently fetch himself water. The urgency to find a replacement depends on the number and age of the children, and on the alternative womanpower available, either in his own household or readily to be borrowed. An older man with a resident daughter-in-law is in no hurry, and may not remarry at all, whereas a man with young children and no woman in the household may be in a desperate plight.

In the whole area, old men with daughters-in-law apart, I knew of only one man without a wife. He did his own cooking and chores. He had two sons, said to be 13 and 15 years old, the elder of whom would soon be able to bring in a daughter-in-law. Perhaps he preferred to keep his resources, which were very limited, for his son's marriage. His behaviour was however decidedly eccentric.

Normally, urgency precludes careful choice and preparation. A widower has a home in running order, and desperately needs a competent housekeeper. Public display is out of the question; he does not want a large trousseau, and is not usually much concerned about physical attractiveness or honour. He is very likely to take a widow or a divorcée, and the market for second-hand wives is always brisk. Sometimes a widower takes an unmarried girl for a rather higher bride price, but he will be allowed to have her only as a favour because she is a close kinswoman or because her honour has been sullied; or because her father is poor or not unduly concerned with his own honour.

People say it is the duty of the deceased wife's family to supply a sister, for a reduced bride price and without a full wedding. Very often, of course, this is impossible, and I only met one case among the existing marriages, but there were one or two more recorded in genealogies. In a number of other cases, widowers had taken kinswomen or close neighbours for a second wife.

More often, however, secondary marriage is with a stranger, even someone fairly remote. A middle-aged head of a simple household with young children in Sakaltutan, who lost his wife just before I moved in, replaced her within a week by a stranger, an unmarried girl from a nearby village. He paid T.L.500, which he was compelled to borrow. During 1949–50, he was working as a shepherd, and using his eldest daughter to help with ploughing, in order to earn extra income to meet the debt. Another man Musa (K), lost his third wife in April, but he was very poor, and even strenuous efforts both among kinship contacts and strangers failed to discover a suitable and willing woman at a price he could afford. He spent four miserable months. At first, his married daughters by his first wife came to keep house in turn, but they could not stay more than a few days each because of their own domestic responsibilities, and after this his household was run by a twelve-year-old daughter. His late wife's tiny baby daughter died. In the end, he took a girl who turned out to be almost blind (p. 184). By 1955, after a steady job in the mill (p. 71), he had divorced her and taken an unmarried girl, for a normal bride price.

A widow is not in the same situation. She depends on her husband not for immediate day-to-day tasks but for long-term support – for tilling the fields, for defending her, for making necessary contacts with towns and officials. She may remain in her husband's house, either more or less independently, or under the protection of his or her own father or brothers: or she can return to her own father or brothers. Naturally, what she does depends on her personality, her age, what kin and affines she has, and how they are placed. Quite a number of widows maintain their late husband's households intact, either shouldering the burden of tilling the land, or letting it out to a share-cropper. In this case, a woman needs male kin to protect and help her in her business arrangements, and with some of the toughest jobs in the annual cycle of work. Growing sons are of course a great asset.

One young widow in Elbaşı, who had four daughters, had

remained single. She declared herself against husbands, and absolutely independent. But no man would lightly take on a woman who had four times failed to produce a son, not to mention responsibility for the four failures. Hayip (B) (p. 144), her father, farmed her land as a share-cropper, and regarded her as an annexe of his own large household. She certainly relied on him for her outside contacts. An older woman in Sakaltutan, who had married out of the village, had lost her husband when her son was an infant, and had returned with him to her father's house, remaining there unmarried. In 1950 she was living in her son's household. One other widow in Sakaltutan and three in Elbaşı were bringing up families.

Most marriageable widows remarry. Unless they have a number of children, they are much in demand; and women often remarked that life without a man is hard. They may remarry within the circle of their husband's kin. In the genealogies, widows often married their husband's brother, occasionally polygamously. In two cases, barely adolescent boys had been married to an elder brother's widow, and in one case to mother's brother's widow. Equally, a widow may return to her father, who will arrange for her remarriage. Her children may remain with her husband's kin, or with her own natal household, or may go with her to her new husband, according to circumstances. The villagers are aware that according to the Şeriat a child belongs to its father, but should remain with its mother until it is seven, but they seem to attach remarkably little importance to formal rights in this matter. This is understandable. No one wants daughters, and other people's sons, even a brother's, are a limited asset. They are likely to cause trouble over inheritance, and in any case to leave the household at their most useful point – at marriage, when their labour, their children, and their obedience should serve to build a joint household.

Polygamy is still socially acceptable. Successful polygamy is a source of prestige, but it is also a frequent subject for jokes, and a polygamist is close to ridicule. It appears to be becoming rarer. It is not of course legal, and polygamous marriages are never registered with the State. Only four cases existed in Sakaltutan and seven (perhaps one or two more) in Elbaşı. I know only one man with a healthy and fertile first wife who had taken a normal marriageable woman as a second. He was a well-to-do man of another village, who presumably had wanted to enlarge his household with more sons. In all other cases, except for two in Elbaşı on which I have no information, some special reason existed for the second marriage.

The commonest reason for taking in a second wife is the inability of the first to produce surviving male children. A man without male heirs is expected to take another wife, with or without divorcing the first. Even when a first wife has had children, but can have no more, a second wife is quite justified. Secondly, a first wife might be incapable of doing her duty. One man seriously considered taking a second wife because his first was crippled with rheumatism; instead he married his fifteen-year-old son to his sister's daughter of about seventeen. Two men in Sakaltutan and at least two in Elbaşı had been married to widows much their senior. Each had married in middle-age a younger woman, in order to continue their procreative life.

Thirdly, polygamy is sometimes the result of widow-inheritance by brothers. A man is said to be the most suitable stepfather to his brother's children. Moreover, his brother's land is felt to belong to the agnatic group, and adjoins his own. Left to her own devices, the widow might marry a stranger, who would take over the land, and might even disinherit his stepsons. It is far better for the dead husband's brother to take over, temporarily adding the land to his own, and if any disinheriting is to take place, to make sure he benefits by it; in the past, it seems, orphans very frequently lost their land, often to their fathers' brothers.

Elbaşı provides a most interesting example of the possible complexity of such arrangements. Sefer, an old man in 1951, had married first his elder brother's widow, after she had borne two sons, Haşım and Şevket. She then bore Sefer himself another son, Ahmet. Haşım and Şevket were thus maternal half-brothers and also father's brother's sons to Ahmet. Sefer, about 1939, had also married his younger brother's widow, who already had one daughter, Ayşe. Sefer married his own son Ahmet to this niece-cum-stepdaughter. At some point, Haşım had separated from this household, taking with him his own wife, who was his father's sister's daughter from another village, his full brother Şevket and his mother. His eldest son was fifteen in 1951. Quite recently Ahmet had died, and after a delay, Haşım had married Ayşe in his place. Thus both Sefer and Haşım were bigamously married, both had married brother's widows, and each had a wife living in the other's household. Both households owned land, and since Sefer was old, Haşım was likely to end up in control of all the property of both households. The only cloud on his immediate horizon was the strenuous opposition of his first wife to his second marriage; she now only had him at home on alternate nights. But more serious disputes are likely in the long run. How will the whole estate eventually be divided between Haşım, his full brother Şevket who shared his household, their children, and his deceased half-brother Ahmet's children?

Haşım visited his second wife in her own house. In this, he constituted the only contemporary example – and an exceptional one – of a fourth type of polygamy. In the past, a man might contract a marriage with a widow who had her own established household, and visit her at night. She would thus take turns with his existing wife – or wives. Three old women in Sakaltutan were widows of the same man, two of them had maintained their own independent households as widows. In cases like this a polygamous remarriage seems to be a matter of convenience. The woman gains help and protection, but retains a good deal of independence; the man gains temporary control over more resources, and the chance of begetting more sons, without the expense and inconvenience of keeping two wives in one household on one holding of land. Three wives at a time appears to be very rare. Two men in Elbaşı, one dead and one still living, were said to have had three at one time. I heard tell of a man in a distant village who had four.

The villagers often speak of the religious injunction to treat all wives exactly equally. The only man in Sakaltutan with two young wives boasted of the care with which he had carried out this rule. But normally the villagers laugh, because they recognise that in most cases such equality of treatment is out of the question.

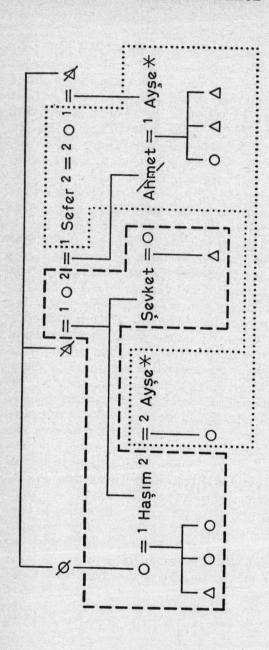

* *The same woman*

— — — *Current members of Haşim's household 1952*

.... *Current members of Sefer's household 1952*

9 Genealogy: Sefer and Haşim

The Range of Marriage : Kinship

I have already discussed the choice of bride from the point of view of the chooser. Let us now look at the results of these choices, that is at the actual marriages which I was able to record. My data are incomplete, but such as they are they are set out in the accompanying tables. For the most part they speak for themselves.

Some interesting conclusions emerge. More than half the marriages are between people with some kinship ties. Marriages with recognised agnates seem to be between one-fifth and one-quarter of all marriages, but actual father's brother's daughter marriages are only about one in ten. Marriages with other cousins are only a little less common, although no preference other than that for father's brother's daughter marriage are ever stated. The noticeably lower figures in both villages for mother's sister's daughter marriages are surprising. They perhaps reflect the frequent physical separation of sisters after marriage, or perhaps more the relative absence of social contact between the husbands. Less strikingly, mother's brother's daughter marriages seem a little more numerous than father's sister's daughter marriages. This difference may be accidental, but there is a possible explanation. People may prefer, if the choice is open, to bring together as mother-in-law and daughter-in-law a woman and her brother's child, rather than a woman and her husband's sister's child, to whom she is less close and with whom she does not share a common domestic tradition.

Since the two villages were twenty miles apart, and differed in size, wealth and degree of outside contact, the similarity in pattern is striking. My inquiries and discussions in other villages confirm that these tables present an overall picture typical at least of this area.

The Range of Marriage: Distance

Tables 10 and 11 (Appendix A) show for each of the two villages the number of village born wives, and the number who came from or went to other communities. The data was gathered as opportunity offered. On contemporary marriages in Sakaltutan, it is virtually complete, but on women marrying out, some

Table 7

SAKALTUTAN: RECORDED MARRIAGES BY KINSHIP OF WIFE TO HUSBAND[1]

	Existing Marriages 1950			Past and Broken Marriages			Total			Women marrying out (alive)		Women marrying out (dead)		Total		Overall Total[3]
	No.	Per cent (a)[2]	Per cent (b)[2]	No.	Per cent (a)[2]	Per cent (b)[2]	No.	Per cent (a)[2]	Per cent (b)[2]	No.	Per cent	No.	Per cent	No.	Per cent	
No information	47	35	—	118	64	—	165	51	—	29	—	16	—	45	—	210
Non-kinship	34	25	39	30	16	45	64	20	42	28	56	7	55	35	57	
Fa bro da	7			5			12			—		—		—		
Fa fa bro son da	8	18	27	4	6	18	12	11	23	—	—	—	—			
Other agnates	9			3			12			1	2	2	15	3	5	
Mo bro da	5			3			8			4		2	15	6		
Fa sis da	0	10	15	4	8	21	4	9	18	4	22			4	20	
Mo sis da	2			2			4			2				2		
2nd Cousin (non-agnatic)[4]	6			5			11			1				1		
Affines[5]	11	8	13	5	3	7	16	5	10	8	16	2	15	10	15	
Kin[6]	5	4	6	6	3	9	11	4	7	2	4	—		2	3	
Total (information)	87	100	100	67	100	100	154	—	100	50	100	13	100	63	100	217
TOTAL	134	100		185	100		319	100		79		29		108		427

202

Table 8

ELBAŞI: RECORDED MARRIAGES BY KINSHIP OF WIFE TO HUSBAND[1]

	Existing Marriages 1951-2		Past and Broken Marriages		Total		Women marrying out		Overall Total[3]
	No.	Per cent	No.	Per cent	No.	Per cent	No.	Per cent	
No information	124	—	102	—	226	—	29	—	255
No kinship	47	40	12	33	59	38	9	50	
Fa bro da	10 ⎫		5 ⎫		15 ⎫		⎫		
Fa fa bro son da[4]	1 ⎬ 22		1 ⎬ 27		2 ⎬ 24		— ⎬ —		
Other agnates	15 ⎭		4 ⎭		19 ⎭		⎭		
Mo bro da	9 ⎫		⎫		9 ⎫		⎫		
Fa sis da	5 ⎪		⎪		9 ⎪		⎪		
Mo sis da	3 ⎬ 19		4 ⎬ 9		3 ⎬ 18		2 ⎬ 11		
2nd Cousin (non-agnatic)[4]	6 ⎭		⎭		6 ⎭		⎭		
Affines close[5]	10	9	3	8	13	8	—	—	
distant	4	3	—		4	2	—	—	
Kin[6]	8	7	8	23	16	10	7	39	
Total on which information available	118	100	37	100	155	100	18	100	173
TOTAL	242		139		381		47		428

(Notes over the Page)

203

Notes:

1. These tables give a good indication of magnitudes but are not reliable in detail. The census material on which they are based was collected, deliberately, as opportunity offered, and the results are incomplete and may contain a few inaccuracies.

2. The sample is haphazard, since I used any sources open to me to augment information, including occasionally deduction. In Sakaltutan, I was able to work out that some marriages were between close kin, and I am fairly sure that I missed no marriages between agnates. Of the marriages on which I have no recorded information about the kinship relationship of husband and wife, most, therefore, are likely to be between non-kin, and very few, if any at all, between agnates. For this reason, I have given the proportion of marriages between various types of kin both as percentages of all recorded marriages (column a), and as percentages of all marriages on which I have definite information (column b). For marriages between agnates, column (a) is reliable; for other marriages the truth lies between the two figures.

   For the cases of girls marrying out of Sakaltutan, and for all marriages in Elbaşı, my information on the kinship network of the individuals was far less complete, and hence the cases on which I happen to have recorded information are less likely to represent a biased sample. I have not therefore given both sets of percentages in these cases.

3. Figures for marriages of women of the two villages who married out are not typical of figures for all marriages—they form a highly biased sample. To add them on to the figures for internal marriages would be to bias the overall total. In particular, the number of marriages with non-kin between villages is obviously likely to be higher than within the village; and the marriages with agnates between villages are almost non-existent. The class of marriages between spouses from different villages is already fully represented by the cases where spouses have married in. The last column is therefore only for overall totals and is otherwise left blank.

4. Since women normally attempt to use the full span of their fertility, even the children of one mother may differ widely in age. Since elderly widowers or divorcés frequently re-marry, paternal half-siblings differ even more widely – up to forty years. Hence marriages between cousins of different generations is not uncommon. First cousins once removed I have counted as second cousins, and second cousins once removed as other agnates or kin. The difference of generation may have no effect on the quality of the relationship.

5. Affines include all cases where a link through an existing marriage was part of the chain, from cases where people married brothers or sisters-in-law, to cases of much more remote connection.

6. The category 'kin' includes both cases of known kinship more remote than those specifically mentioned, and cases where I knew that a kinship tie existed but could not make a reliable guess at its nature.

omissions are inevitable, and I did not always ask if they were still alive, – hence the words 'presumed living' and 'presumed dead' in Table 10. From the totals, it appears that Sakaltutan had a net export of women, and Elbaşı a net import, but this interesting conclusion is doubtful.

In the two diagrams (Figs. 10 and 11) based on these tables, each line represents one village. They show how marriages linking villages decline in number with distance, and virtually cease above five to six hours away.

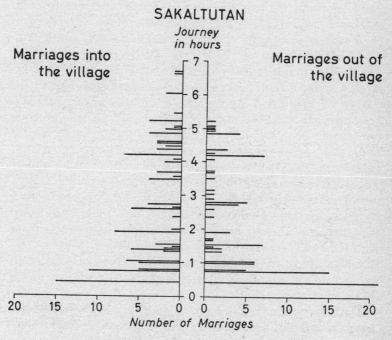

10 Range of marriage: Sakaltutan

On Fig. 10, it appears that in Sakaltutan in the past, only half the marriages were within the village, whereas now the figure is two-thirds. Possibly the rising population offers a greater choice of brides within the village. In Elbaşı on the other hand, a larger village in the first place, the proportion has remained more or less constant at just over half.

Sakaltutan men had recruited very few wives from distant sources. One man had taken a young second wife from a group of tribally distinct villages (*Avşar*) some eight hours to the east. One old woman in the village was said to have been an Armenian refugee. Only one girl marrying out had gone to any distance, to a village beyond Kayseri, said to have been founded about 1870 by a migration from villages near Sakaltutan.

With these exceptions almost all marriages were within the range of five hours' walking distance, and roughly, the closer the villages the more numerous the marriages between them. For Sakaltutan the two villages within half an hour provided strikingly more than any others. But for remoter villages once close contact is established further marriages may result. For example, Sakaltutan and Kölete, to which agnates of a village lineage (K) had moved two generations before, were tied by more marriages than other closer pairs of villages (Fig. 2).

West of Sakaltutan lay a group of villages whose marriage customs were based on those of Kayseri. These villages contained some people of more education and they spoke scornfully of the area round Sakaltutan as *köy*, village. Their women were more formally polite, and expected more comfort and less hard work. No respectable family in these villages would permit a girl to marry to the *köy*, and no woman would consent to such a drop in standards. Hence marriage ties with these villages are very rare, and where they occur, they consist either of marriages with less respectable women from these villages (there are no recent instances of this), or of cases where men of Sakaltutan had moved to their wives' village. Such marriages do not result in active affinal relations.

The distribution chart for Elbaşı is less tidy. A few households are more sophisticated and wealthy than any in Sakaltutan. These, and also a few of the poorer households with portering or other connections with Kayseri, contracted marriages further afield than any people in Sakaltutan. The fifteen refugee households from eastern Turkey, beginning with no established local social links, and no resources, had to find wives as best they could. Once again we find cases of a concentration on a particular village resulting from one or two socially close ties. One household alone in the last two generations accounted for six marriages with Söksün (Fig. 2).

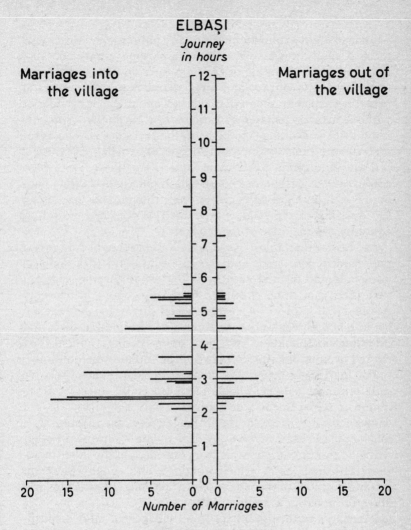

ELBAŞI

*Journey
in hours*

**Marriages into
the village**

**Marriages out of
the village**

Number of Marriages

11 Range of marriage: Elbaşı

But the general picture, with over half the marriages within the village, and most of the rest to places within a few hours' walk, is much the same as that for Sakaltutan. Once again evidence from the surrounding villages indicate that this picture is typical.

The Range of Marriage: Social Rank

Marriage is not explicitly linked to any notions of relative social rank. A man owes his wife's parents personal respect because they have, by consenting to give him their daughter, done him a very great favour. People may marry across differences of rank; in particular a man may take a woman who is his inferior without incurring shame or ridicule. But normally, especially if a full-scale wedding is to be held, the two sides have to agree on terms, and this requires some degree of equality of resources.

Two weddings in Sakaltutan, while I was there, involved a comparatively prosperous household in an alliance with a poor one, but in both cases the girl's father, though poor because of the dividing of the land, was treated as respectable and an equal by the majority of the villagers.

In view of the rapidity with which a household could in the past gain or lose land, and the ease nowadays with which a household can acquire cash by skilled wage-earning, it is not surprising that some existing affinal connections bridge very considerable gaps in the present social hierarchy. But though leading households were sometimes tied to middling ones, and middling households to very poor ones, no direct affinal links existed even in Sakaltutan between the top and the bottom.

For marriages outside the village, considerations of relative rank are more complex. Some men, especially when forced to obtain a replacement wife without ready resources, are not concerned with her standing in her own village. Moreover, a few men had obtained wives by elopement, or cheaply in other ways, and most of these came from outside. On the other hand, those few households which obtained and sought to retain leading positions in the village often intermarried with similarly powerful households in other villages.

Marriages to towns – or for small villages, to more sophisticated villages – are rare. Women very seldom marry down across community frontiers, respectable women never. But village girls may go to town. While we were in Elbaşı one girl of refugee family married, by arrangement through kin, a young Istanbul architect. In another case, a village woman's sister was married to a judge. Plainly, influential affines are useful and bring prestige; but they are rare.

Law and Sanctions in Marriage

In all societies, marriage involves rights and duties which are sanctioned by reciprocity, by self-help, and by public morality and opinion. In societies in which centralised states exist, the central government usually takes formal note of the establishing of a marriage, and provides formal sanctions and judicial machinery. In a great many societies – the Turkish educated urban class, for example – public morality accepts the State formality and the two sets of sanction more or less complement each other. But in some cases, a formal State procedure may not be accepted by the local community, and the formal sanctions which support it fail to have any effect at all.

The Turkish Civil Code of 1928 lays down the procedure for registering marriage. The couple must establish their identity by the production of valid birth certificates, they must submit to a medical examination, and the marriage must be registered by the appropriate official. Divorce by a court is not difficult to obtain, except in so far as anything involving lawyers and courts is always difficult. The Civil Code completely replaced Islamic law, so that all religious ceremonies are legally irrelevant.

But to the villagers it is the Civil Code which is irrelevant. They do not regard people who have been through a civil ceremony as married, they never have recourse to courts for settling disputes over the rights and duties of spouses, and nowhere in Turkey did I find a villager who had divorced a wife by legal process. Officials bring pressure to register first marriages which are celebrated with conspicuous weddings, and if any kind of welfare rights – marriage allowances, for example – are involved, then the villagers register their marriages cheerfully. But whether they do so or not makes not the slightest difference to their view of the morality of a union. To them, registration is not a rite within their system, but a meaningless piece of bureaucratic mumbo jumbo.

Legitimacy for the villages still rests solely on the *nikah*, the religious rite performed by anyone of sufficient religious learning to know the formula. They claim to marry according to the Şeriat, and to regulate the rights and duties of spouses accordingly. In fact, they do not do so, not even to the point of their own knowledge of Islamic Law.

According to Islamic law, a man may divorce a woman by pronouncing any words of repudiation or dismissal. He may recall her twice, but if the words are repeated three times, he may not marry her again unless she has in the meantime been married to someone else. Normally, a man divorcing a woman repeats the words three times on the spot to make sure. Once a woman is divorced under Islamic Law, she should wait a period of one hundred days – *iddet* – before marrying again, or if she is pregnant, until forty days after she has borne the child. All this the villagers know. They claim to practice this system of divorce. Yet they do not in actual instances bother whether a woman separated from her husband has been formally divorced or not, and I never heard of anyone refraining from marriage because of the *iddet*. When I raised this issue, they asked 'And who will cook bread and take care of the children while we wait?'

Nowadays no one adjudicates disputes according to the Islamic law. No formal pressure exists which can coerce a man, and thus the whole system rests on the built-in sanctions of reciprocity, self-help and public opinion. Before 1926, courts did exist which enforced a code based on the Şeriat. Before such a court it was even possible, on very limited grounds, for a woman to obtain a divorce from her husband.

So long as formal sanctions existed for breaches of the rules – formal sanctions which carried the authority of both State and Prophet – it was in theory possible to enforce one's rights. In practice, it is obvious that large areas of the society of the Ottoman Empire – most rural and tribal areas – must have fallen outside the direct influence of the courts and made little if any use of them. I cannot therefore decide whether the present disregard for the Islamic rules, and certain abuses arising from this disregard, were normal in these villages in pre-Republican Turkey. Perhaps people in the villages always ignored the Şeriat when it suited their book. But I suspect that so long as people believed that the rules they recognised were the same as those enforced by urban courts, at the very least, these rules would carry more weight and be more effectively sanctioned by informal local sanctions. If I am right, then in this type of area, Ataturk's reforms have so far increased disorder in marital relationships.

The sanctions which in fact hold spouses together and en-

12 The punching dance. The men take turns to be punched. (p.182–3)

13 A wedding prank: above the victim is a dead dog and a small boy armed with green paint. (p.182)

14 A guest of honour beside the walled up hearth of a guest room. As it is summer, the seat of honour has returned to its traditional place. In winter it is by the stove. (p.238)

15 Village election. A committee of villagers supervises the election official, who is a townsman and a stranger. (p.259)

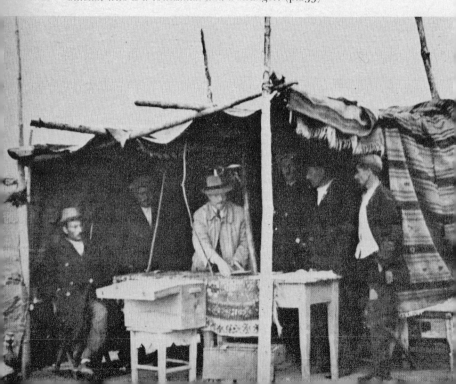

force their duties are reciprocity, self-help and public opinion. The way these work in detail will be largely implied in the discussion of adultery and divorce which follows. By reciprocity, I mean the mutual dependence and in some cases affection between man and wife, and between the couple and the two sets of close kin. By self-help, I mean the use of violence to defend honour and to avenge disgrace. By public opinion, I mean the concern with family reputation and the pressure thus exercised by the community towards conformity with the rules recognised by a consensus of village opinion. The first of these depends on the personal relations between the spouses; the second and third depend on the degree of each family's concern with its honour, and are more effective for those who lay claim to respectability and probity; less effective for those with no pretensions who accept a place at the bottom of the village hierarchy.

Adultery

Self-help is the recourse of any man whose honour has been tarnished by an approach to or insulting of his women folk. The most serious case is adultery. A wronged husband is expected to kill lover and delinquent wife. A man released from gaol in 1950 under an amnesty was greeted and presented to me as a hero because he had done just this. Clearly, the successful execution of this duty requires arms, courage and strong feelings. Not every adulterer is killed, nor does every husband wronged in this way attempt double murder. One man in Sakaltutan had divorced a wife for adultery without violence; and one woman in each village was said to be a runaway wife from elsewhere, with no mention of violence. Nevertheless, the danger is genuine.

People have obvious motives for keeping their own adultery a close secret, and equally obvious motives for concealing known cases from an outsider. Nevertheless, some people also have reasons for denigrating their neighbours, and others are at times indiscreet. I am confident that adultery was in fact rare. This is the more remarkable because some wives are left alone for months, even years. Thus two young wives in Sakaltutan, sharing a household because their husbands were brothers, lived by themselves with their young children. One husband had been away for four years, and the other for one. All questions about the wives were met with the standard answer that adultery was unthinkable, and that it involved the risk of death or at least being run out of the village. In another case, a younger brother was sharing a not very adequate house with his absent brother's wife, yet all questions met an equally steady front of denial. Not even the women, who are much less concerned about preserving the village reputation, breathed a word of scandal to us about either of these two cases.

Scandals about married women do of course occur. After I had left Sakaltutan, two lineages accused each other of making approaches to their own young wives, and this quarrel led to two deaths and one serious injury. On one occasion in Elbaşı, a child's reported claim to have witnessed a married woman with a lover behind a wall in a field was discussed and rejected as *a priori* highly improbable, and, in the light of relations between accuser's parents and the people accused, likely to be a malicious fabrication.

The Definition and Measurement of Divorce

In theory, a village marriage is dissolved in village eyes by the husband dismissing the wife, according to the Şeriat. Village informants told me that witnesses were required, though strictly they are not (Vesey-Fitzgerald (1931) p. 73). But in specific cases, people do not discuss the formal validity of a divorce. Indeed, the village has no distinct words for the 'separation' of married partners and 'divorce', the complete ending of all rights and duties. In most cases, separation constitutes divorce, and in those cases where a couple are regarded as still married though separate, it may be necessary to state this circumstance in full to make the situation clear.

The procedure is as simple as it can be. If a man is dissatisfied, he expels his wife, and she returns to her nearest living male kinsman, normally her father. If a wife is dissatisfied, she simply goes home. Quarrels between spouses are often complex, and it may not be clear who is responsible for a separation.

What happens next depends on circumstances. I have not been able to make a reliable count of cases, but village informants regard marital quarrels as normal, and usually solved by reconciliation. A man with a household full of children and no alternative woman will sue for peace quickly, by coming to fetch his wife back. No one would ask awkward questions about the legal propriety of remarriage even after a full triple-declared divorce. If the woman and her kin wished to end the marriage she would refuse to return, divorce or no divorce. Short-lived separations are dealt with as rapidly and as secretly as possible.

Married women who are separated from their husbands are often in a sort of limbo between marriage and non-marriage. One old woman in Sakaltutan and two in Elbaşı were living apart from their current husbands with sons who had separated from their father's household. In all three cases, the husband had another wife living with him. All these were regarded as married to their husbands, and were too old to be of interest to widowers and divorcés. One widow in Sakaltutan had two children by her first husband, and maintained a separate household in her father's house, apart from her second husband, who was her first husband's brother. They were not on speaking terms, but she refused offers of marriage from others and by 1952 had become reconciled and returned to her husband. Another girl newly married left her husband for some weeks and was still separate when we left, but people assumed this case to be normal and thus certain to end in reconciliation. No other married women were living alone to my knowledge during my field work. I heard of one or two similar cases in other villages.

If a dissatisfied wife cannot return home, either because she is not acceptable there, or because she has no home to which to return, then clearly she is in a difficult position. One unfortunate man in Elbaşı had lost two wives through suicide, of whom the more recent at least took her life because her father had sent her to the man against her will, and she could neither stand him nor return home. Another girl who eloped to escape from an intolerable stepmother only to find that her mother-in-law was just as intolerable, attempted unsuccessfully to drown herself (p. 193). The only way out is to find a man willing to take her as a wife. Her husband might, in theory, attempt violence, but a woman knows the seriousness of the risk, and she will always move to another village. In such cases, the new couple would normally have a technically invalid *nikah* performed, and be accepted as married though with some loss of face for all concerned.

In this society, then, a divorce is any separation which terminates a marriage. Whether or not a given marriage has terminated is not always easy to decide. If either party has firmly declared it to be so, or shown a definite intention to marry someone else, then it is terminated. But any eligible woman living apart from her husband is likely to be sought as a wife by widowers and divorcés.

Apart from the problem of definition, measures of divorce which could be used for comparison with other societies would require data collected with a systematic care that I cannot retrospectively apply. Barnes (1949) makes clear the practical and statistical complications; and as he says (p. 58) 'it (divorce) is a social process which has many aspects, some of which we can measure and some we cannot'. I therefore simply give such data as I have in some detail.

Cases and Causes of Divorce

I knew of roughly 450 marriages in each village, past and present. Whereas in Elbaşı I recorded only eight specific cases of divorce, in Sakaltutan, where I was able to gather much more detail, I recorded twenty-six. Besides these I assume plausibly but arbitrarily that one other man, who had nine wives altogether, had divorced at least two of them; this makes twenty-eight in all.

I have more reliable figures for the marital histories of living husbands in Sakaltutan. Including the presumed case just mentioned, of 129 living husbands, eleven had been involved in fourteen divorces; of these nine had divorced one wife each, one three, and one probably at least two. These 129 living husbands had married 178 wives, of whom only 132 were still current wives, so that forty-six marriages had therefore terminated, of which at least fourteen had terminated in divorce; but a large majority of the 132 current marriages were extremely unlikely to end in divorce.

It is probable that a more careful enquiry into the marital histories of these husbands might have revealed one or two more divorces; it is also true that some of the current marriages would probably end in divorce. Indeed by 1955 one had done so. Even so the divorce rate does not strike me as high, and I would describe marriage as stable.

An analysis of the circumstances of divorce in the Sakaltutan cases confirms this impression. Of the twenty-eight cases, five did not directly involve men of the village. One rather slow-witted young girl had returned home from four different attempts to marry her off, and was rather precariously married for the fifth time while I was in the village. One wife imported into the village had apparently walked out on a previous husband in another village. Seven of the twenty-eight cases involved deceased men of the village, six being accounted for by the marital histories of two of these, who were not regarded as altogether reputable. Two other cases involved living men born in Sakaltutan who had migrated with their Sakaltutan-born first wives to marry bigamously more sophisticated second wives in villages nearer Kayseri. In both cases the first wife had returned home and married someone else.

Of the fourteen cases which involved resident men of Sakaltutan, two are guesses, as I have said. Of the twelve better established cases five wives had been divorced because they failed to produce sons, three in succession by Haci Osman (H) (p. 126). In a further five cases the divorced woman was a secondary wife. In one of these five cases the cause of divorce

Table 9

DIVORCE CASES IN SAKALTUTAN

129 married men, 132 married women

Poor girl running home	4
Women leaving for her natal village	1
Deceased men. Divorce of replacement wife (at least)	4
Deceased men. Unknown causes	3
Failure to produce male children	5
Replacement divorces (including one for alleged adultery and two guesses)	7
Men leaving the village for bigamous unions	2
Co-wife deserting bigamous household	2
Total	28

was straightforward – the wife was reported to have committed adultery during her husband's absence on military service. In one of the two remaining cases out of the twelve, one of two co-wives simply left her husband (p. 219). In the other case a man took in his brother's widow, and after a year his first wife deserted him for a man in another village.

It is striking that in no single case did a normal fruitful first marriage end in divorce, except for the case where a brother's widow was introduced as a co-wife. One recently married young couple were apart when I left the village, but it is safe to predict that they were reconciled later. The weight of evidence from gathered impression, and discussions in this and the neighbouring villages, supports the conclusion that if a marriage is traditionally solemnised and fruitful, it is highly probable that it will not end in divorce unless the household runs into untoward difficulties.

This stability is not surprising. The sanctions holding a couple together are strong although they vary in kind. No young people expect to be able to choose a partner, and normally parents do not force a marriage against strong resistance, so that most first marriages are between people who know each other although only superficially, and have no strong feelings either way. The public ceremonial of the wedding involves them in acceptance, and in exposure to ridicule if they desert immediately. In addition, all concerned, both households, their kin and neighbours have invested considerable effort, money and public commitment in the marriage, so that the couple are under strong pressure to remain together. At the beginning they have no joint responsibility since the running of the household is the affair of their elders, and they therefore have no occasion for contact by day; they are not allowed to have any intimate contact except in strict privacy, and privacy by day is non-existent. The girl is under great strain at this point, not so much because of her relations with her husband but because her whole way of life has been disrupted. She may desert, but the pressures on both sides against a permanent breach will soon force her back. She herself wants a child as much as everyone else concerned, and this gives her another motive for enduring.

In time the new bride adjusts and mutual dependence begins to develop. Once children arrive successfully they form strong anchors since both husband and wife are dependent for their future happiness and status on a thriving family. Slowly the young couple take on more and more responsibility for their own affairs until they establish an independent household. By this time reciprocity becomes the main sanction; each has more to lose than to gain by deserting the other, and they are united by the bonds of habit and common interests, and maybe even by affection. Public shame remains a sanction. Although a man can send a woman home whenever he likes, to do so without a good reason is both shameful, *ayip*, and a sin, *günah*. People even try to avoid publicity for their quarrels, though in a village this is all but impossible.

These sanctions hold only so long as the wife carries out her duties satisfactorily. She must preserve her honour; she must do her share of household work, and she must bear sons. Failure in any of these duties destroys the reciprocity between her and her spouse, and removes the sanction of public opinion since he becomes justified in seeking to replace her. Sullied honour is in fact seldom a ground for divorce. A wronged husband should not divorce but kill. I knew of only one case, in another village, of a first wife divorced for adultery. Equally divorce for inefficiency is rare. One man of Elbaşı divorced a wife because she went blind. More often a wife unable to work would be retained and supported either by a second wife or by a daughter-in-law. The failure to produce sons is a far commoner ground for the termination of a first marriage. Indeed a man is expected to take steps to ensure that he begets sons. He may of course take a second wife without divorcing his first, and if feasible this is in fact regarded as a better solution.

In Sakaltutan three men had divorced their wives for not producing sons, two of them one wife each, and one of them three. Two other men without sons had taken no steps and were extremely unlikely to do so, both being poor and old. A third man with one daughter had had two wives; he was old and sick, and clearly had no intention of making any further effort to beget. In two other cases the husband had taken a second wife without divorcing the first; one of these had deserted, leaving her son behind for her childless co-wife. Besides these, one man with a fairly long standing marriage had no children but clearly still had time to remedy the situation. No fewer than thirty-six other marriages lacked male offspring, ranging from newly-weds to marriages of a few years standing. In all of these there were still reasonable grounds for hope.

To sum up: of 129 living husbands nine had apparently faced the probability or certainty of having no sons by their current wife. Of these three had had recourse to divorce, two to bigamy and four had taken no steps at all though one was still likely to do so. Thirty-six marriages, including two remarriages after divorce, had still grounds for hope. The rest, eighty-six, had sons. These include cases where a man had had two wives, because the first had died, but sons by only one. We can then say that roughly nine-tenths of men achieve male heirs either by their first marriage or by wives married as replacements when their first dies. Of the remaining tenth some divorce and remarry, more than once if necessary, some marry polygamously, and some take no action at all.

The stability of secondary and replacement marriages is markedly less. Of thirty-eight recorded, four ended in divorce, that is about one in ten. The reasons are not difficult to understand. The same grounds for divorce still hold, but the additional one of personal incompatibility is added. By definition at least one partner in a secondary marriage has been married before. Very commonly a bereaved widower is bringing a woman of whom he knows little into a functioning household which she has to take over and run. They have no time for gradual adjustment to each other's idiosyncracies. True, in a culturally homogeneous society the possible differences in household routine are limited, but even so it would be surprising if there were not a multitude of small frictions between the man and his new housekeeper and bedfellow, and between her and her predecessor's children.

Among secondary marriages there are also a number of special cases. Sterile men are likely to try a number of wives before they give up hope of producing children. Some of those who have abandoned or divorced spouses have already lost their honour, or most of it, and are not subject to the pressure of public opinion. Some of the wives available for replacement are available precisely because they have already proved unsatisfactory. The girl who had deserted four husbands by the age of twenty is an extreme example.

The dependence of stability in marriage on sanctions is illustrated by a particular abuse of which I came across several examples. Women normally pay routine visits to their natal home. In a number of instances, including one wife in each village in which I worked, the wife's father simply took advantage of such a visit to marry his daughter to someone else. He collected a bride price, and sent little or no trousseau, so he was certainly in pocket. In all the cases of which I heard people denied that there had been any kind of quarrel and the husbands declared themselves surprised, defrauded, and angry.

In the Sakaltutan case the wife in question was the second of two coeval wives, brought in with the active help of the barren first wife; she had borne a son. She herself was the only literate woman in the village, and coming from the *nahiye* centre to which Sakaltutan had previously belonged, regarded the village as uncivilised. In spite of his public indignation, the husband was left with his first wife, a less quarrelsome and expensive home, and a son, so he did not suffer unduly.

In all the other cases the wife was already herself a widow or divorcée before the marriage which she thus abandoned. I have no means of knowing whether the initiative came from unhappy wives or greedy fathers. One man had done this twice with the same daughter, and my informant unequivocally blamed his greed.

In all cases of this type the normal sanctions were more or less inoperative. The three households concerned, those of the two husbands and the woman's father, were separated by considerable physical and social distance, so that gossip in the first husband's village was a matter of indifference to the father and the new husband. Violence was not attempted, partly perhaps because in these cases honour was no longer pristine, but mainly because an attempt to use force in a strange village would be suicidal. The marriages had been arranged to provide a replacement, primarily a housekeeper, and the affinal link between husband and father-in-law was socially unimportant. The wronged husbands had no remedy.

These cases are perhaps more remarkable for their rarity than for their occurrence. They are only possible because when the normal built-in sanctions fail, the formal system can provide no alternative; its rules and institution are irrelevant.

The stability of marriage, then, depends entirely on sanctions built into the local community, and is totally unaffected by the State laws. For fruitful, honourably celebrated first marriages these are effective, and the divorce rate almost nil. Failure by the wife to fulfil her duties does give respectable grounds for divorce, the commonest and most pressing grounds being failure to bear and rear sons. Misconduct in such marriages is apparently extremely rare. Owing to the relatively high death rate, and to a few justified divorces, secondary marriages form a considerable proportion of all marriages. Among the more respectable of these divorce is still rare but among a minority whose marriage was less honourable in the first place, or who were forced to contract a secondary marriage at very short notice, divorce is commoner, and cases of this kind account for a considerable part of the relatively modest total of divorces.

Since no formal procedure, enforced by higher authority, is recognised, nothing can prevent a couple performing a religious *nikah*, even if in strict Islamic law they are not permitted to do so, so that no one in the villages lives in a state of concubinage. All unions are marriages in village eyes.

CHAPTER TEN

RANK

Rank

In every human group some members are more, some less admired and respected; some more, some less able to impose their will on others. Description and discussion of this universal hierarchical arrangement relies heavily on the word status. It is used to mean both a place on a scale, high and low status; and also, on the analogy of legal usage, a social position with its concomitant rights and duties, the status of husband or headman (e.g. Homans (1951) pp. 11–12, 179). Because of this ambiguity I prefer to avoid the word, and to use *rank* for the one meaning, and *social position* or *rôle* for the other.

In this wide sense, rank is partly a matter of an individual's place in a scale of prestige, and partly of an individual's place in a hierarchy of power. In practice the two scales largely coincide. Discrepancies certainly occur. A man may exercise power yet be despised for the ways he acquired it, while another may be admired for moral qualities yet exercise little power. The two scales tend to coalesce in time; power earns increasing respect, and respect brings increasing influence.

A scale of prestige is a matter of what people think of each other, and varies with the person who is doing the thinking. We must also distinguish admiration for personal qualities from deference given to social position. Personal dislike or pretension may prevent people from explicitly admitting, or even recognising, deference which they nevertheless display implicitly in their behaviour.

In spite of these difficulties it is possible to establish a rough overall hierarchy among the village men. In the guest rooms, in the mosques, at wedding feasts, people arrange themselves publicly according to a more or less generally accepted scale (Stirling, 1953).

I have avoided the terms 'stratification' and 'social class'. In Sakaltutan people occupying similar positions on the prestige scale do not associate more with each other than with people below or above them, nor do they develop common interests or common customs to set them apart. Thus it is incorrect to speak of classes or strata In Elbaşı one or two of the village leaders did tend to set themselves apart from and above the rest of the village and adopt elements of urban middle-class culture which their neighbours totally lacked. But this development had not gone far enough to justify speaking of a separate social class or stratum.

Three Scales

The grounds on which people rank each other are numerous and varied, and the order varies with the context. It is theoretically possible to construct a series of different scales in different contexts: one for religious observance, one for neighbourly co-operation, one for honour, one for landholding, one for agricultural skill, one for overall income, one for generosity, and so on. I have grouped these different scales more or less arbitrarily into three sets.

To put the same idea in different words: a man's position in the overall ranking system is determined by an indefinite number of factors, which I have for descriptive convenience divided into three main groups. One group comprises age and the position of a man in his own household, lineage, and kinship network; the second comprises landholding, occupation, income and patterns of spending; and the third, piety, religious learning, and moral respectability.

This list omits two factors commonly important in ranking in other societies – nobility of birth, and the holding of formal office. Let me explain. I am always tempted to describe village society as egalitarian; this is perhaps misleading, but at least people are not respected for their ancestry. Young members of respectable households obviously inherit village respect. But there is no notion that belonging to one line rather than another confers inherent superiority. This is rather what I would call a 'chip-on-the-shoulder' society. No one is willing to admit any-one else's superiorty, let alone an inherited right to issue orders. People are always saying that 'we are all the sons of Adam', implying that we are all therefore equal. In daily intercourse they treat almost everyone with the same formal politeness. If any adult man enters a guest room he will exchange salutations with everyone in turn. No one is ever barred from a guest room on grounds of social inferiority. Of course, men normally avoid guest rooms in which they are likely not to be courteously received. The only exceptions to this general politeness are one or two of the poorest and most personally disreputable members of the community.

Formal offices within the village are mainly those of village servants, such as the herdsman, and these carry no prestige, rather the reverse. Even the headman himself was not treated with formal deference. Religious office holders are accorded deference only in certain contexts, and in these villages there are no local hereditary *sayyids* (holy men) or *şeyks* (sheikhs) such as one finds in other parts of the Islamic world.

Age

The village roughly divides the male population into four age groups: children, unmarried youths, 'young men', and the old. The village terms do not correspond quite to current categories either in Istanbul or in England. The term for youth is *delikanli*, (lit. 'mad bloods'), and the term for married men in their prime is the word normally translated 'youth', (*genç* cf. Lat. *iuvenis*). The only formal mark of change from one stage to another is marriage, which moves a man from *delikanli* into *genç*, although a man married very young might still be called *delikanli* for a while. The passage from child to *delikanli* is not marked by any formality except that a *delikanli* must have a moustache. Circumcision is normally, though not necessarily, held much earlier, and appears not to make any formal dif-ference in a boy's standing or to involve any principle of social organisation, though it is a necessary condition for marriage and for respectability as an adult.

The passage from *genç* to *ihtiyar*, (old man), is also vague. The moustache becomes a beard, and if economic circumstances

223

allow, or health compels, an old man spends his time sitting in his home, in a guest room or in sunny places in the village, and does little or no work except perhaps at the harvest. Very roughly this change seems to occur about the age of fifty although individuals vary greatly according to health, resources and inclination.

These are no more than stages in a man's life. They do not correspond to any kind of formal organisation, and the people described by one of these terms do not form a single group. Of course, people are at ease with their equals, and informal gossip groups, especially out of doors, tend to consist of co-evals. Relative age is always important since deference to elders is strictly enjoined at all age levels.

In the long winter evenings when almost all the men sit in guest rooms, the young are expected to keep quiet in the presence of their elders, and children are sent out if they giggle or make a noise. Youths do not speak, and the younger married men speak little, especially in the presence of their own fathers. A younger man is expected to sit in a respectful posture, that is, not to cross his legs if sitting Europeanwise with his feet on the floor, and to keep his feet tucked underneath him if squatting on the divan. Smoking in the presence of father is forbidden. Every guest room has a drinking cup and a filled wooden water bottle always ready. If a seated man wants a drink he will demand it simply and unceremoniously, and one of his juniors, usually a boy, will bring the cup, wait respectfully with his hands crossed while his elder drinks and then take it back.

Position in Household and Lineage

Closely tied to age as a factor in rank is a man's position in his own agnatic group. The senior male member of a household always speaks for it; even a man of mature years will normally keep silence publicly in his father's presence. To disagree publicly with his father is a declaration of rebellion. His relative position in the village rises sharply therefore when his father dies and he is in charge of his own household. Even then, the eldest of a group of brothers tends to speak for the others and to carry weight as their representative. I have already described the wedding feasts in Sakaltutan attended by 'the great ones', *büyükler*, a term also used less precisely in other contexts.

A man's age, his position within his own household, and that within his agnatic group all operate together to determine his overall standing in the village. Over these factors he has no control. His position on the age and kinship scale is ascribed and not achieved.

A man's family brings him prestige in one other way, namely by the number of his progeny. Though this element is in fact also outside his own control, it is seen by the village as a matter of personal prowess. The mere begetting raises a man's prestige, and the existence of many sons increases the power and wealth of his household.

The Scale of Wealth

Wealth is the single most important factor in village ranking though it is only one among others. Wealth enables a man, with traditional generosity, to succour the poor and the sick; to contribute in money and kind to expensive celebrations, mainly weddings; to lend free of interest to others in need. When he spends within the village society he is a customer or employer. He will employ labourers on his land especially at harvest time, and he will have a say, perhaps a controlling say, in the choosing of some of the village herdsmen. He can afford to entertain visitors, and establish contacts with important people outside and above the village hierarchy. A man who is able to hand out charity, to provide jobs, to offer loans, to control appointments and to influence the outside world is not likely to be offended. Haci Osman (H) paid for the wedding feast for 'the great ones' for a neighbour of his, thus putting the man under an obligation and displaying his generosity to the whole village. In Elbaşı, I saw a wealthy man enter a poorer neighbour's house and request the services of his daughter for a day's harvesting at a low wage. The neighbour was in no position to argue.

Wealth can exist in many forms. In the more traditional type of behaviour just described, it is expendable wealth that counts, an income convertible to influence by judicious giving. But wealth may exist in land which is not exploited, or in the ownership of animals, or even, nowadays, in modern enterprises such as a share in a lorry or a mill. It may even consist simply of a skill which confers a high earning-power.

The wealth of a landowner is the most highly regarded and the most effective. People see it as reliable and permanent. The head of a landed household either controls a large household or at least has dependent share-croppers anxious to retain his goodwill. His income is in kind, earned by the work of others, and he is able to be generous out of well-filled granaries or well-stocked flocks. Almost without a dissenting voice, migrants and farmers alike told me that farming was by far the best occupation.

The migrants, whose income is mainly in cash, wear suits, watches and fountain pens; their houses are often better stocked with rugs for the guest room, pressure lamps, gaudy cups and glasses, painted mirrors. Yet they count for much less in the village. In part this is because, however successful, they do not normally have an income comparable to that of the larger village landowners. But it is also because the village regards such wealth as transitory and uncertain, because craftsmen are often away from the village scene for long periods, and because they spend less freely on their neighbours' needs, not readily converting their personally earned cash into the more nebulous commodity of neighbourly obligation.

Plainly all incomes are highly variable. Not only does the crop yield vary with rainfall, but even the sown area varies with the sickness of people and animals, or misjudgements in the time of ploughing. The earnings of the migrant labourers are even more chancy. It would be quite impossible to draw up a list of village households in order of income.

Over longer periods, as I have explained (pp. 134 ff.), the income of a household head depends largely on the manpower available; and the death of a household head results in considerable redistribution of resources. Striking changes in the ranking order of the village therefore take place within one generation. One result of these changes is that the recent poverty of the rich, and the recent respectability of the poor, are remembered and affect people's prestige. Haci Ismet's (T) household, the richest in Sakaltutan, was neither the most powerful nor the best thought of; similarly Hayip's (B) one of the more pretentious households in Elbaşı, had recently been poor and people thought the less of him for it. Two household heads with similar incomes, even with similar landholdings may rank very differently.

Skill and Occupation

Most of those who work on anything but their own land fall into two clear-cut classes: the skilled and the unskilled. This applies whether or not they are migrants.

Skilled men earn from twice to three times as much as the unskilled. Labourers are generally paid by the day; skilled men by the job. Traditionally, men of skill, carpenters, smiths and masons, are known in the village as *usta*. The distinction between skilled and unskilled was sharp. No single word in normal usage covered both; a man was either *amele* or *usta*. The word *usta* is often used as a sort of title, for example Ahmet *Usta*, with an implication of dignity, and I was sometimes called *usta* because of my skill with a pen. Quite apart from the great financial advantage young men were anxious not to remain *amele*, though the village was not in practice prepared to accord the title *usta* as a matter of general usage to every young man who became a migrant plasterer or painter.

I expected at first to find that the skilled migrants would be those with little or no land, those, that is, who had nothing to keep them in the village; and that the unskilled would be those with land who needed relatively little extra income and had little time to spend learning crafts. But in fact the migrants from better-off households tend to become skilled, and the migrants from the poor or landless households to remain unskilled. A few of the better-off farmers, when they face special needs, go to work, shamefacedly, as unskilled labourers, and one or two of the poorest households have sons who become skilled men. But on the whole the correlation holds.

The retail trade covers a wide range of social positions. At the lowest end, peddling with a donkey for example, it was definitely a despised occupation. But the well-dressed outsiders who arrived on horseback to sell cloth – including a man of Sakaltutan resident in a village nearer Kayseri – were obviously persons of higher standing. Again some of the shopkeepers who had no other source of income seemed to rank at the lower end of the village scale, but some shops were run by men with land

and other resources who were toward the top of the village hierarchy. Buying and selling were regarded as necessary evils, not perhaps degrading, but certainly not intrinsically honourable like farming. Perhaps a certain ambiguity was due to the fact that a more rigid traditional disapproval of trade was declining under economic pressures and incentives. (Turhan (1951) p. 100; Salim (1961) pp. 141–3.)

Elbaşı contained a few men who earned official salaries (p. 58). By their dress and behaviour these State employees (singular *memür*) demanded a certain amount of respect, but they did not rank all that much more highly in the village for their official status. The holding of a salaried post certainly did not give a man rank above a villager with adequate land and the ability to maintain the same standard of living.

A certain level of power and prestige, provided it is derived from land, gives a villager the right to be regarded as an *ağa* (pronounced roughly 'ah!'). This familiar Turkish word was very commonly used in the villages in several different senses. It was, for example, normal in addressing a neighbour to call him, 'Ahmet Ağa' or 'Mustafa Ağa' as the case might be. Sons and younger brothers often addressed their fathers and elder brothers as *ağa*. But a man of eminence was spoken of as an *ağa* in a slightly different sense. Thus Kara Osman (Ax) (p. 145) has been an *ağa* without any question. One very poor but intelligent informant when speaking of one or two wealthier men whom she personally respected would add this title after their names, but she once remarked that since Kara Osman died the village no longer boasted a true *ağa*, only a collection of pretentious nobodies.

Occupation and wealth can be treated as a single scale. The wealthiest and most highly respected households owned plenty of land, yet often combined agricultural with other skilled or commercial activities as sidelines, often profitable. At the other end of the scale are households, generally small ones, of which the head is a landless unskilled labourer or herdsman. But it would be almost impossible to sort out a significant order of rank for the majority of villagers in the middle of the scale.

Religious Rank

Religious ideas enter every aspect of village life. Everyone is measured on a religious scale in terms of piety and learning. *Cahil*, ignorant, is a common term of abuse; stronger still is *gavur*, infidel. A few people have reputations for special religious or magico-religious knowledge, and one or two hold specific religious positions. Moreover, since moral rules are seen as directly ordained by God, moral judgements are also to a large extent religious judgements.

The village imam or *hoca* always receives a minimum amount of deference and politeness because of his office. Formally he is required to hold a licence from the Mufti of the province, appointed by the Presidency of Religious Affairs, a department of government directly under the Prime Minister. When he is acting in his religious capacity, conspicuously at Friday prayers, he leads the whole village and all must listen to his words. On less formal occasions he is welcome as an honoured guest in guest rooms in the evenings, and normally encouraged to discourse on a religious theme or tell a religious story. Nevertheless his office does not automatically confer influence or personal prestige. His own personal learning and piety, and his character are the main determinants of his standing.

In Elbaşı and Sakaltutan, during the years I knew these villages, a new imam was appointed each year, and none of them was satisfactory to the villagers, nor highly regarded. The men appointed were ordinary villagers from local villages, not conspicuously more learned than the rest. Their objective in seeking office seems to have been the attached income.

Other villages had different arrangements. In Kanber the imam was permanent, a local man with his own land, and apparently of some weight in the village. In Kölete, on the other hand, the imam was also permanent, but was a landless immigrant and of little account. Çevlik had a young man of Sakaltutan as its imam who remained in office for several years. In Alışar, according to Morrison (1938, Chaps. II and IV), the largest landowner was the son and heir of a man who had arrived in the village as a stranger and remained as permanent imam.

In every village there are a number of men who can read the Arabic script, and are able to intone, though not to understand, the Koran. Many of these are capable of leading Friday prayers. Their learning earns them some prestige, and they are often given a courtesy title of *hoca*. Those few who have been on the pilgrimage to Mecca and who bear the title *haci* are regarded as sacred, and receive deference.

Traditionally, the only purpose of learning was religious. Even now villagers say that the great benefit of being able to read is that it enables one to acquire religious knowledge. I was asked why I spent so little time reading works on religion. For religious reasons, learning itself acquired prestige; and thus, paradoxically, modern secular education earns reflected respect as learning although it is considered dangerously irreligious.

One class of expert remains: the man who has special knowledge of Koranic charms. The main forms of magic, rites for healing, for punishing thieves, for arousing illicit passion, and so forth, are based on what are believed to be Koranic texts written on pieces of paper which are then swallowed or worn on the person, or intoned like spells in incomprehensible recitative. Experts in this field are not highly regarded, but are recognised as knowledgeable, useful, and slightly dangerous.

In some of the villages some of the men were members of the dervish religious orders, normally spoken of as *şeyklik* by the villagers. These orders are formally illegal, and were not prevalent in either of the villages in which I worked. No clear view of their activities emerged from my questioning. On the whole most people regarded members as specially pious, but tinged with dangerous or foolish heterodoxy. Many regarded the whole business as socially low-grade, and a few as positively wicked.

Morality and Honour

To report accurately on the way in which behaviour is assessed, on the concepts used and the relation between moral behaviour and moral ideas is a task of great difficulty. When I did the field work for this study I had not learned to suppress my own assumptions about good or bad behaviour, and I sometimes failed to ask important questions because I assumed I already knew the answers. Moreover, systematic collection of data on the way in which concepts are used requires more than a good working knowledge of a language; I was often too busy grasping

RANK

what was being said to reflect on subtle differences and changes
in implication from one context to another.

Nevertheless, people are eternally assessing each other's
conduct, and by living among people one learns much more
than is to be found in one's notebooks. Yet it is almost impossible, even with impeccable information, to discuss concepts
of this kind without implying that they are a great deal more
consistent and explicit than in fact they are.

Two sets of concepts are used side by side for assessing conduct, which although not explicitly distinct are yet not altogether mutually consistent. One is a scale of sin (*günah*) and
merit (*sevap*) backed, according to belief, by God's authority
through the Book. This set of concepts is itself complex.

Moral decency, compassion, kindliness, neighbourliness,
forgiveness, longsuffering, honesty, a proper respect for the
rights of others, these are good because God ordained them so –
they are *sevap*, meritorious. Ritual duties, the performance of
regular prayers, of ablutions, of the major anniversaries of
Islam, of the fast, are also good, meritorious, because God
ordained them so. It appears to follow that the villagers do not
distinguish moral virtue from ritual conscientiousness. Certainly, in discussion they sometimes asserted or implied that no
distinction can be made. In practice they know a mean, sly
man who is meticulous in all religious duties from a generous
reliable man who is not. But they see the whole business of sin
and merit as a single balance sheet on which ritual merit can
outweigh moral failures; one's ultimate fate at the Last Judgement depends on this balance, tempered by the Mercy of God.

Overlapping yet in some points contradicting this measure of
conduct, is another based not on religion but on the notion of
honour, *namus*. An honourable man is ready to fight, resentful of
insults, able to keep his women pure from all taint of gossip, if
necessary by killing them, and incapable of underhand and
deceitful practices. The opposite of *namuslu*, honourable, are
namussuz, without honour, or *ayip*, shameful. These two words
are in constant use, mainly for reproving children or for critical
gossip. Except in jest, they are not said lightly by an adult to a
social equal. They imply both internal personal rottenness, and
at the same time a loss of public face. They are used to children
to inculcate conventions – for example the correct greeting for

231

elders – as well as for the really serious matters of uprightness and sexual propriety.

On one occasion, two men were arguing more or less rationally, if heatedly, about the rights and wrongs of a piece of land to which they both laid claim. Then one used the word *namussuz*. The other immediately flew into a rage, threatened violent reprisal for such an insult, and broke off the discussion. He resented the implication that he was resorting to deceit and underhand arguments to make out his case. This aspect of honour clearly overlaps with religious injunctions to honesty and uprightness. But in another matter the codes are in clear contradiction. Honour requires intransigence and implacability; insults must be pursued and avenged, and never taken lying down. On the other hand, God is merciful, and it is the duty of a good Muslim likewise to be merciful, and to live in peace. When people are seeking to compose a quarrel, as they often are, they use the arguments from religion against the arguments from honour.

Peristiany and Pitt-Rivers have pursued these concepts of honour in other parts of the Mediterranean seaboard far more thoroughly than I have.[1] Both point out that virility and a man's honour are closely connected. This holds for Turkey too. Sexual prowess is discussed, mainly measured by procreative success. But whether a man earns a reputation by successful extra-marital sexual adventures, I find it very hard to decide. Within the group of kin and neighbours, certainly, to approach other men's women is dishonourable; urban whoring is not an honourable activity, though many adopt a neutral attitude towards it. To make approaches to the women of known enemies or outsiders would be manly and courageous, perhaps even honourable in some contexts. On the whole, virility seems to be no more than one element in the concept of male honour.

Women's honour is more closely tied to sex; that is to modesty and an undefiled reputation. *Namus*, honour, is said to be the most important quality of a bride. The whole social system with its segregation of men and women, and its insistence on constant companionship, especially among the women, makes it

[1] Papers delivered to a conference held in 1959 at Burg Wartenstein, publication of which is promised in Pitt-Rivers (Ed.), *Mediterranean Countrymen* (1964), p. 5. see also Campbell (1964).

difficult for a girl to show any interest in boys or men without immediately losing *namus*. Women who fail to show respect for elders, or in other non-sexual ways defy custom, might be called *namussuz*, but in general for a woman *namus* is very largely a matter of sexual modesty.

Specific accusations of dishonour or moral slackness, especially by known enemies, have little effect on a person's standing. But households, generally poor households, may become known as ritually slack, or worse, as careless of their honour, while others, sometimes also fairly poor, may conversely earn a reputation for morality, or for nobility and generous conduct. These two extremes apart, the majority of villagers are impossible to distinguish in terms of morality and honour.

The Overall Scale

It would be impossible to rank everyone in the village because it is impossible to know exactly what weight to give to the various scales or factors. The three main scales I have described are each made up of several others; there is no finite number and one could argue academically for more and more minute distinctions.

Moreover, the scales or factors influence each other in complicated ways; indeed, they are not in practice always distinguishable. The word *iyi*, for example, is used both for a morally good person, and for a moderately well-to-do household. Theoretically a well-off man can be wicked and a good man poor. Yet there is always an implication in village thinking that to possess the physical means to live respectably confers moral respectability, and to be squalidly poor is morally disgraceful. Theologically, a link between the two meanings is provided by the theory that God rewards the virtuous and punishes the wicked in this life; or alternatively by a much less Islamic doctrine loudly pronounced by a successful sheep breeder from Elbaşı, who preached that wealth was the result of virtuous hard work and foresight, and poverty of sloth and neglect. In the context of rural Turkey I found his version of the protestant ethic unconvincing. Wealth and morality affect each other in a more practical way. On the one hand, the possessor of a commanding position can get away with minor or even not so minor transgressions without his reputation suffering. If a man has been to Mecca, is pious in word and deed, and judiciously generous, the fact that he has robbed his sisters' sons of their inheritance is unlikely to be mentioned. On the other hand, the less a man has the lower is his rank and the less he has to lose by public dishonour, so that the poor are generally more shameless than the rich.

Yet a rough overall ranking scale does exist. The three scales frequently coincide, and where they do not, the individual's position on one scale is drawn up or down towards his position on another scale. In all this, wealth is the single most important factor; but it is certainly not a simple determinant. The relative rank of men of middling means varied greatly on the other two scales. The wealthiest household in Sakaltutan was neither liked nor respected, despite the fact that its old head had been to Mecca. He was not a native, having come to the village as an orphan, and acquired his land in one lifetime (p. 127). The man who appeared to have most influence was third or fourth in terms of wealth; his holdings were largely due to inheritance and he was the head of a sizeable lineage group. In Elbaşı equally, the wealthiest were not always the most respected, and at least one of those who in terms of manpower and land was best off, and who frequently entertained important guests, was generally held in low regard. Another man in the village who was quite comfortably off was generally ignored because he was thought to be mean and sanctimonious.

In the middle of the scale even considerable differences of wealth between one household and another were less important than honour, decency, neighbourliness and position within a lineage. One of my informants was a very poor man, but he was respected if not liked because he was given to showing a chip on his shoulder. One very poor old man who peddled with a donkey was treated with politeness because of a reputation for goodness and piety.

The religious scale correlates least with the others. A reputation for genuine religious knowledge carries great weight even for a poor and unimportant man. Yet on the whole it is the more respectable households which insist on a proper religious training for their children, and among which the few who have had formal religious training are found. The elderly are in general more pious in their personal conduct than the young, and it is only the wealthy who can afford the greatest religious glory of all – the journey to Mecca.

Even the factors which are independent of personal control, age and lineage position, fit more or less into the overall scale. An old, poor, and shameless man will be thought little of, but treated with respect for his age. A young man who has no senior kin and who commands ample resources will be listened to and given respect, but his youth will limit his standing in the village. Between those roughly equal in other ways seniority is of great importance.

The existence of a very roughly agreed scale or rank in the village is clear from the seating arrangements in the guest rooms. The position nearest the fireplace or stove is that of greatest honour. When people assemble in guest rooms they arrange themselves roughly in order. It is polite to be self-effacing and men manoeuvre to force their approximate equals to take a place above them, so that the final order is roughly a result not of claims but of imposed public opinion. If a fairly highly regarded man enters a crowded guest room, someone near the fireplace will leap up and offer his seat, himself being immediately offered someone else's, and so on until everyone is seated again.

The guest room groups are fairly constant (p. 240) and thus the order is one among regular associates. People cannot make claims for themselves, but if they are afraid of being slighted in a given guest room then they avoid it. The mosque on the other hand is a meeting place for all the village. In a mosque people stand in long parallel lines, precisely to symbolise the equality of all before God. Yet the senior men always stand in the front row and the place of honour is in the centre. In this context, age and a religious reputation count highly. Young men and boys stand at the back. But in the middle rows the egalitarian principle of Islam works, and in any case late-comers have to remain at the back, unless they are visitors to the village of particularly high rank, in which case they may be ushered silently forward. I was always left towards the back in the mosque as a very doubtful believer, whereas in other contexts I tended to be pressed to a position of honour.

CHAPTER ELEVEN

GROUPS, FEUDS AND POWER

Groups

Nothing about these villages surprised me more than their apparent amorphousness. People did not seem clearly to belong to distinct groups nor was there any clear hierarchy of power or authority. Village households are largely economically independent of each other, and none is dominant. Most adult men are proud and egalitarian, at least in theory, and unwilling to take orders. Competitive intriguing and manoeuvring in such a situation is complex, and since I did not know the full details of their own intimately shared past, and since the current moves are kept as secret as possible, unravelling is not easy. Because of the complexity, the discussion necessarily embraces a number of topics: formal and informal groups, violence and feuding, and village leaders and their followers.

Only two types of group in rural society are corporate, exhaustive and mutually exclusive, namely the household and the village itself. The tiny percentage of individuals whose membership is temporarily uncertain is insignificant. As I have already shown, the existence of a unilineal kinship ideology gives rise to a third set of groups which theoretically could be of this type, but in practice are neither corporate nor exhaustive.

The remaining types of group are few in number and all vague in their criteria of membership; none provides an exhaustive or a mutually exclusive set. The two villages contained only three types of voluntary associations. First, the religious orders, the dervishes, had some members in the area. They had very little importance in one village and none in the other. Secondly, in theory, every village had 'hearths' (sing. *ocak*) of the main political parties, but none of them had a fixed body of supporters, and membership had little influence on village organisation. Thirdly, in the winter of 1951-2, Elbaşı, in response to a special situation, produced a Union of Youth which I will discuss below. More informally, a number of other groups exist. All of them consist of a fairly distinct core, with a periphery of other people attached with varying degree of tenousness.

First, the villages are divided into quarters, and people use the physical layout of the village socially. Secondly, in the intervals between work, most of the time during the winter, the men sit and talk. In the summer they collect in the open air, roughly by neighbourhoods, but in the winter they foregather inside guest rooms where a stove is burning. Thirdly, even more vaguely, the poorer members of the village depend on the richer and more influential, and the village may be divided into one or more factions with a shifting and overlapping membership.

Sakaltutan had only two quarters, upper and lower, though sometimes the centre of the village was spoken of as the Mosque quarter. This vagueness extended to the boundary; it was not clear where one quarter ended and another began. But the two ends of the long thin village were sharply contrasted and expressed their rivalry in ceaseless jokes, in quasi-serious running down of each other to me, in the hiring of separate shepherds; they even spoke of fighting, though fighting between quarters is in fact fighting between lineages under another name.

Elbaşı had several recognised quarters, some actually called after lineages, others by geographical names – the lower quarter, and the *karakol* quarter (the *karakol* is the government building which housed the gendarmes). Once again the boundaries were not precise but the quarters were at least distinguished by the division of the village flocks between five shepherds. Fighting here was never spoken of in geographical terms but explicitly in lineage terms.

Even in Sakaltutan, the distance from one end to another was sufficient to discourage casual visiting between people at opposite ends, and in Elbaşı, kinship apart, people's close neighbourly relationships did not extend beyond a circle of nearby households.

Guest Rooms

Every household contains a living room but only the better off can afford a guest room. The full name of such rooms is *misafir odası*, guest room, but in practice the villagers simply call them *oda*, in contrast to *ev*, the women's part of the house. Traditionally, a guest room was a fairly large room with a built in *sedir* or divan but nowadays many households are building smaller guest rooms.

To possess a guest room of any kind is a mark of wealth and standing. They are normally built by craftsmen and hired labour, and in Sakaltutan, in 1950, a new *oda* was said to cost at least T.L.1,000 (£250, $700). Moreover, the owner must be able to provide fuel, either wood which is scarce and very expensive, or a plentiful supply of cakes of dung and straw, which depends on a fairly large household with surplus materials and female labour. The standard word for putting or keeping a guest room in use is *yakmak*, to burn or kindle.

A count of guest rooms is a little misleading because some of the better-off households had rooms built on the guest room pattern, that is with *sedir* and without *tandir*, but used them as a part of the ordinary household living space, as a room for a young married couple and their children, or for storage. Sakaltutan possessed roughly sixteen guest rooms in 1950, though several people wanted to build them, and by 1955 at least six new ones were in use. In 1949–50 the greatest number of these sixteen in use on one occasion was twelve. One large, old, guest room standing by itself was never used at all, and one or two of the others hardly ever. All were owned individually except the unused one which was owned by two brothers, and one other, an old one which was jointly owned by a lineage.

The guest rooms are used at any time of the year for special occasions such as weddings, meetings, and for entertaining important guests, and some also serve as the male part of the households to which they belong. But primarily, they are clubrooms for the village men. In autumn, as the evenings get chilly, the men retire to the guest rooms after their evening meal, which they take at sundown in the *ev*, or in their own guest room. They normally sit till the time of the last prayers, formally one and a half hours later. As winter draws in, work both in the village and in the towns grows less. More migrant labourers return to the village, and the guest rooms are used more and more, even in the daytime. In January and February, when conditions become really severe, men often sit all day, leaving only for meals, for the essential routine of feeding the animals and for any special business of their own.

Attendance at a guest room in mid-winter is the only alternative to sitting in one's own household with wife and children. Not only is this uncomfortable and undignified, it automatically cuts a man off from male company since his male kin and neighbours will not visit him at home. Men attend a guest room for warmth, company, and information, and they usually choose one close at hand. Most of them attend one particular guest room regularly. In Sakaltutan, a few used more than one according to daily inclination. Very few used none at all. Regular attendance has social implications, and for some, choosing a guest room may be a difficult matter.

I made no count of guest rooms in Elbaşı. The overall situation was similar. The wealthier households possessed guest rooms, the humbler and poorer ones on the whole did not. Few guest rooms seemed to be very old. One household at least possessed a guest room for the women to entertain in as well as for the men, but it was not used much. Hayip (B) whose rapid rise to wealth I have described, built a guest room before he built a new house. The tax collector's guest room, though small, was more elegantly furnished, and contained tables and chairs. But on the whole the provision and use of guest rooms was, in proportion, similar to that in Sakaltutan.

All over the Middle East, the guest room, or guest tent, is an important institution; attendance implies political submission to and support of its owner (Barth (1959) pp. 52 ff; Salim (1962) pp. 76 ff; Musil (1928) p. 66, etc.). To a lesser degree in these villages too, to accept a man's warmth day after day is to put oneself in his debt, and to admit his superiority in rank. The less a man is concerned about his rank and reputation, the more freely he accepts comfort where he can find it, and the more readily he switches allegiance. No one is ever barred from a guest room, and scarcely anyone fails to receive a full-scale greeting on arrival. Men of position or pride are more chary and may even prefer to attend nowhere rather than to accept regularly the hospitality, and implied superiority, of men they regard as equals or inferiors. Certainly, no one would enter the guest room of a man he regarded as an enemy except for specific and pressing business.

Guest Room and Gossip Groups

In the winter of 1949–50 in Sakaltutan, I went to the village guest rooms in rotation, and am able to give a fairly accurate analysis of the groups attached to particular guest rooms. Twelve were in use, though not all of them all the time. In all of them males from about nine or ten years of age and upwards came to sit, the young usually in silence; there is no strict lower age limit and I have seen baby boys and occasionally small girls of the household left in their father's care in the guest room. Older children usually, but by no means invariably, go to the same guest rooms as their fathers or father's brothers.

One may divide the people to be found in any guest room on any given occasion roughly into four classes: the members of the household, regular attenders from other households, occasional attenders whose presence or absence does not call for remark, and those whose presence is unexpected. These last may be paying a social call or they may have special business with one or more of the regular members.

Of course these four classes grade into one another along a continuous scale. In the following analysis I am concerned with the regular attenders. I begin with guest rooms serving mainly the household to which they belong and work towards the larger groups.

The guest room of Haci Ismet (T), after the first rush of visitors in November on his return from Mecca, was used only by the household. His two sons, and their sons, were often to be seen in the other more sociable guest rooms. Their own guest room was always warm because the old man was sick and could not leave it, yet no neighbours ever came to sit there.

The guest room of Abdullah (M) was used up to a point by members of his lineage though only occasionally. I have also seen his cross-cousin (mother's brother's son) in it, who is also his sister's widower, a man I have never seen in any other guest room except for strictly business reasons. There was no group centred on this guest room, and once when I visited it in mid-winter I found the whole household, women and girls as well, gathered in it, presumably in order to save heating. Two neighbours were also present.

Mehmet (M), Abdullah's father's brother's son's son, had his own small guest room and was a rare visitor to Abdullah's. His own, situated in the Lower quarter, drew more on neighbours than on kinsmen. One son of Ismet (T) visited occasionally – his sister was Mehmet's daughter-in-law. The members of K lineage also went there – Mehmet's recently deceased wife had been a member of K. The hostility between V lineage and M lineage barred members of V lineage. When, early in January, the guest room of K came into use, Mehmet's went out. One night I caused consternation by marching in to find it full of the women of the household. The sole revival of this guest room was during heavy rain in the spring thaw which flooded Nureddin's, making it suitable, as he remarked, 'only for ducks'.

Haci Ömer's (D) guest room, after the period of open house during November to celebrate his return from Mecca, was at first used by a small clientele consisting of some members of D and F lineages. In January the large and ancient guest room, the common property of the D lineage, was opened and Haci Ömer's lost its outside following. Because, I suspect, their pride would not allow them to accept others' hospitality, neither he nor his brothers and their sons went to sit in the other guest room.

Hüseyn (F) kept a guest room for his own use. Here one always found his companion and immediate neighbour Yahya (p. 149); and sometimes another neighbour, a member of K through his mother (p. 164), and Hüseyn's wife's sister's son; and a lonely old man, close neighbour but not kin. Hüseyn's own father's brothers' sons were often there.

Ziya (S) the carpenter, used his guest room as a work shop, and so it was always open and warm. Early in the winter a few neighbours, besides his brother, and their children would be found there. One was a cross-cousin, two others were unrelated; Yakup (p. 129) an occasional visitor was brother to the deceased wife of Ziya's deceased brother, whose orphan daughter lived with Ziya. The 'kindling' of the guest room next door by Ziya's father's brother's sons, Kemal and Süleyman, on their return to the village from work in the town, attracted these visitors away from Ziya's. The new company included also another young agnate, and one or two other occasional visitors. I never saw Kemal or Süleyman in Ziya's guest room, nor he in theirs, though his brother who more or less shared his household and his own sons were often there.

Very near to this guest room was that of Haci Osman (H). Several neighbours were regular visitors, including two agnates, but of his sisters' sons (p. 163), only the one he had adopted as a member of his own household. Between this group and that centring on the guest room of Kemal and Süleyman (S) there was some overlap. Moreover, besides these, many men of the Upper quarter came casually, including Ziya the carpenter himself, though none of them were close kin. Haci Osman's old mother of about ninety, and sometimes his wife were to be found in this guest room. They said nothing when the men were talking, and no one took the least notice of them except occasionally during the day when it was almost empty.

All these guest rooms were used as part of the household living space; male members of the household ate in them and the old men and unmarried boys slept in them. This was also the case with Zeynel's (G), which I shall discuss last, but less so with the other three.

The four remaining guest rooms all had larger and more regular attendances. One, belonging to an elderly member of V lineage, was used mainly by members of that lineage. Small, airless and lit not by a proper oil lamp, but only by a small one-candle-power lamp made locally out of petrol cans, it was nevertheless always crowded. Those of the lineage living at some distance did not use it. The households on the spot, on the other hand, attended regularly almost to a man. One young and two old men, close neighbours, but not kinsmen, were regular visitors. Before Nureddin's guest room opened several of the men from the Lower quarter also went there, especially members of K lineage. Ismet's son (T) was seen there, but on one occasion it was to play cards, on another to get advice from old Hamit (V) on his water buffaloes' constipation.

The communally owned D lineage guest room also had a very definitely lineage following. Hither came all members of D and their children, except for Haci Ömer and his brothers; and also one entire branch of F lineage, except for one man who lived some way off in the Lower quarter. This branch of F lineage was linked through maternal and marital ties to D. The only other guest room in which I ever saw any of these men was Haci Ömer's before their own opened. They explained that when they had done sufficient honour to the newly returned Haci Ömer they had moved because they were ashamed to use his hospitality night after night, because he was ill, and because they could not take their children there. They seemed to have very few occasional visitors.

By far the most crowded guest room in the village was Nureddin's which lay beyond the main road. This did not open in the autumn, because, after a disastrous harvest, no one could afford fuel, and there was much complaining about this. In January, enough fuel was contributed from various sources, and the room was put into use both as a social centre and as a shop. Here again the core of the regular attendance was the lineage, none of whom, after it was opened, went anywhere else, except rarely to play cards; but almost the whole of the Lower quarter was to be found in this guest room. It was not a grand building, and the village leaders never came, but those who did included heads of households which were not on speaking terms with each other, and many who were not related to each other or the owner. Ömer (G) often came here in preference to sitting with his agnates in Zeynel's (G) guest room, and so did the adult sons of a pair of brothers who themselves preferred Zeynel's.

Only four grown men in the village segment cut off by the road did not attend this guest room, apart from Hüseyn (F) who had his own. One never went to a guest room at all, though his own small guest room was not in use, and one went if at all to Hüseyn's. Two others went regularly to Zeynel's.

Only Zeynel's (G) guest room remains. His son was the headman during my stay, but except on one or two special occasions this made no difference to the composition of the group that met there. Only Ahmet (K), in his rôle as village scribe, went there frequently on official business, because the headman himself could neither read nor write. Only one of Zeynel's close agnates, Ömer (G), ever attended, and then irregularly. Two pairs of brothers, neither of very high standing, were closely related, one pair to Zeynel's wife, and the other to his son's wife. All were close neighbours. One other apparently unrelated neighbour dropped in occasionally. The remaining regular attenders consisted of three brothers from one end of the village and two men from the other, none of whom had more than tenuous kin ties with Zeynel, and all of whom had some distance to walk.

In some guest rooms the regular group is more sharply defined than in others. The D guest room for example was attended by three related lineage segments almost to a man. Any visitor would have been an outsider. In Haci Osman's guest room, or Nureddin's, people dropped in and out and a visitor was much less conspicuous. But all the guest room groups except Zeynel's were collections of people who were close kin or neighbours, or both. The Zeynel group puzzled me a good deal. Here the explanation seems to be negative. Some who were neither kin nor close neighbours went to this guest room because they felt even less welcome and less comfortable in any other, and the alternative, sitting evening after evening with the family, was grim. One guest room had to rank lowest and to collect the left-overs. The only guest room whose owner ranked lower in the village hierarchy was Nureddin, a less pretentious and more jovial character, whose guest room was organised in response to popular demand, and not on his private initiative for his own prestige or political purposes.

In the autumn of 1951 I attempted a similar enquiry in Elbaşı, but the number of guest rooms and room groups was greater, the time shorter, and the season not properly begun. I myself was still an object of curiosity, so that my arrival in a guest room drew in neighbours who would not otherwise have come; and I was still unable to identify everybody readily by sight.

Nevertheless, it is plain that a similar system operated, though with a larger margin of non-attenders, and a proportionately larger number of guest rooms in use, making for smaller groups. Five guest rooms appeared to draw mainly on five main lineages, but with varying degrees of completeness and varying numbers of other kin and neighbours. Several of the better-off villagers used their own guest rooms, but seldom had more than one or two visitors, some of them none. Some guest room affiliations were surprising, as in Sakaltutan, and again are probably due to personal reasons for avoiding hospitality in the guest rooms which they did not attend rather than for seeking hospitality in those which they did.

In Elbaşı some of the shops were rivals to the guest rooms. One or two shops were started in guest rooms. Conversely, a shop in a separate room of its own tended to draw a group of men together to chat, offering the advantages of warmth and shelter without the social implications of guest room hospitality.

In both villages similar groups met the whole year round. Once winter is over, everyone is busier, and the weather makes it possible and pleasant to sit out of doors. The guest rooms are left empty. People gather in the evenings, and even during the day, except at harvest time. But no hospitality is implied and it is easy to join or leave such a group. People choose a group near at hand. Moreover, whereas in the winter the young men and children attend in the guest rooms for the sake of warmth, and are expected to behave respectfully, as soon as the weather permits they prefer to form their own groups, according to distinctions of age.

In spite of the greater informality, the groups had recognised sites and a fairly steady membership. In Sakaltutan one such group formed in the Upper quarter, another in the central space by the headman's house, a third by the mosque, and a fourth at the roadside in the Lower quarter. I was not in Elbaşı at the right season to observe the corresponding groups. I would guess that in a larger, more heterogeneous, village the meetings are more casual still; and that some of the wealthiest men would keep their guest rooms open and use them all through the year. In the heat of the summer at this altitude guest rooms are cool by day and keep off the evening chill.

It is impossible to sort out of this complex data any simple principles of attachment to groups. The lowest and poorest were prepared to accept warmth and company more or less anywhere they could find it; the nearer home the better. People who regularly attended a guest room can be assumed to have friendly relations with the owner, and where a person avoids the guest room of a close kinsman or neighbour some hostility is probable. Large lineages normally congregate in the guest room of a senior member, and most of the larger guest room groups were built round a lineage core, though often outnumbered by neighbours, affines and other kin. Household heads of some pretension may prefer solitude in their own guest room, or even their living room, to accepting regular hospitality. Personal inclination and convenience had a lot to do with where people went; and only limited conclusions could be drawn from their guest room affiliations about their loyalties in village politics.

Violence

People, particularly the men, are quick to anger, and quick to draw knives or guns. Even the boys carry knives, and hardly any adult villager goes unarmed. On one occasion a twelve-year-old lad was brought into us with a severe cut across his fingers. He had attempted, exactly like his elders, to intervene between two comrades who had drawn knives in anger, and had caught one knife by the blade. This incident provided the villagers with a peg on which to hang public denouncement of the folly of village violence. I was to grow accustomed to these self-accusations of wildness, barbarity and trouble making, but the harangues seemed to make little difference to the realities of village life.

My nine months in Sakaltutan were comparatively peaceful, and I assumed at first that the one or two acts of violence of which I heard were exceptional. But over the years of which I have evidence the total number of acts of violence is considerable, and enquiries in other parts of Turkey lead me to suppose that it is not in any way untypical.

Among the men of Sakaltutan, from 1948 to 1955, fighting or assault with knives or guns took place on at least six occasions. Five people were wounded and one killed; and in addition one elderly woman died two weeks after an assault by another woman, but the court exonerated her attacker from murder. In nearby villages I heard by chance gossip of four deaths and two woundings in the years 1947 to 1950, without making systematic enquiries. Two different men to whom I was introduced by friends from Sakaltutan boasted to me of occasions on which they had killed in a quarrel.

In Elbaşı one killing and one wounding happened during the period of my field work there; the killing while I was present in the village. Fighting had taken place on apparently three occasions in the recent past, and one man had been knifed in the thigh. A boy was shot dead by his mother's brother's son (who was also an agnate), apparently by accident when they were playing with a rifle, but the family of the victim had refused to make peace and the killer's father had moved away from his own house to a cave in another part of the village to avoid vengeance.

No one regarded these events as abnormal, and the evidence I have supports the view that this rate of violence seems quite typical of the less suburban parts of rural Turkey.

In all these cases, except for the children's accident, people apparently used arms with the intent to kill. But of course quarrels of a less violent character happen constantly. The seriousness of a quarrel depends partly on the degree of violence which has been used, partly on the nature of the disagreement, and partly on the social distance between the two sides.

Feuds

The primary function of lineage groups, defence in quarrels, is no minor matter. Normally it is regarded as the duty of a man to side with his agnates on all occasions, and to be prepared if necessary to fight for them. People said that the two causes of lineage hostility which can never be settled are homicide and insults to women.

This violent hostility between lineages exists only within villages. In no case did the killings I have listed take place between villages. Sakaltutan had, it is true, been involved with a village near by in fighting over land on the border about two years before my arrival, but there had been no casualties. I heard of another case of inter-village fighting in the area, but had no details. It is possible that in the past such clashes were more frequent and people were killed. On the other hand, so long as each village had a smaller population and enough arable land and pasture to meet its needs, it is equally possible that fighting between villages as such was rarer.

Whatever may have been the case in the past, in 1950 to 1952 effective and serious long-term hostility was always between lineages of the same village, and on the rare occasions when men left their natal village for their wife's village they seem, *de facto*, to have shed their duties to their agnates and acquired quasi-agnatic rights and duties towards their wife's kin.

When two persons quarrel they are said to be *küs*. This word is constantly heard. On one occasion a grandmother left to cook and to mind her baby granddaughter while the rest of the household went out to harvest in the fields, remarked jokingly at the end of the day that she and the baby were *küs*. The dictionary meaning for this word is 'sulk', but this is too un-dignified a word. It implies the behaviour of Achilles in his tent, a formal breaking off of social relations, usually in the interests of honour. Its converse is the word for speaking together, *konuşmak*.

This formal state of hostility often exists for longer or shorter periods between individuals or households. A man may be *küs* with his parents-in-law, or husband and wife may be *küs* with each other. But if it is established between two normal non-kin households then the agnates on each side are likely to be involved.

No recognised machinery exists in the village for the settle-ment of such quarrels. It is always possible for people to decide to resume social relations, and this may be done simply by a single formal visit. Sometimes third parties with ties to both sides may attempt to bring them together. But if the matter in-volves violence or interference with the honour of a woman, then in theory no reconciliation is possible. Revenge is necessary to satisfy honour and in turn leads to further revenge. Not even time was recognised as a palliative. Even after fifty years, people said vengeance may still be exacted. This absence of machinery for reconciliation or compensation I found astonish-ing, and I made persistent enquiries with no success. In the short run at least the evidence seemed to support the village theory of implacability.

It is always the duty of bystanders to intervene to prevent violence; once moved to anger people will quickly resort to violence and must be prevented. On one occasion I myself lost my temper with a young lad, chased him across the village and punched him on the jaw. A large pack of villagers pursued me and laid hands on me for fear we should injure each other.

On another I was severely censured for not leaping to the defence of a wife who was being physically threatened by an angry husband. This pattern I saw repeated many times. It is the duty of everyone to prevent violence, even at considerable risk and even in intimate relationships.

I was explicitly told that if fighting breaks out between two lineages, then other lineages should intervene to stop it. One informant in Elbaşı denied this. As far as Elbaşı went he was at least realistic since, in the fighting reported there in the recent past, the whole village was split into two factions. But many others confirmed the traditional duty of intervention in the interests of peace even during a major clash. Yet such intervention is always *ad hoc*, and no formal or recognised procedure exists. It is unlikely to achieve more than the immediate separation of the contestants. The state of *küs* persists.

Vengeance likewise seems to lack a formal or recognised procedure. No one lays down even in theory who is responsible for carrying it out, or who is a proper victim of vengeance. On four occasions, two in each village, one of the principals in a dispute was the object of an attack, twice by day and twice by night. On one occasion the attacker was said to be unknown, but it seemed to be generally assumed that it was the man with whose son's betrothed the victim had eloped a year or two earlier. In the other three cases, the aggressor was also definitely a principal. Premeditated attacks on close agnates of the principals are said to be within the rules, but in fact they did not happen to my knowledge. On the other hand, if two lineages are in a state of *küs*, any minor quarrels involving members of the two sides will easily lead to fresh violence.

Feuding between lineages is a matter of years; in theory, of generations. Acts of violence are often separated by long periods of uneventful *küs*. It is therefore impossible to unearth reliable details in a stay of a few months, particularly as people are very unwilling to discuss quarrels and fights, and when they do talk, they give highly tendentious accounts. Even in Sakaltutan, in spite of considerable knowledge of the village people, I found the complexity of quarrels and alliances baffling.

The largest lineage in Sakaltutan, V lineage, had two quarels in progress, one with S lineage, and another with M lineage (pp. 162 ff.). Both were of long standing, and both produced violence soon after my departure from the village.

V and S were *küs* during my stay, and I heard a lot from each about the short-comings of the other. Bekteş (V) told me that, the year before, S lineage 'attempted to kill us', but I did not establish any clear details. In the summer of 1951 a plumber who was a member of S, was knifed on a building site in a city by a member of V. A young man of S was accused of having approached the wife of a young man of V. Next, according to his own account, the plumber advised an employer in Adana against employing a plasterer, without knowing that the man in question was from V lineage. When V lineage found out, they assumed the act was deliberate. They caught him on a site and knifed him in the stomach. The youngest amongst them confessed and received a light sentence because of his age. According to the story the blow was actually struck by another young man of a different lineage, whose father had been wounded in a fight with S in the village the year before. No further major violence had occurred between these lineages by 1955. S declared themselves to be willing to make peace but I doubt if this is to be taken seriously.

During my stay at the village V and M lineages were also *küs*. Both lineages used the K guest room, but no member of V lineage ever used either of the M guest rooms. Then at some point after I had left a young man of V 'insulted' the wife of a young man of M, perhaps in retaliation for some previous affront. Close young agnates of the household of the aggrieved young man attacked the house of the young man of V by night, and shot him in the jaw. Some time later, Durdu of V fell into a public dispute with a member of the other main M household. He went and fetched a gun, and was standing outside his opponent's house challenging him to come out, when another villager (T), not concerned but an affine of M lineage, came along and urged him to stop. Durdu, I was told, turned his gun on the newcomer but failed to release the safety catch. This brief delay enabled the intervener to draw his own gun in self-defence. He shot Durdu dead and duly went to prison for homicide. The day after the shooting the victim's daughter, who was married within her own lineage, beat up the mother of the man of M who had refused to come out. Two weeks later the woman died, but her assailant was subsequently exonerated by the courts. People said vaguely that Durdu's son might well take vengeance when he grew up.

Two cases from Elbaşı also illustrate lineage feuds; one of these involved the whole village and will be dealt with in the next section. The other was a purely limited lineage quarrel. The Z lineage were a well-knit and self-conscious group. But one household head, Melik, had quarrelled with the rest of the group at some time in the past and was *küs* with the lineage as a whole. He was next door neighbour to a poor member of B lineage, which figures in the major dispute described in the next section.

Melik made a window in a wall overlooking a patch of ground which belonged to his neighbour Hasan. Hasan allowed this to pass. Melik then made it into a door. Hasan objected, but Melik took no notice. Hasan collected his agnates, about a dozen young men, who 'surrounded' Melik's house, presumably intending to block up the doorway by force. Melik and his three grown sons opened fire from inside and the attackers withdrew. Some days later, Hasan chased Melik's eldest son, and shot him in the back. The victim recovered, the door was blocked up, and there the matter rested, except that Hasan himself was worse off than ever, since he was now compelled to remain in hiding in the village caves to avoid arrest by the gendarmes. For a specific affront, Hasan was able to collect most if not all of the younger members of his lineage, whereas Melik forfeited the support of his, because he had previously quarrelled with them, and was *küs*. Once the mass action which followed ended inconclusively, one principal set out premeditatedly with his gun to attack a principal on the other side. Why he took so drastic a step I do not know. Possibly after being driven off, he felt himself both publicly humiliated and in danger of losing his case.

In this institution we find many of the typical ideas and customs of the feuding situation: the solidarity of close agnates, the duty to seek revenge, the notion of honour, the importance of 'insults' to women for whom the men are responsible. Yet compared with many examples of feuding it is highly informal and unsystematic. In practice, not all agnates feel themselves committed; revenge is not necessarily specific or immediate; no system of compensation or reconciliation seems to exist and

9*

it is not precisely laid down who is and who is not involved. The system is similar to that found by Barth among the Kurds, and unlike that of the Arabs or of some African peoples. (Barth (1953) p. 74 f; Peters (1960) p. 31; Evans-Pritchard (1940 p. 150; Colson (1962) p. 106.)

After an act of homicide the tension is notably great. Those involved in a hot feud walk in daily fear of their lives. People said that men at enmity normally avoid each other's part of the village, and that in fact it is not easy to kill a fellow villager. My own observations indicate the direct opposite. As far as I can see nothing could be simpler than to surprise a man and shoot him, given that one is a close neighbour and that time is on one's side. I have recorded four attacks of this kind although admittedly only one was fatal.

It has been commonly argued that the existence of unsettled blood debts within a small community of this kind is intolerable. Evans-Pritchard, for example, says of the Nuer, 'a feud cannot be tolerated within a village', (Evans-Pritchard (1940) p. 159) and a similar argument is used by Colson (1962) p. 119 f. The argument, *a priori*, would seem to have equal weight when applied to these small, tightly-knit Turkish communities. Why does it not fit the facts?

The disorganised and unsystematic nature of the feud may itself provide an answer. Everyone fiercely insisted on the duty of revenge. But this may be indefinitely postponed. In the course of years the implacable may become less implacable. There is some evidence to show that after a time the offer of a woman in marriage to the victim's lineage to provide heirs to replace him, and to establish a political alliance may end the state of open hostility. Moreover, new quarrels are constantly happening. Each new generation is likely to see new elopements, new arguments about land, and so on. Old enemies may well find themselves on the same side. If every serious quarrel lasted for ever no lineage would be on speaking terms with any other. In fact, therefore, in time reconciliations must take place. In some cases a chain of killings may follow a homicide, but in others the threats do not materialise, and after a number of years social relations return to normal. People did not normally speak of wrongs done in past generations. It does not follow that they were not remembered, but if they were I am sure they would

252

be selectively remembered, that is, they would be remembered if they reinforced existing hostilities, and forgotten if they cut across existing alliances.

This argument assumes that the feuding situation has been steady for a long period. In fact the great extension of State interference and the recent improvement in police and judicial institutions can hardly have failed to alter the working of the feuds. The hypothesis that feuds such as I have described could not exist unresolved in small communities over long periods could be saved by arguing that in fact some more efficient means of settling village quarrels existed in the past but has disappeared. It would seem improbable that a highly formal machinery would be forgotten, but shifts in power could have some effect as I have myself suggested elsewhere (Stirling (1960) pp. 73, 74).

One fact undoubtedly favours this view. The increased efficiency of the government has greatly decreased the autonomy of the village communities, and has weakened the strength of their indigenous leaders. It is therefore conceivable that, in the past, it was more often possible to forestall serious quarrels, and also to bring more pressure for settlement on feuding lineages. But it is impossible to prove this, because no evidence exists which could provide an accurate measure of violence in the villages in the past, or a detailed analysis of political relations between villagers.

Instead of arguing that the present situation is *a priori* improbable and cannot therefore represent a stable state, it is also possible to re-examine the *a priori* argument itself. The argument as presented by Colson (1953), and expanded by Gluckman (1956) Chap. I, is an economic one: the daily supply of food depends on co-operation, and a state of hostility calling for homicide renders this co-operation impossible. In the Turkish village, on the contrary, supplies of staple foods are stored in each household behind stone walls and locked doors, and even animals can be cared for for short periods without co-operation. In any case a feud between two lineages does not prevent the member households on both sides sending their animals to the same village herdsmen. Further, within a state armed with police and a system of justice, however remote from the village, the village is not a political unit in the way Nuer or

Tonga villages were political units. Segments of a village can maintain hostility over long periods without destroying the political system because this does not depend on village unity. The danger that one's enemies will attempt murder makes life difficult, but in practice even this applies only to the principals of the feud, and these usually absent themselves, or are in gaol, or move to another part of the village and take special precautions. A fresh quarrel is always possible, but in a quarrel everyone is, or pretends to be, sure he can look after himself. Feuds therefore may be exceedingly unpleasant to live with, but they do not render life impossible.

To sum up then, every village contains a number of active lineages involved in blood feuds with other lineages of the same village. In theory, vengeance is mandatory and the feud unresolvable. In practice some cases of feud are allowed to die out, and reconciliation is possible, often by giving a woman in marriage. Often a relationship of hostility depends on chance incidents for its continuance, though in fact it makes these incidents more probable. But an absence of incidents may in time permit social relationships to be re-established. Moreover, new quarrels are likely in time to set up new alignments in the village which may force people to make allies of their old enemies.

The Headman

One of my surprises during my first visits to Turkish villages was the youth of the headmen I met. I had expected the headman to be the most senior and powerful man in the village, yet I met few headmen over forty and several much younger. The turnover in headmen was high. The term of office was four years before 1950, when it was reduced to two. Many failed to last it out; I only ever knew one man who took a second term. The reasons for all this became obvious. The headman was no longer the top of the village but the bottom of the official State hierarchy. It was not a pleasant position to hold.

The headman's immediate senior in the hierarchy was the District Officer, *Nahiye Müdürü*, a high school graduate who shared the values and prejudices of the educated governing class. The headman, who was often illiterate, belonged himself to the traditional society of the village. His main concern was to keep out of trouble both with his superiors and with his neighbours. Since some of his legally imposed duties were complex, and some unpopular, this was very difficult.

The headman's duties were in theory very numerous; a few of them were either inescapable or important, or both. He was supposed to report any trouble in the village and any strangers who could not give a good account of themselves. He was also supposed to see that the Registrar was informed of all births, deaths and marriages. He was responsible for seeing that conscripts answered the call to the army. Any special jobs fell on his shoulders, for example, the preparing of the village register of voters for the 1950 election. The headman in Sakaltutan had on one occasion to renumber all the houses in the village, extracting 10 *kuruş*, (about 3d.), from each unwilling household for a useless tin number plate.

He was expected to receive and assist all official visitors to the village – medical officers, court officials, veterinary officers, tax collectors, agricultural officials and so on. On these occasions he usually served food, and sometimes had to provide a bed. In return for this duty he received an allowance, decided by the village, towards the cost of entertaining. Perhaps his most unpopular task was the collection of dues to the village chest. This fund he was supposed to collect, supervise, spend and account for to higher authority. The collection was extremely difficult; he was invariably accused by the villagers of eating it himself; and even if not actually illiterate he was unlikely to be unable to keep accounts, and was thus in permanent danger of trouble from above.

The official policy was to recruit young men as headmen. Plainly a literate, sophisticated young man, if one could be found, would do the job better. The most suitable young men in the village were the migrant craftsmen, whose visits to town gave them the chance to use their literacy and learn something about townsmen. But they were unwilling, indeed unable, to bind themselves to stay permanently in the village as the headman was required to do.

The job was unpopular. Yet it did bestow advantages, particularly that of direct contact with the authorities. Not only was the headman the official channel for his neighbours but his privilege of receiving all officials in his guest room enabled him to hear official news first, and also to establish personal contacts which might be useful later, even after his term of office.

Leading villagers did not want to be headmen; but they did want to be able to control the headman, and to entertain important guests. Thus one found that the headman was usually a young member of a substantial village household, or the nominee of the head of such a household. Without such support a young headman could not entertain. I knew a considerable number of headmen, and most of them fitted this pattern. In Sakaltutan there were three headmen during my field work. The first was the adopted son of Haci Osman (H) (p. 103); the second was the son of Zeynel (G) (p. 243); and the third belonged, by an accepted affiliation, to the lineage of Haci Ömer (D), and used his guest room. His rival at the election, and others mentioned as possible candidates in the village, all fitted into the same pattern. All were under forty.

The headman in Elbaşı in 1951–52 was the youngest of four brothers who used a common guest room that formally belonged to the eldest. These four were the leaders of Ay lineage (p. 165), and also of one of the two village factions. All were comfortably off. The eldest had had some experience as a building contractor, and the headman himself had had a share in a village lorry, and at the time had an interest in a hotel in Ankara, in common with a partner from a neighbouring village.

The headman in Sakaltutan never to my knowledge exercised authority except in so far as his neighbours recognised that he as headman had to take official responsibility. On one occasion a woman was struck with a piece of iron by a neighbour and kinsman. The headman was called but decided to do nothing. If a stranger arrived in the village the headman would automatically be sent for, or failing him, his deputy, to entertain the guest, though sometimes, if the guest was worth capturing, anyone with an adequate guest room might invite him in before the headman arrived on the scene.

The headman of Elbaşı made rather more attempts to assert his authority. Near the harvest time the village shepherds came to him daily for instructions on pasturing their flocks, and he also supervised the activities of the field watchmen. I came across him, on one occasion, in the middle of an altercation with a fairly wealthy agnate, a man on his own side in the village quarrels. Two of this man's animals had been found among the crops and impounded, and the headman refused to release them unless he paid a small fine for each beast. When he paid one fine and received only one beast the man grew really angry but the headman stood his ground. On another occasion I found him in his guest room trying to mediate in a disputed case of inheritance (p. 129). I was compelled to admire his sagacity when I found him sitting in the headquarters of the Credit Co-operative, beside the manager, collecting the village dues from each man as he received his annual loan. With a bundle of notes in his hand, it was impossible even for a villager to argue that he had not got the money.

In general the headman of a Turkish village exercises no more influence, outside his specific duties as headman, than he exercises before and after being headman. The exceptional efficiency of the Elbaşı headman was due to his standing in the village as an individual. In any crisis the only advantage the headman has is the opportunity to act as government contact man, but in purely village matters his office lends him no extra weight.

Leaders in Sakaltutan

In every village a few men have greater wealth, greater outside contacts, and greater internal influence than the rest. Generosity is expected of them. The less fortunate are bound to look to them for help and support, and to offer in return deference and perhaps political support. The terms patron and client hardly apply where an open etiquette of equality is carefully maintained, and where many households are self-sufficient and can cope with their emergencies by the exchange of reciprocal services with equals. No formality attaches to relationships of dependents, but nevertheless, openly or covertly, vaguely defined followings do attach to certain leading men.

Both Elbaşı and Sakaltutan were divided in this way into two groups. In both villages the rich helped the poor with special problems such as wedding hospitality and loans of food or cash, presents at festivals and so on. In Sakaltutan however, the violent lineage hostilities cut across these groups, which were centred on a mild rivalry between two leading men. In Elbaşı on the other hand, the split was sharper, more violent, and, with complicated exceptions, lineage quarrels coincided with what may be fairly called the village factions which I shall discuss in detail in the next section.

Two men stood out in Sakaltutan; Haci Ömer (D) and Haci Osman (H). They were openly on good terms, and had been companions on the journey to Mecca in the autumn of 1949. But they very seldom visited each other. I had the impression that in 1950 Haci Ömer was more accepted as village leader than Haci Osman, but he was a sick man. He did not normally give definite orders, although on one occasion, in the absence of the headman and against his wishes, he ordered the watchman to make a public announcement about the government distribution of seed.

Haci Osman was a fitter and wealthier man. He wisely made a point of saying that he was a man of peace, and was always gentle and pious as became a pilgrim to Mecca, a genuine Haci.

He cultivated a collection of sisters' sons. He had two in the Upper quarter who had been away from the village for a long period, one for a year and the other for four years. He made the long journey to Izmir in person to find them and bring them back. Three other sisters' sons lived in the Lower quarter. When one of them lost his wife Haci Osman helped financially and personally in the attempts to find a replacement. When he was one of a syndicate which organised the building of a diesel mill in the village, this man and his younger brother were employed first as building labourers; later as millhand and mechanic. Haci Osman's sister's daughter's husband was Ömer (G). Ömer and his six sons, three of them grown up, were on excellent terms with him and called him *dayı*, (mother's brother). In the winter of 1949–50 most of these sisters' sons went not to his guest room but to Nureddin's (K) in the Lower quarter. Although technically they all had rights to some of the land on which his wealth and influence was based, none of them showed any signs of raising this embarrassing subject publicly.

Plenty of people in the village belonged to neither following. Several men were more or less their equals in standing, and others were prepared to befriend both sides. They were not

overtly hostile to each other, and very few issues arose to divide
the village. Indeed, only once during my stay was the village
split, and then fairly peacefully and casually.

The occasion for this was the election for headman which
took place in 1950. For the first time ever the headman was to
be chosen, not by confabulation between the leading men, but
by a formal democratic election. Two candidates stood,
Nureddin (K) from the Lower and Ibrahim (D) from the
Upper quarter. Neither had a close elder kinsman to provide
entertainment and a guest room for official visitors and village
business, and hence Nureddin was backed by Haci Osman, his
father's brother's wife's brother, and Ibrahim by Haci Ömer,
a not very close pseudo-agnate. Both candidates repeatedly
declared their unwillingness to stand at all, and no one involved
regarded the matter as one of much importance. When Ibrahim resigned after a year in office, it was, by an electoral
accident, Ömer (G), Haci Osman's sister's daughter's husband,
who succeeded.

These two men then were no more than the most influential
among their neighbours. They were not in sharp rivalry, and
neither held any office nor exercised any sanctions which gave
them power to coerce unwilling villagers. Sakaltutan was conspicuous for the absence of authority.

Factions in Elbaşı

Elbaşı resembled Sakaltutan in the absence of a single source
of authority armed with coercive sanctions, and in the independence and neutrality of many households. Some of the
leaders were further removed in wealth and power from the
village poor and more inclined to issue orders. Instead of two
leaders one could name some eight or nine, or more, according
to the criteria used. The situation was more complex than that
of Sakaltutan, and I had less time to unravel it.

In one way Elbaşı was sharply different from Sakaltutan.
The village was seriously split, and fighting had taken place
more than once in the years immediately before my visit. I
failed to realise fully the importance and nature of this split at
the time of the field work, and the account which follows is
partly based on deduction and interpretation. The detailed

arguments to support it have already been published in a much fuller account (Stirling (1960) pp. 63–9).

I have already (p. 145) spoken of the pre-eminence in the village of Kara Osman (Ax). This man had taken over a great deal of fertile irrigated land, belonging formerly to the next village, and had become pre-eminent in the area, not merely in the village. I met him first in 1949 in Sakaltutan. Sometime during or after the war others had begun taking over village pasture on a large scale. The eldest son of Hayip (B) (p. 144) had been headman about 1946: a fact undoubtedly related to the extent of his father's land at the time of my field work. B lineage had been allied to Ax the lineage to which Kara Osman belonged. Hayip's son was, it seems, deposed on charges of misuse of his office. The two headmen who followed him were opponents of Ax, and during this period several fights seem to have taken place. The main issue was the taking over of yet more village pasture for private arable land. On this issue the faction opposed to Kara Osman eventually won the day with the support of the government authorities. Kara Osman himself died in 1950. When I reached the village it was divided into two camps, Ay leading one and controlling the headmanship, and Ax backed by B leading the other. There had been further fighting at the election of the headman in 1950.

While I was in the village two interesting events took place. A senior member of Ax betrothed his daughter to the son of a senior but slightly marginal member of Ay. At the same time the factional dispute became entwined with a personal quarrel. Yusuf, a young man of Ax, had quarrelled with a young wife at the fountain, and struck her. This girl was a sister of the four leading men of Ay, one of whom was headman. Her husband Mehmet (C), away on military service, was the son of a leading member of C lineage; his father had given him in infancy to a childless brother. Mehmet had inherited a house and lands from his mother by adoption, and was a close neighbour of his wife's four brothers (Ay). The quarrel on this occasion led to general fighting, but no one was hurt. When the husband Mehmet returned from military service he is said to have threatened dire action to avenge the insult to his wife. His opponent Yusuf clearly took these threats seriously, as well he might.

At this time the betrothal ceremony for the wedding between Ax and Ay was celebrated. Yusuf was father's brother's son to the bride, and though engaged himself to a daughter of Hayip (B), he took upon himself to intervene with the traditional and forceful protest; he fired shots over the heads of the departing guests (Salim, (1962) p. 50).

He declared that he would stop the wedding at all costs, but the parties showed no signs of being cowed. Three days later, close to sundown, in the centre of the village, he drew a gun and shot Mehmet at short range. Mehmet died a few minutes later. Yusuf fled, under fire, to be arrested in another village. This act separated the two sides again; or rather it created a new split, between C lineage and Ax. Up to this point C lineage had not been involved. People said that reconciliation was impossible, and revenge sooner or later certain. Yet by 1955 nothing further had happened; the two original sides Ay and Ax were more or less reconciled, and the wedding had taken place. But C lineage maintained an attitude of general non-co-operation, and remained hostile (*küs*) to Ax.

This case illustrates a number of points. First, it is perfectly normal for a village to have a definite split into two factions. In one other village I was told that one large lineage had the previous year, 1948, fought the whole of the rest of the village, again over the headmanship. One man was killed. But as far as I could judge from the outside, most other villages in the area were more like Sakaltutan in having a complex structure of rivalries and loyalties which did not easily break down into two sides.

Secondly, it illustrates the possibilities of settlement, and the much tougher problem presented once a death has taken place. Thirdly, it illustrates the way in which an incident between members of already hostile lineages can lead to serious trouble. And finally, it makes it clear how difficult it is to sort out personal fear and resentment, notions of personal and lineage honour, and factional struggles for power in the village.

Disputes

The interweaving of village matters and personal quarrels in this story illustrates some of the typical disputes that arise in a community of this kind. The stream is constant. Children fight, buffaloes fight, young men are accused of showing interest in, or insulting girls, debts are said to have been unpaid, favours are unreasonably refused. The most lasting of these disputes are those concerning women, and those concerning land.

The villages themselves say, and it seems to be *a priori* probable, that in the past the village was more able to deal with its own internal troubles. Though not generally held for life, the headmanship was traditionally an office of some power and importance, and the headman was able to bring pressure on disputants and to punish offenders.

Disputes over women stand apart. Interference with a man's womenfolk calls for violence, and arbitration or litigation are beside the point. Adultery may lead to murder but not to recognised claims for restitution or compensation. In a sense the word dispute itself is inappropriate. If people feel strongly enough they will act; otherwise the matter remains unsettled. In either case it is a possible source of future trouble.

Nowadays a young headman carries no weight as an arbitrator, still less as a judge. He has no coercive sanctions at his command nor the necessary prestige or skill. Among the senior men no one holds any recognised office, and no one normally stands out as an acceptable arbiter. Thus the village lacks any internal machinery for the settlement of disputes except the informal pressures of neighbours and the self-interest of the parties, which sometimes lead to negotiation and a formal reconciliation. On the one occasion on which I found the headman of Elbaşı attempting to arrange peace between the heirs of a recently deceased villager, he had no great success (p. 129). His only weapon was the argument that failure to reach agreement would be to the disadvantage of all.

Under the Village Law (p. 271) the headman has the right to settle disputes up to a certain value (in 1950 T.L.50 equivalent to about £6, $18) in collaboration with the Council of Elders (p. 31). In theory he could use the coercive sanctions of the State to insist on this right. In practice no headman in his short term of office is likely to be foolish enough to call in State sanctions against kinsman and neighbours among whom he has to live out his days; if he is already so powerful in the community that he can do so with impunity, he would not need to.

Above the headman the District Officer and the Kaymakam also have authority to settle disputes of a limited value *ad hoc*, subject to the right of the disputants to appeal to the courts. I have no record of an actual case in either of the villages but I am assured that such cases occur fairly frequently, and I did sit in on an informal hearing of such a case in another village. This procedure allows a wise official to make decisions on the basis of village public opinion, and to ignore strictly legal arguments which often do not coincide with equity. But on the whole, though many disputes do come to the authorities and even to the courts, a very much larger number of disputes simply remain unsettled.

Formerly land was freely available for cultivation (pp. 134 ff.), and in those days disputes about land must have been far less frequent. But as soon as land becomes short and cash-cropping normal, it is plainly prudent to establish rights to land whenever possible. Claims were constantly made on a wide range of grounds. Traditionally sales of land took place between kin and even neighbours, but transfers were never registered and the village assumed that the vendor had the right to buy the land back for the purchase price whenever he chose. In an inflating economy people make frequent use of this right, usually demanding the land back, as a cover for obtaining a further payment to match the increased money value of the land. Others claimed that land was originally lent to kin as a favour, sometimes in return for an annual gift or on a share-cropping basis. Cultivators counter-claim that the original gift or sale was outright, or sometimes that since the dues paid on the land exceed its value they have acquired it by purchase. The varieties of argument are endless and the facts exceedingly difficult to establish.

This growth in the frequency of disputes has coincided with the weakening of the village's own political system brought about by increased governmental interference. A large number of grievances and disputes over land simply remain unresolved, and possession is usually ten-tenths of the law.

It does not follow that in the past the village authorities settled disputes efficiently or finally. Although marginal land was once freely available it is highly probable that the village has always been full of claims and counter-claims, and that what land a household has been able to control, at any given point, has depended at least as much on the balance of village power as on recognised rights.

The village then is full of unresolved disputes. The strong are safe so long as they are strong. Now that violence is suppressed with ever increasing efficiency by the State, and straight filching or recovery of land by force is well-nigh impossible, most claims simply lie dormant. In the past disputes were settled by strength, either the relative strength of the contenders, or in some cases, the perhaps slightly less partial strength of the village leaders. Not, of course, that recognised rights had no moral weight. The ability to mobilise strength depends at least to some degree on public approval and acceptance. A reputation for impartiality and respect for others' rights is often one element in the strength of the leaders. But nevertheless the weak had no guarantee, and even nowadays strength and wealth carry their own moral justification, and usually have things their own way.

Order

The village as I have described it is a collection of households of different degrees of strength, wealth and prestige, living together in close intimacy, and with enough co-operation and mutual tolerance not only to survive, but to form a strong and stable community. Yet it lacks any effective formal structure of authority, and any undisputed informal leadership. In spite of the truculent independence of most respectable household heads, the existence of innumerable unsettled disputes and quarrels, and constant jockeying for influence and prestige between the leading households, the village leads an orderly life; people are constantly visiting, helping, advising, co-operating and intermarrying.

This calls to mind the paradox, 'ordered anarchy' (Evans-Pritchard (1940) p. 181), applied to a very different society. The order in fact depends on diffuse or informal sanctions: reciprocity, self-help and public opinion. People can only enjoy the help, social intercourse and friendliness they need if they offer help, social intercourse and friendliness to others. They are tied to each other by all kinds of relationship; by agnatic, non-agnatic and affinal kinship, by share-cropping, by loans and credits, by the generosity of the rich and the deference of the not-so-rich, by sharing shepherds, by common occupations, by employing or working for each other. Offensive conduct in one of these relationships may dislocate others. Any quarrel will not only affect the principals but will pull apart other people in other relationships; pairs of friends are always liable to be divided by new disputes among other friends or kin. Behind good behaviour lies the knowledge that to give offence, at least to those more powerful and intransigent than oneself, is to invite trouble. And no one who is tied for life to a small community by economic and social bonds of land-holding, family and kinship, wants to invite its scorn or ridicule.

Outside and above this local order stands the State, with its overwhelming superiority in force. The State should be able to intervene not only to put down major breaches of the peace but also to right the minor wrongs of the weak; to correct the defects of the village's own rough and ready system. As things stand, it does the first effectively, but it cannot do the second; in spite of a weakening of village coherence and of the strength of internal authority, the village still maintains its own order within itself more or less independently of the State.

CHAPTER TWELVE

THE VILLAGE AND THE WORLD

The Urban-Rural Divorce

Villagers live in a national society, which they share with people far wealthier, far more educated, far more powerful than they are themselves. In Turkey this wealthier and more powerful section of the society lives almost exclusively in towns. The villages are dependent economically on the national economy and formally subordinate to the administrative and party political machinery of both local and national government; and they are well aware of their dependence and subordination. Yet they have comparatively little to do with these people who control their existence, and see only a tiny proportion of them. Moreover, most urban people know little about the villages and fill the gap of their ignorance with unshakeable misconceptions. In a country where four-fifths of the people live in villages, where government expects and is expected directly to control the economic life and the general welfare of these four-fifths, and where they have the vote, these misconceptions have interesting consequences.

One of the most often repeated statements about Middle East society is that town and countryside are completely divorced. Yet obviously both sides are dependent on each other economically and politically, and the rulers must have a machinery for enforcing their rule, a machinery whose complexity and efficiency grows with the growth of the functions of government. All this implies considerable and complex social relationships. What is it then that people who assert the divorce of town and country wish to say? Firstly, they are struck by the great difference between relations between Middle East intellectuals and the countryside and the corresponding relations in Western

Europe, even those before the industrial revolution. Secondly, they are struck by the wide cultural differences between the westernised and sophisticated Turks of Ankara and Istanbul, the ones the foreigner meets, and the pious, hospitable, often illiterate villagers. Thirdly, they see that often, as I have said, the city dwellers really know nothing, unless it is a little romanticised folk-lore, about the actual life of the villages.

But none of this justifies the simple theory of the two separate worlds. Officials and orders reach the villages in an ever-increasing stream, and villagers visit towns for business, to find work, to make purchases and to sell their goods, and even to seek entertainment, also in an ever-increasing stream. A few even move to towns and marry with townsfolk. The question to be asked is not whether or not town and village are divorced, but how the significant relationships between them work.

The frequency of face-to-face contact through visits is one important measure of urban/rural contact. But it is quite possible for the town to be dominant in shaping village ways of thinking, and symbols of prestige, and even the village social structure, without great frequency of face-to-face contact, without the village being a direct imitation of the town, and without the town knowing much about the village. The most frequent contacts of the villagers are with the lowest ranks of town society; those which affect the village most profoundly are with the top.

The Government in the Village

The traditional Ottoman government, like most pre-industrial governments, was concerned with two main tasks: the maintenance of order, and the collection of taxes. For both, armed forces were indispensable, and were maintained by the taxes they helped to collect. Both also required a political hierarchy, a bureaucratic organisation and, at least in the towns, legal and judicial institutions. To the peasants such a government is a kind of legitimate robber, legitimate because of the superior social rank of its agents, and justified because it is ordained by God. Political obedience and loyalty is owed not to a social entity, the Empire, nor to specific officials, but to a remote individual, the Padishah.

The War of Independence created for the first time a Turkish nation state, demanding a new loyalty. Many villagers even today speak of this war as a religious conflict, a victory of Islam over infidels, but the Turkish government does now symbolise to the villagers a social entity to which they belong, their nation among the other nations. Nevertheless it is still seen as a legitimate robber and arbitrary interferer in village life.

The Republic added a new function to government; a concern with welfare, a duty to help and care for the people. In so far as such ideas existed at all at the centre in Ottoman governments, they were largely ineffective, and even under the Republic the new function took time to show any concrete effects. But now the state provides a great many benefits: roads, schools, waterworks, credit, seed, stud animals, public health and medical services, hospitals, factories, and so on, and people expect the government to do things for them. Sometimes, of course, what the government regards as welfare the village regards as wanton interference – forestry control, for example.

These government benefits are not seen as conferred by an impartial machine. No villager doubts that officials are all primarily interested in their own advantage. With some notable exceptions they are right; most officials in all bureaucracies are necessarily more concerned with their relationships to their immediate superiors than with anything else. For the villagers it follows that one has to please officials personally in order to get them to use their powers on one's behalf. And it is largely true that in order to get things done in Turkey it is best to use personal contacts.

The relations between village and hierarchy were greatly complicated by the introduction of party politics. Before about 1946 party and government were identified. Most villagers were more or less indifferent or ineffectively hostile to the Ataturk reforms. Some co-operated more actively than others. It was, for example, taken for granted that all officials, headmen, schoolmasters and so on had to be, at least outwardly, party supporters. The appearance from 1946 onward of a legitimate opposition party campaigning in the villages, and then the subsequent change of ruling party in 1950, confused the issue. The villager assumed that a system of rival political patronage was about to be introduced. Party and government were still to a large extent regarded as one. Stories were current immediately after the election about Republican People's Party supporters losing official jobs. It is more significant that these stories circulated and were believed than that, in many cases, they were founded on fact.

From the government end, once elections had become politically important, winning village votes became a major aim of policy. Very noticeably, after 1950, officials in villages became more polite, more concerned to please, more willing to discuss village needs and desires, and less peremptory and paternalistic. In other words, to the rôles of maintainer of law and order, legitimate robber and arbitrary universal provider, the government added that of vote catcher.

Peace, Tax and Conscription

A sergeant and four gendarmes (p. 11) were stationed in Elbaşı to control seventeen villages. Sakaltutan was over four hours' walk, and in 1950 a good hour by car or lorry, from Talas where their gendarmes were stationed. Most villagers possess firearms. Yet the gendarmes are able to intervene to end fighting, to arrest murderers when they can find them, to enforce sequestration of property and so forth. The villagers are armed against each other, not against the gendarmes, and respect the forces that they represent rather than their four rifles. They have no direct quarrel with the state as such.

In 1949–50 the villagers had to pay considerable animal taxes, a small land and house tax, and in addition every adult male had to pay a 'road tax' of T.L.12 a year, in effect a poll-tax. The Democrat Party abolished the road tax and the animal tax; the land tax, being a fixed proportion of a 1939 valuation, had become negligible by the operation of inflation, so that farming was left, and remained until 1961, virtually untaxed. But even in 1949 the tax collectors, unwelcome as they were, were treated with reasonable cordiality. I knew two while in Sakaltutan. Both were willing to give the villagers as much latitude as they reasonably could, but both claimed not to be fooled by village pleadings, and both were prepared, indeed I suppose forced, to take measures to distrain on property as a last resort. No one ever suggested they were corrupt or corruptible – a remarkable fact, since accusations of this kind are easily and frequently made. The villagers showed no personal resentment.

Every man was called up at the official age of eighteen for service in the army or the gendarmerie. The responsibility for seeing that those called reported for duty rested on the headman. Some people sought to evade conscription by not registering the birth of sons, many to postpone it by registering it late. Some young men evaded the summons by going away, for shorter or longer periods, to take casual labour in the towns. Official postponement was granted in certain circumstances. But on the whole everyone did his military service and most young men looked forward to it. Those who had served remembered it with pride as an exciting and interesting period of their lives. Military attitudes were common. The villagers gave the sergeants and officers of the gendarmerie military respect; they called villagers who had become sergeants or corporals by these titles for the rest of their lives; they played soldiers at wedding festivities; they frequently gloried in Turkey's military record, and in their national prowess in Korea. Ataturk's official policy of firmly separating the military and the political functions had had little effect on the village view of government. Officials visiting the villages were given quasi-military respect, and they discussed with anxiety the dangers of exchanging the soldier Ismet Inönü, hero of the War of Independence, for the banker Celal Bayar, in 1950, as Head of State and ex-officio Supreme Commander of all national armed forces.

Undoubtedly military service was a major cause of the village's unquestioned identification with the national state, and a source, through indoctrination, of glory in Turkey's achievements. Almost all had an opportunity to see more of Turkey, and a few learned literacy and technical skills. None of this, in 1950 to 1952, made any great impact on village life.[1]

The Law

Villagers frequently talk about law, *kanun*, usually in the course of explaining institutions or behaviour, or in arguments about rights. These references imply a finality; the law is the

[1] Robinson and Lerner (1960) pp. 34–36 take a more positive view.

law and that is that. On the other hand they know that the law is often ignored in the villages, and are not impressed when an opponent uses law as an argument. '*Kanun manun yok köyde*, there is no law and all that stuff in the village' one of the men of Sakaltutan once remarked.

In fact, of course, the law affects the villages profoundly and in many ways. The main obvious impact is threefold. First, administrative law and regulations, and especially the Village Law, sets out the formal arrangements for village institutions and for relations between village and state. Secondly, the villagers are frequently charged in the criminal courts, mainly for breaches of the peace and acts of violence. Thirdly, rights to land can only be finally decided by the civil courts. As I have shown (p. 209) the effect of those parts of the Civil Code that govern marriage and the family have at present almost no bearing on the village.

All bureaucratic and political institutions are shaped by law, even though what happens never corresponds exactly to the intentions of the legislator, or even to the provisions of the law. The impact of general constitutional and administrative law on the village is relatively indirect; but one law does directly shape village formal institutions. The Village Law (No. 442), of March 1924 (Robinson, (1949) letter 24) was one of the earliest acts of the Republic. With a few important exceptions the law is remarkable for its irrelevance. It serves rather as a document of the attitudes to the villages of a paternalistic ruling class than as the legal basis of village organisation.

After a section defining a village and laying down regulations about boundaries, the second chapter contains two lists, one of things villages must do, and one of things which villages may choose to do, with legal power to coerce defaulters. This first list contains thirty-seven items, including such matters as the building of a covered drain, the type of privy to be used, the building of two village streets to cross in a village square, the separation of all living-rooms from stabling by a wall, the construction not only of a school but of a mosque, the proper maintenance of the land and property of orphans by the village authorities. It is even forbidden to tire animals unnecessarily.

The list of permitted activities, thirty-one items long, includes the setting up of various trades in the villages, the provision of books, help for the poor, and the organisation of sport. The law then proceeds to detail methods of election of the *muhtar*, headman, and the council of elders, *ihtiyar heyeti;* the sources, uses, and administrative control of village funds; the settlement of disputes in cases involving up to T.L.50; the arrangement for village watchmen and for a village imam; and a few miscellaneous details, including the requirement that the law itself should be posted publicly in every village and learned by heart by every village child.

This law is almost wholly ignored in the villages which I knew. The election of a headman and a council of elders, and the appointing of a watchman are enforced by the administration and are carried out. Boundaries are in fact registered. The headman's duties to arrest criminals and to question any stranger who appears in his village are known and enforced. But for the rest the law is a dead letter. The few points of the law that the village carries out, it carries out from custom, and not because they are in the law. I have never heard anyone in Turkey raise the question of the village using its powers under the law to enact local regulations. Even the District Officers did not give the impression of knowing the contents of the law. They did not even use it, as they could easily have done, to bring pressure on the village by threatening to enforce its more awkward prescriptions. In fact no one I met seemed to know more about it than that it existed.

Most prosecutions of villagers before the criminal courts are for assault or violence, and on the whole sentences are light. On one occasion the topic of Kayseri jail came up in the course of a guest-room conversation. Almost all the seven or eight men present had had experience of it, all for breaches of the peace. They complained of the discomfort, especially the sanitation, but prison has no social stigma, and a short sentence is a trivial matter. The social sanctions within village society which require a man to be intransigent and virile are incomparably stronger than the state sanctions against violence and disorder. Young men generally receive lighter sentences than older men, so young men are encouraged to carry out any necessary lineage business of a violent sort. Sometimes they are put up on false evidence to answer for the acts of their elders.

Under the Turkish Civil Code, as under the Swiss Civil Code

on which it is based, legal rights to land depend on a cadastral register. In Turkey no cadastre exists, and though registration deeds exist, in rural areas they are seldom up to date or complete (p. 51). Many villagers have expanded their cultivated holdings at the expense of the village pasture (p. 135) but they are in no hurry to register new holdings and thus incur tax; indeed, strictly, they cannot do so since the land only becomes legally theirs after twenty years of undisputed possession. Hence a legal title to land is often, indeed usually, very difficult to establish. The complications are greatly increased by the *ad hoc* nature of village settlements of inheritance (pp.121 ff.). These seldom if ever correspond to the Civil Code. This legal confusion tends to be self-perpetuating since purchasers and heirs do not go to lawyers to register changes, because, apart from the trouble and expense, there would be too many questions to answer.

Turkish legal procedure for sorting out the confusion is itself complex and bureaucratic. Decisions are made on written evidence in Ankara, where all records are kept. This leads to slow and lengthy correspondence, and cases frequently last for years. The young men who act as judges in the local areas are in fact the subordinate investigating officers of a centralised judicial machine.

Village opinion condemns resort to the courts. It is shameful for kinsfolk to be unable to reach a compromise among themselves, and foolish to give lawyers a chance to eat their property. The range of questions and investigations, the time the whole business takes, and the numerous visits to the court, generally make it far more bother than it is worth.

A more serious objection which one might have expected from the villagers is that the decisions of the courts do not correspond to village notions of right and wrong. It is certainly true that legal rights seldom correspond to acknowledged customary village rights. But the villagers never complained on this account, and it is not hard to find reasons why they did not do so.

First, any one village uses the courts so seldom that the discrepancies do not become obvious. Secondly, in any dispute over land, both sides have a claim under village custom and believe themselves to be in the right. Whichever side wins will be delighted and not bother itself with the reasons the court gives for its decision. Thirdly, the main provisions of the Code, equal division between children, with one-quarter for a widow, are not strikingly different from traditional practices. Fourthly, the villagers regard landholding to a considerable extent as a matter of power and luck, and not as a matter to be settled exclusively by the precise application of rules. A powerful and incomprehensible arbitrator provides an enforceable and final decision; they would not expect this decision to correspond to their own notion of justice. Fifthly, law has prestige, and a decision of the courts even if odd is nevertheless *kanun*, law.

Threats to resort to law are extremely common. In argument villagers normally speak of the law as the source of all land rights, and of the courts as the source of justice. The imperfections in the Code, and in the judicial process, have not apparently undermined the respect for Law. Occasionally, when the stake is high or when the parties are more interested in victory over enemies than in economic advantage, villagers do go to law, and cases of this kind are sufficient to clog the national machine and keep it permanently in arrears. But in most cases the threats are idle, and only a tiny percentage of land disputes actually reach the courts.

Because of the total lack of village interest in official registration of marriage – less than half of all marriages were registered (Timur (1957) p. 35) – many respectably born village children are legally illegitimate. Special laws have, from time to time, rendered the legitimisation of such children extremely simple, but many village wives remain without legal claims on their husbands or on their husbands' estates. In practice, so far, because the villages have recourse to law so seldom, the illegitimacy of many wives and widows has no consequences that I could discover.

School

Traditional village education was religious and local. The *hoca*, or imam of the village was expected, among his duties, to teach the young; indeed *hoca* means teacher. He taught them Islam, especially the correct performance of prayers and rituals. He taught them to recite suras from the Koran in uncomprehended

Arabic and sometimes he taught them to read the Arabic script, so that they could read old Turkish, and read out without understanding the Arabic version of the Koran, pronounced according to local convention. In the past therefore, probably a few men in each village were literate. In Sakaltutan, in 1950, eight of the older men could read the old script.

The Republican government had very different ideas about village education. It set out to provide a state-imposed system of schools teaching modern subjects in the new infidel script. Up to 1949 religious teaching was specifically forbidden, and since then it has been a reformed and modern version of Islam which has been found in the official textbooks of religious knowledge (Lewis (1961) p. 412).

Teachers of the new sort were necessarily urban-educated, and mostly young. They were also few in number – 28,000 for the whole of Turkey in 1940, of whom 21,000 were primary school teachers (Ann. Stat. (1951), Tables 117, 119). Those who were available were mostly unwilling, indeed unable, to live in villages because of the vast cultural differences between town and village.

The government made two experiments to meet these difficulties. As a temporary expedient, suitable men doing their military service were picked out, given short courses, and sent back to their villages to teach. They took the village children in single three-year batches of mixed age, mainly in reading and writing. For these men this occupation was mostly a winter sideline to the main business of working their land. Ahmet (K) (p. 24) was doing this job in Sakaltutan in 1949–50.

The second experiment was on a much grander and more permanent scale. Between 1939 and 1946 twenty-one special boarding schools for village children were built, known as Village Institutes. All except one were outside towns and away from urban influences. Much of the construction work was done by pupils and teachers, some by more or less voluntary village labour. The programme aimed to give the boys practical as well as academic training and to send them back to the villages as leaders and reformers. The early Institutes worked at their task with enthusiasm and idealism. The boys who entered had to have completed five years of elementary school and were given a further five years, bringing them to at least seventeen years of age. In spite of the strict régime and heavy timetable – they were only allowed two months at home in the summer each year – five years was too short a period to cover adequately the great range of subjects in the curriculum. Learning by rote was the rule rather than the encouraging of intelligent and critical thinking.

Among a body of teachers and pupils all in close contact with the desperate poverty of ordinary village life, it was not surprising that radical political ideas caught on. How strong these really were I do not know, but the government was alarmed. It first slowed down the growth of the Village Institutes, and then officially abolished their separate identity and merged them with the urban teachers' training colleges.

These Village Institutes were successful in rapidly producing a body of young men legally bound, able and in most cases willing to become village teachers. All the trained village teachers I knew, except the Travelling Headmaster resident in Elbaşı, were products of these Institutes.

These young men had been taught that they were to act not merely as schoolmasters but as general missionaries of scientific enlightenment and progress. In fact they were far from adequately trained for such a task, and the social problems they faced would have daunted highly trained social workers. The point of the spartan regime and relatively remote position of the Village Institutes was to prevent the young men becoming irretrievably attached to urban life, and thus unwilling, even unable to settle back in the villages. But the result of this system was to teach them about a way of life very different from their own village upbringing, without giving them any first-hand experience of it. They were aware of ideals and values which made them despise the village, and yet had little realistic notion about urban life or about the possibilities of village reform, still less about Western society.

To the rest of Elbaşı, the three young teachers were still members of the village belonging to familiar village households. Yet they had lost intimate contact through five years of almost continuous schooling. Their new ways and ideas and their pretensions created a social barrier between them and the village, and they symbolised to the village the hostile, outside urban world which had trained them and sent them back as its apostles. They were of the village and yet not of it. The duty laid on them of acting as school attendance officers did not make their position easier.

These teachers faced a dilemma. Either they took their modernising mission seriously, caused offence without making any impression, and withdrew into ineffective resentful isolation, or they tried to lead a normal social life, yielding to the conservative pressures of the village community, and living as much like a traditional villager as the job of actually teaching the children allowed. Their difficulties are graphically portrayed by one of them, Mahmut Makal, who wrote a series of books, the first of which was Turkey's best seller to date (Makal 1950, 1952, etc.).

The primary course which they taught officially lasted five years, from seven to twelve, since altered to run from six to eleven. Children often began late, partly due to the irregularity of registration of birth, partly to the opposition of some parents to school altogether. Many failed to finish the course. The curriculum included reading, writing and arithmetic, history and geography, civics and some elementary science. But the subjects were taught largely by rote, and in spite of lip service in high places to making village education relevant to village life, in fact it appeared to the villagers to have no relevance at all. Reading, writing, and number apart, what was taught was largely mumbo-jumbo to the children. Education was something which belonged not to the village but to the outside world, where the skills and the knowledge it taught might conceivably serve some purpose.

Traditionally, knowledge is religious knowledge, and the learned in village eyes are always religiously learned. One hears stories of village sages in the past whose knowledge of books was so great that they could work wonders, and knew what was happening in other places without being informed. The new secular teaching in the infidel alphabet is not well regarded. But the recent production of cheap religious pamphlets in the new script which enables the new literates to memorise religious texts more easily has helped somewhat to make for its acceptance. And even in 1950 the strongest opponents of the new teaching had no serious hope of its disappearance.

Within the village literacy served little purpose. No newspapers reached either village, except accidentally and occasionally. Yet people's attitudes were not uniform. Almost everyone admitted the advantage of being able to add up and subtract because one could avoid being cheated. And most households had young men away in the army or in the towns with whom they wished to correspond. Some of the children who could read were fascinated by old American or European magazines because they recognised the letters, and even more so when they found something in Turkish which made sense. Literacy is a great advantage to a young man during military service. A few families even thought in terms of the promotion of their young into the urban literate world. One ordinary middle-run villager in one village had sent a son to Kayseri schools by using kinship ties in the town and then eventually to Istanbul University, and several young men had been to the Village Institute to train as teachers. As a new largely literate generation grows up, the uses of literacy in a rapidly developing economy will surely become more obvious and education more acceptable. At the same time the status benefits of achieving higher education will become plainer.

Government Services

Education, once a community matter but now a government service, has far more direct effect on the villages than any other, and for this reason I have given it separate treatment. From the point of view of Sakaltutan and Elbaşı in 1950–52, the remaining government services fall into three groups: public works, agricultural and veterinary services, and health services.

Government interest in providing villagers with roads and water supplies became conspicuously greater after the election in 1950. Public buildings, particularly schools which had once been village responsibility, were undertaken at government expense. This system provides the village not only with improved facilities but with paid employment, and became a major topic for lobbying the local powers through one's influential friends. A village like Sakaltutan stood to gain little from the new system since its contacts were few, but Elbaşı had far more opportunities to play the game. While I was there the Public Works department paid for work on the village approach road, the last two hundred yards or so of which were so appalling that the lorries ran through the fields on either side to avoid the quagmire. Funds unfortunately ran out before completion, and the officials left with promises to return after the next year's budget.

I have already described the State Office of Soil Products (p. 73), which buys the grain crop and thus controls prices, and the generous working of agricultural credit. Neither of these involved more than direct face-to-face relationships with minor officials, and both institutions were taken very much for granted.

The much more formidable problems of raising technical efficiency, and thus productivity, were hardly being tackled seriously in the area in which I worked. Clean, good quality seed was provided on credit, help with disease control was available for both crops and animals, and stud bulls, stallions and rams were provided to improve local stock. Except perhaps for curative veterinary services for animals, on which people commented favourably, these services though accepted as of right, and even used to some extent, are regarded with scepticism and constant criticism. The villagers had no conception of the possibility of a revolution in their techniques and economy, and did not expect the government to produce one.

Village health services had even less impact, with one major exception. As in many other countries malaria has been virtually wiped out in Turkey. One village which had suffered had been Elbaşı. Malaria control continued in 1951 but quite divorced from other medical activities.

The main health interest of the villagers is in cures for current illness. Here the government did virtually nothing. Free hospital services existed in Kayseri but the resources were so limited that villagers did not even think of using them. When they wanted a doctor they had to go and find one in Kayseri. An official doctor resided in Bünyan (Fig. 2), but the village disregarded him. In Kayseri there were about fifty. The fare to Kayseri, the doctor's fee, and the expensive medicines, often involving injections, which were normally prescribed, provided a strong deterrent in all but urgent cases. If the cure was not noticeably and rapidly successful, the patient would try another doctor rather than go back to the first. The notion of a family doctor was completely lacking. The doctors, overwhelmed with patients who were mostly poor, suspicious and unsophisticated, can hardly be blamed for not offering a better service.

Around 1950, the government was attempting to provide health workers for the villagers. These were of two kinds, Health Officers and midwives. No trained midwives had been posted to the area in or near which I worked, but those of whom I heard were not highly successful. Being young, unmarried, and without training in the social and educational problems they would have to face in the villages, they had little hope of leading a normal social life in a village, let alone of establishing influence and inspiring trust.

The Health Officers were young men who had undergone the same initial training as the teachers and been selected for special courses in hygiene and related subjects for the last two years. Their job was vague. It included some specific tasks, vaccination and inoculation for example, and the giving of injections when necessary. In fact some of them, so I was told, charged illegally for these services. It also included supervision of sanitary arrangements, latrines for example, the destruction of superfluous dogs, and general health education. But they had neither efficient repressive sanctions to back them up in enforcing irksome regulations, nor the slightest training in, or equipment for, persuasion and propaganda. A young man with seventeen villages to attend to had little hope of achieving anything; indeed it was impossible for him to know where or how to begin.

The main health need from the village point of view is immediate and cheap relief from illness, both chronic and short term. We ourselves faced an incessant demand for medical help, to meet which we could do very little. But a Health Officer who was not even permitted to carry aspirins, and who could do nothing about illness, was completely disregarded by the village. The only Health Officer I knew personally appeared to me to do in fact almost nothing at all, and to be acutely unhappy about his ineffectiveness.

The Political Parties

The villagers had been asked to vote for Deputies to the Grand National Assembly regularly every four years since the foundation of the Republic. Before 1946 the candidates were all approved by the Republican People's Party, and very often there was no choice at all. In 1946 a genuine opposition was permitted, but the villagers, confident that the result was a foregone conclusion, had not apparently taken the election seriously. As the 1950 election approached, it became clear that the Democrat Party was truly to be allowed to make a serious challenge to the government. Both sides visited the village and seemed more eager to explain that the law had been changed, and that the election would be genuine and the ballot really secret, than to win votes for their respective parties. Sakaltutan had recognised but ineffective village leaders of local sections of both main parties. People discussed the matter ceaselessly, but the new line-up did not coincide with any existing social divisions. Very roughly, the skilled migrant labourers tended to be supporters of the Democrat Party; those who remained permanently in the village as full-time farmers tended to support the Republican People's Party, partly perhaps because they did not see any point in changing, partly because they were impervious to the current argument about more private enterprise and economic freedom, and partly because they were more afraid to oppose the established government. But people were quite willing to waver openly, and members of a single household would argue opposite cases. At a wedding which took place in the winter of 1949–50, the men dressed up as Democrats and People's Party and played a game resembling 'cops and robbers'. This argumentative and lighthearted attitude was not typical. Elbaşı, if my conjectures are right, represents a more normal case. Two sharply defined factions already existed. The reigning faction had necessarily already identified itself with the existing government, so that the headman and his supporters were automatically R.P.P. Those who opposed them were thus committed to the D.P. No one can be certain in a secret ballot how people actually voted, but on the whole it is probably safe to assume that most votes follow public affiliations, and affiliations for most villagers follow, not national lines, but local ones. So long as the two-party system continues, the votes of each village and small town are likely to be split in this way, giving the opposition a certain minimum number of votes more or less regardless of national issues.

This conversion of existing local factions into local sections of the national parties made possible the very rapid establishment of a two-party political system in full-scale activity. Outside urban intellectual circles, the R.P.P. was an alliance of all factions who happened to be on top in 1950, the D.P. an alliance of all the local oppositions. During the time of the election rioting or disturbances between the parties were reported in the press, as though these were due to the new political activity. In fact, it is highly probable that in almost all cases these were old local factions with new political affiliations for whom the election provided an excuse for active hostility.

This analysis implies that the D.P. in fact captured the support of most of the local oppositions which existed in every town and village in Turkey. Once this had happened third parties had relatively little chance of becoming established in rural areas on a national scale. Most communities have two main rival factions, even if these are loose confederations of smaller groups and somewhat unstable. If third forces exist in some communities they are neither numerous nor strong enough to enable a third party to weld them into a national force offering serious rivalry to the two main parties.

Of course, this analysis is not true for all people nor for all communities. Some people in every community would be un-committed, and some vote in national elections differently from their explicit affiliation. Some communities possess internal structures permanently or temporarily unlike the simple two-faction model I have assumed. Moreover, if the system is to function in this way the people must feel a reasonable degree of confidence in each of the two parties and in freedom from persecution for political activity.

The system as I have outlined it strengthens the tendency towards a local spoils system. If people support a national party because they want the existing office holders in their local community out of office, then when that party wins they expect to replace them. The motive for remaining loyal to one party is not intellectual conviction, but the realisation that in order to reap political rewards, one must not only be on the winning side, but have a reputation for being a trustworthy supporter. So the parties, like the parties in the U.S.A., become alliances of local factions each contending in its own area; overall ideology and national policy become relatively less important.[1]

Urban and Rural Social Rank

Social relations between a particular villager and a particular townsman are plainly a matter of the structural position each holds, both in his own section of society and in the larger society of which town and village both form a part. The most important single element in this relation is rank. In some contexts people speak as if the village ranked below the urban system altogether. Even the poorest of established townsmen is proud of his urbanity, and the words *köy* village, and *köylü*, villager are used as terms of opprobrium. Villagers are well aware of this collective inferiority, and are often explicit about their lack of civilisation, *medeniyet*, and their uncouth, *kaba*, way of life. Yet it is obvious that this simple model of a single scale ending in the town, and beginning its downward path again in the village is absurd. The bulk of the town population, petty traders, artisans, porters, labourers, overlaps in rank the bulk of the rural population. Only the high school and university graduates, and the owners of really substantial property, that is, every one from the middle-range officials to the cabinet ministers and the Istanbul élite, rank unequivocally above the village. Roughly one might say that the village poor correspond to the labourers and porters and the urban unemployed; the better-off villagers, those of middle position in Sakaltutan and Elbaşı, correspond to the artisans, the stall-holders and petty traders, and the upper end of the village, especially the upper end of Elbaşı to the lower end of the educated stratum, the junior officials, the petty merchants, the contractors, the small hotel keepers.

In spite of this correspondence the ranking systems are very different. The total span of social distance between the top and bottom of the village hierarchy is much less than the corresponding social distance between the corresponding ranks in the towns. This is fundamentally a matter of a shared way of

---

[1] Turkish politics since 1960, in spite of the army, have tended to return to the basic division between R.P.P. and the successors of the Democrat Party; this trend strengthens my analysis, in that the two-party system is re-emerging in the teeth of attempts to break it up; but national factors are perhaps more important than my model allows.

10*

life and culture. The village watchman visits the guest room of the village *ağa*, just as his wife uses the same methods of cooking, fetching water, bedmaking, child care as the *ağa's* wife. Both are interested in the same gossip, the same set of people. Both see themselves primarily as members of their village. In the town, by contrast, the poor and the rich live different lives in very different styles, with different interests, a different material apparatus, and a different language. A single village household may occasionally have kin ties which span the urban hierarchy, without any feeling of embarrassment. But if these same persons through their village connection bring their urban worlds into contact, the class differences will at once assert themselves.

I have already said (p. 222) that ranking differences in the village do not produce social classes, but rather pyramids in which vertical relations of sociability are as easy as horizontal ones. Ranking differences in the towns on the other hand, inhibit vertical relationships of sociability.

This difference in quality between rural and urban stratification, is, I think, at least partly responsible for a phenomenon commonly remarked by foreign observers, and spoken of with pride by the Turks themselves. Villagers often conduct themselves with remarkable dignity and self-respect, and are outspoken in the presence of important people. These egalitarian manners are said to prove an absence of social class, or class consciousness. This is a false conclusion. Such behaviour is typical only of a minority of vocal village leaders: the majority are respectful, silent and unnoticed before their urban betters. In fact, Turkish society is almost military in its hierarchy. But to the villager social intercourse and hierarchy are not mutually exclusive, because in the pyramidical structure of the village, hierarchy is not the social barrier it is in the towns.

In spite of this widspread impression of egalitarianism, the general inferiority of the village to town profoundly affects relations between town and village. The villager, even the man who is pre-eminent in his own village and proud of his urbanity and connections, is in fact ignorant beside his urban kinsman. Most village leaders were not literate in 1950, at any rate not in the new Latin script. Thus, while town and village may meet for a large number of purposes, official business, temporary urban employment, visits of kinsmen to the village, and so on, they do not share a common life. Vertical sociability within rural society is greater than horizontal sociability outside it, and a gulf of mutual strangeness and mistrust is fixed between town and village.

Although, therefore, the village ranking system has a certain correspondence to the dominant urban ranking system, the two systems do not fit together easily. Relationships between individuals on the two sides reflect these somewhat inconsistent elements: the general inferiority of village to town, the rough correspondence of the two systems, and the gulf of unsociability between them.

Villagers and Townsmen

We can divide face-to-face relationships between town and village into two types; the personal relations of kin and friends who treat each other more or less as equals, and the single stranded relations of villagers with officials, merchants, or professional men, where the villager requires one specific service or owes one specific obligation. The first of these two classes of social relations corresponds roughly to relations with the lower strata of the town, where there is the greatest degree of mutual comprehensibility and shared culture; the second to those with the educated, the culturally distant, whom the villagers treat with deference.

Sakaltutan had very few relationships of the first type. One close agnate of K lineage was living in Ankara with an Ankara wife. He visited the village during my stay, bringing her with him. He apparently ran a permanent stall in a street market. He and his wife dressed like townspeople, and he spoke of the blessings of a town education for his children. Otherwise Sakaltutan's social contacts with town consisted mainly of those formed by the migrant labourers (p. 64). As far as I was able to judge, the social life of these migrants in town was largely spent among other villagers. The system of contracting and subcontracting (p. 65) meant that often the immediate employer was another villager. The migrant labourers seem to have formed their own sub-system within the town, and to have lived very largely within it. For the six men who worked in the factory in Kayseri on a permanent basis the situation was perhaps different; yet they too lived in bachelor quarters with other villagers, and none showed any eagerness to move their families to town. A few others had special town connections. One man, old and very poor, regularly went to town as a porter, which implied that he was accepted among the Kayseri porters. Another man with a similar profession had been living for some years in Kayseri; he had had a Kayseri wife but divorced her, and replaced her with a village wife. During my stay he moved his village wife and family back to the village saying that life in town was too hard, but he continued to spend his time portering in Kayseri, allowing his brother to work his land as a share-cropper.

Migrant labour apart, the range of urban contacts in Elbaşı was much greater, both with the local town Bünyan and with Kayseri itself. One past and three existing marriages in the village had brought wives in from Bünyan, and two past and three existing marriages had brought wives from Kayseri. One woman was said to have married out to each of these towns. At least some of the villagers had agnates in Bünyan, and one refugee household head had a brother in Kayseri. Another man who had come as a child with a widowed mother from Kayseri to Elbaşı had a brother who was a secondary schoolmaster in Kayseri. Another villager had a house in Kayseri and a post in the administration, and the tax collector's two sons, both doing their military service as officers, were also from the Kayseri administration. Of the more lowly villagers two had lived in Kayseri, one as driver of a horse and cart, and the other in an attempt to survive on a state disability pension. The first gave up, so he said, on health grounds, though his wife's version was different; and the other because it was impossible to make ends meet. Another villager had been employed by the Kayseri town watch, a locally organised adjunct of the centrally controlled police.

The relationships of these two villages with town were typical. Larger, more central villages have a much more developed set of links with town than poorer and less sophisticated ones. The top people in Elbaşı had links with the local town and with the local bureaucracy. Sakaltutan had no such links. The most urbanised in Sakaltutan were those with established economic connections as migrant craftsmen. Except perhaps for one or two even poorer villages, Sakaltutan and Elbaşı represent the extremes, and other villages in the area mostly seemed to fall in between them in the degree of their urban contacts.

Within relationships of this personal type some degree of intimacy, exchange of ideas, and mutual help is possible. But this is not the case with the single-purpose relations, those with officials, professional men, politicians and merchants. Even these vary according to context. When the villager, often shabbily dressed and usually uncertain of himself and his village manners, visits the townsman he is very much at a disadvantage. It is easy in Turkey for anyone to walk into any office, including that of the Vali, with a request, but a villager is unlikely to receive much consideration unless he has a pull, or an exceptionally well presented case. Doctors, dentists, and lawyers too, treat village clients with a lofty air.

When the official visits the village, where he is more or less compelled to receive village hospitality, he is on more equal terms. He automatically meets the village leaders, men confident of their local superiority, and he is not surrounded by telephones, desks and messengers. Under these circumstances, even the Vali or a member of the National Assembly may appear to be on easy terms with his hosts. But such visits are rare, brief, and so covered by a formal politeness on both sides that the degree of real communication is strictly limited.

While senior officials, especially after the Democrat victory in 1950, were often polite, junior officials were more obviously paternalistic. On my first visit to Sakaltutan, the local District Officer who accompanied me explicitly and publicly spoke of the assembled company of village elders as his children, whom he, on behalf of the government, cared for like a father. After the 1950 harvest, which was poor enough to justify a moratorium on debts due to the Agricultural Bank, the visit of an official commission to assess crops for this moratorium coincided with a routine visit of the tax collector, who complained by way of conversation that he was having some difficulty in a neighbouring village. The senior official of the visiting party promptly lectured the villagers present as if they had been schoolboys, on the moral duty of paying taxes, threatening that if the tax collector had occasion to complain about them he would see to it that there would be no moratorium.

For most villagers, and for the village community as a whole, educated urban people are best avoided. No one likes the humiliation involved in making visits to doctors and lawyers, and everyone is suspicious of and opposed to any official interference in village life. Normally, the outside world is called in only when specific benefits are known to be obtainable, for example the stemming of an epidemic among village flocks; or when specific sanctions are likely to follow a failure to pass on information – about for example serious injury or homicide.

Such an attitude towards social superiors, especially when they are also outsiders, is normal. It has the consequence of preventing all but highly selected information about the villages from reaching the urban world which controls them, and thus aiding the preservation of current illusion and mutual misunderstanding.

The Foreshortening of the Outside World

Understanding is limited by experience. People anywhere can only interpret that part of their society that they do not see, or do not live in, in terms of the society they do live in. They are therefore bound to misinterpret what goes on in other parts of their society or in other societies, in terms of what goes on in their own. People in a small-scale society are bound to fail to grasp the size and diversity of the larger society in which their small-scale society nests. The tightly knit, stable rural communities which I studied constantly foreshorten social distance and underestimate social complexity in the outside world.

In the present-day village, the degree of grasp varies very greatly from individual to individual. All village women know that towns exist, and a few of them have been to Kayseri. Yet they normally asked us what village we came from, and many seemed to find it difficult to take in the fact that we did not come from a home like theirs in a village like theirs. At the other extreme the most sophisticated men were used to doing business in Ankara, and knew a great deal about national and international affairs.

The commonest form of this foreshortening is the constant assumption that one educated man knows and can influence all other educated men. I was believed to be able to obtain favours, if not of all educated Turks, at least of all educated foreigners in Turkey. This implies that the villager sees the educated world as a small network very like his own rural network, in which by kinship and friendship one can find a link with anyone if one only takes the trouble. Disclaimers are not believed. They were convinced that we refused not because we were unable, but because we were not prepared to take the trouble, or out of personal spite.

Most villagers realise more or less clearly that urban educated society contains a very large number of rôles that are distinct both socially and in the skills they demand. Yet they do not apply this knowledge systematically. They expect the highly educated to know everything, to be able to cure the sick, mend radios, give legal decisions and so forth. In particular, they assume that all educated Turks are knowledgeable about Islam, and frequently asked educated visitors questions about religion.

This foreshortening has an interesting effect on changes in taste and techniques. The urban world itself happens to be changing very rapidly, particularly the world of the local towns. In these many people still live more or less traditional urban lives, using the customs and the material culture which the village has for generations associated with the towns. But at the same time Western dress, schoolgirls with uncovered heads, motor-cars, blocks of modern flats and a host of other things represent a new and totally different tradition. This tradition is European and still to most villagers infidel. This unstable blend in urban society is misleading and confusing to the villagers. On one occasion a man of Sakaltutan brought his wife to town. I met him and offered him and two companions tea, and embarrassed everyone by offering tea to his wife also. She turned away into the corner to drink in order to uncover her mouth without being seen. I pointed to two educated Turkish women in Western dress and cosmetics who were passing. 'They are not Turks,' she said, 'they are foreigners.'

One of the villagers had recently completed a new guest room. It was a modern one, with a divan running right round the wall. 'It's the new style,' I was told, 'alafranca (i.e. European), like the towns.' A style of building already out of date among town Turks was justified by a villager as being town-like, and a typical Middle East room was called European.

autonomous life, and virtually to ignore its obvious inferiority to the town.

The effect of the vastly increased contact between town and village which I have just described is two-fold. By greatly increasing the range of social relations even the poorer villagers have with people outside the village it has decreased the solidarity of the village, weakening the strength of the social controls on which village conservatism is founded. The villagers are no longer necessarily dependent on their leaders. At the same time they come to depend on the good-will of a host of other people outside the village with different assumptions and ideas. The village community is pulled apart by multiplying relations between its members and the outside world. This process so far is no more than begun, but it has already brought the village into the nation in a much more definite and inescapable way. Even if he pays his taxes without argument and keeps out of the way when involved in violence, the villager can no longer hope to ignore the authorities. He is constantly, through the radio, reminded that he and his village are a part of a much larger social unit, the nation. He has become aware also that the village is despised by townsmen, and that most villagers have a vastly lower standard of living than the urban educated. The village is all too clearly at the bottom of the national hierarchy. Once the village was a social foothill to the distant urban peaks, proud in its semi-autonomy and more or less able to ignore them by looking the other way. Its social world was centred on itself. Now it is acutely aware that it is only the peripheral lower slopes, uncomfortably forced to face or evade the constant stream of interference and scorn which pours down from the urban peaks of national power.

The old attitudes are not gone. The village is still proud; each village still knows itself to be the best of all communities and, like most rural communities, at times writes town society off as corrupt and decadent. But contradictions are a normal part of any society, and the opposite is heard even more often – that the village is backward, uncouth, poor, dirty and violent. Such contradictions can, of course, live more or less permanently in a society. But though I have no empirical first-hand evidence of the village attitudes two generations ago, I am confident that its pride and independent spirit are declining and its diffidence and sense of inferiority increasing.

Changes in this direction are inevitable, and serve humanitarian as well as national ends. A higher standard of living can only come with more technical efficiency, more controls, more education, more taxes, more intervention by national organisations in local politics, and so on. Eventually the full weight of all this may narrow the gap, and by destroying the tightness of the local community, integrate its members more effectively in the nation. But the initial effect of attempts at reform and betterment, by their more or less unintended transformation of the social structure, are likely to be an increase of tension between the villagers and their urban rulers, both local and national.

APPENDIX

Range of Marriage: Distance

Whenever possible, I gathered information about the origins of the partners to marriages. In the tables attached, I give a summary of the results. The figures for living wives in Sakaltutan are virtually complete and reliable, but those for women married out of the village are less so, and in some cases I am not sure whether women who have left the village are still alive. The Elbaşı figures are based on a more or less complete census of village households, but my data on origins of wives is less complete, and on women who have left the village even more partial. It is obvious that figures for past and broken marriages could only be said to be complete in any sense if one set a time limit, which I did not.

These tables should be read in conjunction with the map, fig. 2 (p. 17), with the diagrams, figs. 10 and 11 (pp. 205 and 207) and with the discussion on pp. 201, 205-7.

Table 10

MARRIAGES IN AND OUT: SAKALTUTAN 1950

| | Sakaltutan Wives | | | | Sakaltutan Women married out | | Total no. of marriage links |
| | Existing Marriages | | Past or Broken Marriages | | Presumed Living | Presumed Dead | |
	No.	Per cent	No.	Per cent			
Born in Sakaltutan	87	67	84	51			
All villages within approx. 1 hour							
Süleymanli	6		9		17	4	36
Ardıç	5		4		7	8	24
Kanber	1		6		6	0	13
Çevlik	1		4		5	2	12
Alayınlı	3	16	0	20	5	2	10
Söksün	1		4		2	3	10
Gülveren	3		3		0	0	6
Kepez	0		2		2	0	4
Vengicek	0		2		2	0	4
Other villages with several marriage links to Sakaltutan							
Kölete (4 hrs.)	1		6		1	6	14
Travşun (2 hrs.)	1		7		3	0	11
Zerezek (2 hrs.)	3	8·5	1	13	3	1	8
Harsa (4 hrs.)	1		3		4	0	8
Koşçağız (2 hrs.)	2		4		0	1	7
Tomarza (4 hrs.)	3		0		1	2	6
Other local villages (32)	11	8·5	22	13	17	6	—
Special cases	1		4	3	1	0	—
TOTAL	130	100	165	100	76	35	—
Unknown	2		15		—	—	—

Based on data on 423 marriages.

Table 11

MARRIAGES IN AND OUT: ELBAŞI 1951

	Elbaşı Wives		Elbaşı Women married out (Existing and past marriages)	Total no. of marriage links
	Existing Marriages No. Per cent	Past or Broken Marriages No. Per cent		
I				
Born in Elbaşı	137 63	74 61	—	—
II				
All villages within approx. 1 hour:				
Karadayi	12 ⎫	2 ⎫	0	14
Zerezek	9 ⎬ 12	8 ⎬ 9	2	19
Zek	3 ⎪	1 ⎪	1	5
Kölete	2 ⎭	0 ⎭	1	3
III				
Other villages with several marriage links to Elbaşı:				
Söksün (2 hrs.)	8 ⎫	7 ⎫	8	23
Hezaksah (2 hrs.)	7 ⎪	6 ⎪	1	14
Kanber (4 hrs.)	6 ⎬ 13	2 ⎬ 16	3	11
Kïzïl Ören (2 hrs.)	3 ⎪	2 ⎪	5	10
Büyük Bürüngüzlü (6 hrs.)	3 ⎭	2 ⎭	1	6
IV				
25 other local villages	16 7	13 9	20	—
V				
Towns and other special cases	12 5	6 5	5	—
TOTAL	218 100	121 100	47	
No information	25	47		

Based on data on 458 marriages.

GLOSSARY OF ANTHROPOLOGICAL TERMS

Affine	Relative by marriage; adj. affinal.
Agnate	Kinsman or kinswoman related exclusively through males; adj. agnatic.
Cognatic	Kinsman or kinswoman related through any link, but excluding links through marriage.
Consanguineal	As for cognatic.
Endogamous	A group which bars to its members marriage with outsiders.
Exogamous	A group which bars marriage among its members.
Jural	Refers to formally and socially accepted rights, whether or not these are part of the law of the State.
Patrilateral	Related through father (unlike patrilineal, this term includes father's kin through female links).
Patrilineal	As for agnatic; used particularly of kinship systems.
Unilineal	Patrilineal or matrilineal.
Uxorilocal	Residing with or near the wife's kin (of a married couple or marriage).
Virilocal	Residing with or near the husband's kin (or a married couple or marriage).

SYMBOLS USED IN GENEALOGIES

△   Male.

○   Female.

=   married to.

⚤ ⚥ Bilal.   Oblique stroke indicates death.

299

GLOSSARY OF TURKISH WORDS

Notes:

Turkish forms the plural by adding *-ler* or *-lar*.

When two nouns are joined (as in *field watchman*), the second takes a possessive suffix, e.g. *tarla bekci-si*, field watchman, *köy katib-i*, village scribe.

A full list of kinship terms used in the villages will be found on pp. 152–3.

Purely local and village meanings are indicated by *vlg.*

aile	family; *vlg.* wife
ağa	title of respect for men (pp. 105, 228)
akraba, akrabalık	kin; kinship
almak	take
amca	father's brother
amele	unskilled labourer
anne	mother
ayip	shameful
baba	father
bacanak	wife's sister's husband
baldız	wife's sister
başlık	bride price
bayram	feast; holy day
bekci	watchman
büyük	great
cahil	ignorant
ceğiz	meadow
çayır	trousseau
çirak	apprentice; resident servant
damat	bridegroom; son-in-law
dayı	mother's brother
delikanlı	young man
dönüm	decare (p. 52)
dünür	own child's parents-in-law
düğün	wedding
düzen	wedding gift
efendi	title of respect for men
elti	husband's brother's wife
emir	command; *Allahın emri*, the Will of God
enişte	sister's husband; aunt's husband
ev	house

evlad	children
gavur	unbeliever
gelin	bride
genç	youth (p. 223)
görümce	husband's sister
günah	sin
güvey (*vlg.* guvah)	bridegroom; son-in-law
haci	pilgrim to Mecca
hala	father's sister; *vlg.* mother's sister
hane	house
harman	harvest
hebe	saddle bag
hecelik	part of the bride price (p. 179)
helva	sweet made of nuts and honey
henna	yellow dye (with religious significance for Muslims)
hoca	religious leader; teacher
horanta (*vlg.*)	wife
iç-güvey	a man living with his wife's kin
iddet	period of three menstrual months (or more) which a widow or divorcée must wait before remarriage under the Şeriat (Vesey-Fitzgerald (1931) p. 52)
ihtyar	old man
ihtyar heyeti	council of elders
iyi	good
kaba	vulgar
kabile	tribe; lineage
kanun	law
katib	scribe
karakol	gendarme post
kayın	brother-in-law; *vlg.* spouse's kin
kaza	administrative division of a province
kilim	a kind of rug
kimsesiz	without anyone
kız	girl
kız kaçırma	elopement
kol	arm; branch
komşuluk	neighbourliness
konuşmak	talk; talk with
köy; köylü	village; villager
kuma	second wife
kurban bayramı	Muslim festival
kuruş	a cent, one-hundredth of a lira
küs	sulking
mahalle	quarter (of a town or village)
medeni; medeniyet	civilised; civilisation
memür	official
misafir odası	guest room
müdür	director; officer

muhtar	headman
nahiye	rural administrative subdivision of a *kaza*
namus	honour
namuslu	honourable
namussuz	dishonourable
nikah	marriage ceremony
nişan	betrothal
nohut	chick-pea
ocak	hearth
oda	room
ofis	office
oğul	son
pekmez	syrup made from boiled grapes
Ramazan	annual Muslim month of fasting
salma	tax (in *köy salması*, village tax)
sandık	chest; fund
satmak	sell
seyit	Muslim saint
sedir	divan
sevap	religiously meritorious
sıhhat memürü	health officer
sura	chapter of the Koran
Şeker Bayramı	Muslim festival at the end of Ramazan
Şeriat	Holy Law of Islam
şeyh	*vlg.* member of a religious fraternity, dervish (compare sheikh)
şeyhlik	office or activities of a dervish
şöför	driver
şube	branch
tandır	fireplace (p. 21)
tapu	deed of title to land
tarla	field
teyze	mother's sister; aunt
türbeh	tomb
usta	skilled craftsman
vakşi	wild
vali; vilayet	provincial governor; province
vermek	give
yakmak	kindle; burn
yenge	bridal attendant; brother's wife; *vlg.* uncle's wife

BIBLIOGRAPHY

Arensberg, C. M. and Kimball, S. T., 1940. *Family and Community in Ireland*, Harvard.

Armstrong, H. C., 1925. *Turkey in Travail: The Birth of a New Nation*, London.

[Ataturk, K.], 1929. *A Speech Delivered by Ghazi Mustafa Kemal, President of the Turkish Republic, October 1927*, Leipzig.

Aran, S., 1938. *Evedik Köyü; Bir Köy Monografisi*, Ankara.

Barnes, J. A., 1949. 'Measures of Divorce Frequency in Simple Societies', *J. Roy. Anthrop. Inst.*, LXXIX, London,

Barth, F., 1953, *Principles of Social Organization in Southern Kurdistan*, Oslo.

——1959. *Political Leadership among Swat Pathans*, London.

Campbell, J. K., 1964. *Honour. Family and Patronage*, Oxford.

Code Civile Turc, 1926. Istanbul.

Colson, E., 1953. 'Social Control in Plateau Tonga Society', *Africa*, xxiii, London. Reprinted in *The Plateau Tonga of Northern Rhodesia. Social and Religious Studies*, Manchester, 1962.

Embree, J. F., 1946. *A Japanese Village: Suye Mura*, London.

Evans-Pritchard, E. E., 1940. *The Nuer*, Oxford.

Faculty of Political Science, University of Ankara, (n.d. 1952). *Economic and Social Aspects of Farm Mechanisation in Turkey*. (Mimeographed.)

Fei, H. T., 1939. *Peasant Life in China*, London.

Freedman, M., 1958. *Lineage Organization in South Eastern China*, London.

Fortes, M., 1953. 'The Structure of Unilineal Descent Groups', *American Anthropologist*, 55.1

Grandquist, H., 1931. *Marriage Conditions in a Palestinian Village*, Helsingfors.

Gluckman, M., 1956. *Custom and Conflict in Africa*, Oxford.

Halide, Edib., 1930. *Turkey Faces West*, Yale.

Herschlag, Z. Y., 1960. *Turkey: an Economy in Transition*, The Hague.

Homans, G. C., 1951. *The Human Group*, London.

International Bank for Reconstruction and Development, 1951. *The Economy of Turkey*, Baltimore.

Jaeckh, E., 1944. *The Rising Crescent*, New York.

Karpat, K. H., 1959. *Turkey's Politics. The Transition to a Multi-Party System*, Princeton.

Koşay, H. Z., 1944. *Türkiye Türk Düğünleri Üzerine Mükayeseli Malzeme*, Ankara.

Lerner, D. and Robinson, R. D., 1960. 'Swords and Ploughshares: The Turkish Army as a Modernizing Force', *World Politics*, XIII.1.

Lewis, B., 1961. *The Emergence of Modern Turkey*, Oxford.

Makal, M., 1950. *Bizim Köy*, Istanbul.

—, 1952. *Köyümden*, Istanbul.

—, 1954. *A Village in Anatolia* (Translation of selections from *Bizim Köy* and *Köyümden*), Vallentine, Mitchell and Co., London.

—, 1952. *Hayal ve Gercek*, Istanbul.

—, 1954. *Memleketin Sahipleri*, Istanbul.

—, 1957. *Kuru Sevda*, Istanbul.

—, 1958. *Köye Gidenler*, Istanbul.

—, 1959. *17 Nisan*, Istanbul.

Morrison, J. A., 1938. *Alişar: A Unit of Land Occupancy in the Kanak Su Basin of Central Anatolia*, Ph.D. Thesis, University of Chicago.

Musil, A., 1928. *The Manners and Customs of the Rwala Bedouins*, New York.

Orga, I., 1958. *Phoenix Ascendant*, London.

Peters, E., 1961. 'The Proliferation of Segments in the Lineage of the Bedouin in Cyrenaica', *J. Roy. Anthrop. Inst.*, 90.1.

—, 1964. 'Aspects of rank and status among Muslims in a Lebanese village' in *Mediterranean Countrymen*, ed. Pitt-Rivers, J., The Hague.

Pitt-Rivers, J. (Ed.), 1964. *Mediterranean Countrymen*, The Hague.

Planhol, de X., 1958. *De la Plaine Pampaylienne aux Lacs Pisidiens*, Paris.

Robinson, R. D., 1948–54. Letters to the Institute of Current World Affairs, New York. (Restricted circulation.)

—, 1954–57. *Developments Respecting Turkey*, Vols. I–IV, American Universities' Field Staff, New York.

—, 1954–58. Letters and Reports to American Universities' Field Staff, New York.

—, 1963. *The First Turkish Republic*, Harvard.

Salim, S. M., 1962. *Marsh Dwellers of the Euphrates Delta*, London.

Schapera, I., 1950. 'Kinship and Marriage among the Tswana' in *African Systems of Kinship and Marriage*, eds. Radcliffe-Brown, A. R. and Forde, D., Oxford.

Srinivas, M. N., 1952. 'A Joint Family Dispute in a Mysore Village', *Journal of the M.S. University of Baroda*, I.1.

Stirling, A. P., 1953. 'Social Rank in a Turkish Village', *Brit. Jnl. of Sociol.*, IV.1., London.

—, 1957. 'Land, Marriage and the Law in Turkish Villages', *Int. Soc. Sci. Bull.* IX.1.

—, 1958. 'Structural Changes in Middle East Society', *Tensions in the Middle East*, ed. Thayer, P. W., Baltimore.

—, 1958. 'Religious Change in Republican Turkey', *Middle East Journal*, Washington.

—, 1960. 'A Death and a Youth Club: Feuding in a Turkish Village', *Anthropological Quarterly*, Washington.

—, 1964. 'The Domestic Cycle and the Distribution of Power in Turkish Villages', in *Mediterranean Countrymen*, ed. Pitt-Rivers, J., The Hague.

Timur, R. H., 1957. 'Civil Marriage in Turkey: Difficulties, Causes and Remedies', *Int. Soc. Sci. Bull.* IX.1.

BIBLIOGRAPHY

Toynbee, A. J., 1923. *The Western Question in Greece and Turkey* (Second Edition), London.

Turhan, M., 1951. *Kültür Değişmeleri. Sosyal Psikolojik Bakımından bir Tetkik*, Ist. Univ. Edebiyat Fakültesi Yayınları, No. 479, Istanbul.

Turkey, Republic of, 1951. (*İstatistik Yıllığı* (*Annuaire Statistique*), Ankara.

—, 1955. Census, Ankara.

Vesey-Fitzgerald, S., 1931, *Muhammadan Law*, Oxford.

Yasa, I., 1957, *Hasanoğlan. Socio-economic Structure of a Turkish Village*, Ankara.

—, 1960. *Sindel Köyünün Toplumsal ve Ekonomik Yapısı*, Ankara.

—, 1956. *Problems of Outlying Rural Administration in Turkey*, Ankara.

INDEX

11

INDEX

Land,
  dispute over, 263
  filching of, 144, 264
  fragmentation, 44-5, 140-1
  freely available, 134-40, 263
  holdings, 51-3
  measurement, xiii, 52
  recovery of, 264
  sales, 49, 263
  share cropping and renting, 65-6
  shortage, 140-1
  tenure, 48-51
  use, 44-6
Last Judgement, 231
Law, 270-4
  commercial and penal, German
    and Italian models, 8
  marriage, and, 209-11, 220
  See also Turkish Civil Code;
    Judicial machine
Leaders, senior members, 31
  Elbaşı, in, 259-61
  Sakaltutan, in, 257-9
  Sakaltutan wedding feasts, 160,
    224
  weakness of, 264, *See also* Author-
    ity
Legal procedure, 274
Lerner, D., 270
Lewis, B. L., 4, 75, 275
Lineages, 27, 158-70
  clustering of, 160
  confined to village, 162
  criterion for membership of, 161
  description of, 158-60
  effective, 161-2
  Elbaşı, details of, 165-7
  exchange of women, 176
  feuds between, 246-54, 259-61
  fission, 169-70
  names, 159
  not corporate, 158
  Sakaltutan of, 125-6
  women, position in, 161
Literacy, 277
  Arabic script, in, 229, 274f
  level of, 24
  Turkish, old, in, 274

Lorries, 23f, 70

Magic,
  bridegrooms, against, 184, 230
  Koranic spells for, 230
  thieves, against, 230
Mahalle, 26
Mahmut (K), 154
Makul, Mahmut, 277
Markets, 72-4
  former difficulties of, 135f
Marriage, Chapter 9
  adultery, 211-2
  age at, 179
  agnates role in, 157
  ceremonies and customs, 178-85
  cross-cousin, 176, 201, 202-3
  Divine intervention in, 191
  divorce, 210, 212-20
  father's sister's daughter, with,
    149, 201, 202-3
  gifts (trousseau, etc.), 179, 180f,
    185-7
  law, 209-11
  normal for all, 42
  numbers known to me, 214
  other villages, with, 204-7
  political reasons for, 191
  range of, distance, 201-7, Appendix
  range of, kinship, 201
  range of, social rank, 208
  registration of, 274
  remarriage, 195-9
  sanctions, 209-11, 216
  secondary, definition of, 184f,
    195-9,
  stability of first marriages, 216-8
  stability of secondary marriages,
    218-9
  uxorilocal, 43
Marriage payment, *See* Bride price
Masons, 60
Measurement,
  area, xiii, 52
  volume, xiii
  weight, xiii
Medeni, medeniyet, 34, 283
Mehmet (C), 260